C

MW00770280

for Architects

The Architecture Briefs series
takes on a variety of single topics
of interest to architecture students
and young professionals. Field-
specific information and digital
techniques are presented in a user-
friendly manner along with basic
principles of design and construction.
The series familiarizes readers with
the concepts and technical terms
necessary to successfully translate
ideas into built form.

Color
for Architects

Juan Serra Lluch

Princeton Architectural Press
New York

Introduction

We architects struggle with color when designing and constructing buildings. Certainly, color is difficult to manage and is left unaddressed in many undergraduate curricula in architecture schools all over the world. Some academics and professionals still believe that contemporary architects should reject color and use only white, black, grays, and the natural finishes of materials. But not even modern architecture was all white! Contemporary materials can be fully colored (enamel glasses, painted steel, colored concrete, LED lighting technologies, et cetera), and architects cannot avoid questions of color. This book, organized in three main sections, answers most of these questions.

The first part addresses color fundamentals and provides a brief overview of color perception and color notation systems. These fundamentals underpin the many perceptual phenomena that influence design. Readers will find practical examples of how to apply these principles in everyday architectural practice. Color harmony and criteria for combining colors are also addressed, introducing readers to a grammar of color while emphasizing that breaking the rules, stretching them, or even choosing random colors might also be effective. Fortunately, there are many approaches to these topics.

The second part of the book discusses color for the architectural project. It starts with a plea to leave aside any prejudices that we might have as a consequence of misunderstanding modern architecture, which is often thought to have used white exclusively. On the contrary, color was used by renowned twentieth-century architects to emphasize their ideas—an essential strategy for our profession. Architectural color is most interesting when it is not merely applied as frivolous decoration but instead is woven perfectly into the essentials of a building: functional, constructive, formal, and aesthetic. Color can be understood from a formal and compositional point of view, leaving aside other subjective matters and reflecting on the nature of the environment, the logic of the architectural object itself, the use of the building, et cetera.

The reader will also find an overview of color and psychology. Color has inherent subjective and psychological effects that go beyond a functional understanding, and many authors have addressed this topic. It is tempting to base color choices on these effects, but architects should avoid trying to assert complete control over inhabitants' reactions and always consider the full range of compositional, artistic, formal, and aesthetic aspects of their color decisions. Nevertheless, the reader will find honest and practical ways to approach color semantics, from a cultural as well as a psychological point of view. Colors have meanings that may be learned in society, influenced by fashion, fed by mass media, or used to represent brands by architects and other designers—all of which are relevant when making color decisions.

The third part of the book provides guidance on establishing color workflow for the office. We all experience difficulties with colors that look different on-screen from how they appear once they are printed or built. Setting up accurate color management across devices, from the original concept to the final design, saves time and worry. Helpful software and hardware are explained step-by-step.

In total, readers will find an introduction to the many aspects of color as it relates to architecture, incorporating the most outstanding findings and the latest discussions on the topic. Lastly, a selected bibliography will help readers to further study the many facets of color—an inexhaustible architectural resource!

Part One

Color Basics

*Color should be used to
underline the internal laws
of the architectonic form of
the building and to make
them visible and artistic.*

Anna and Ricardo Bofill

*Physicists and chemists study the physical properties
of color....Physiologists study the workings of the
human eye and nervous system...At a certain point the
physiologists must yield to the psychologists who are
concerned with the experience of human conscious-
ness....Physical stimuli are the concern of physicists,
biological correlates are the concern of psychologists.
Color experiences are also the concern of artists and
designers. Each group is studying something different,
but all would claim to be studying "color."*

Paul Green-Armytage

1   What Is Color?

Defining color is a challenge, given that descriptions very much depend on
the discipline under discussion. Imagine trying to describe color to a blind
person. Is color a property of the materials? Sooner or later, you would probably
give an example; is it even possible to explain what the color blue is without
giving an example?

Color is a perception, the "sensation produced by light rays that strike the
visual organs and which depends on the wavelength."[1] Color perception relies
on our cognitive organs, and it is all but impossible to share an experience
that is intimately subjective. As the philosopher Ludwig Wittgenstein asked,
"How do I know that I mean the same by the words *primary colours* as some
other person?"[2]

Fig. 1.1 For color to
exist, there must be
a light source, an object,
and an observer. Part
of the light received is
absorbed by the object,
and part is reflected.
The additive mixing of
this reflected light is the
color we perceive.

1.1
Light, object, and observer

Color perception requires three protagonists: a light source,
an object, and an observer. If any of these are missing, we
cannot strictly be sure that color exists. Color is not a static
characteristic of an object but rather a relative circumstance
that depends on the lighting and the observer. If any of them
changes, color will also change. [Fig. 1.1]

Light
Without light, there is no color. We might believe that when
a room is dark, we do not perceive the real colors of objects
(if there is such a thing as a "real color"), but in fact, in that
visual situation, objects either have no color or they are black.

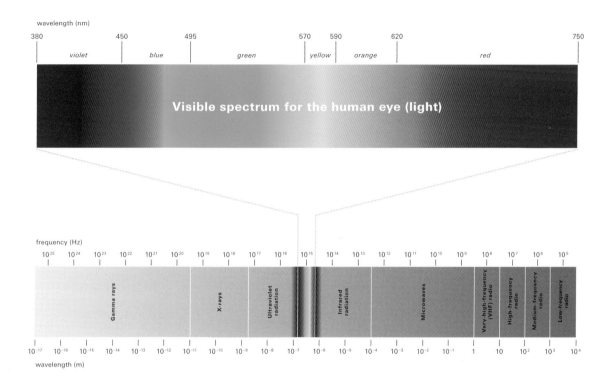

Fig. 1.2 Visible light is just a small part of the electromagnetic spectrum.

In physics, light is considered to be any kind of electromagnetic radiation that spreads in a straight line with undulating movement at the speed of 300,000 kilometers per second.[3] Only a small set of these electromagnetic wavelengths is visible to the human eye. This constitutes the **visible spectrum**, those wavelengths between approximately 400 (violet) and 700 (red) nanometers (nm), with slight variations among observers. [Fig. 1.2] Note that some animals, including cats and dogs, perceive as **visible light** wavelengths that are ultraviolet (under 400 nm), which are invisible to humans. In 1666 Sir Isaac Newton showed that when a beam of visible light passes through a prism, **dispersion** causes a rainbow to appear that includes the following spectral colors, from shorter to longer wavelengths: violet, blue, cyan, green, yellow, orange, and red. [Fig. 1.3]

Fig. 1.3 Light beam diffraction through a triangular prism

Object

When visible light strikes a surface, some wavelengths are absorbed, while the rest are reflected (or transmitted, if the material is partially transparent). The color of that material depends on the light it reflects.[4] The **spectral reflectance curve** of an object is defined as the ratio of reflected energy to incident for each wavelength of the visible spectrum. [Fig. 1.4]

Observer

Without an observer, color does not exist—only electromagnetic waves belonging to the visible spectrum drifting through space. Color is the perception by a living being of the visual light reflected off an object, which is produced on two levels: physiological (retinal) and psychological (cortical). The first depends on the physiology of the eye and visual receptors, while the second depends on the interpretation of nerve impulses received in the cortex of the brain.

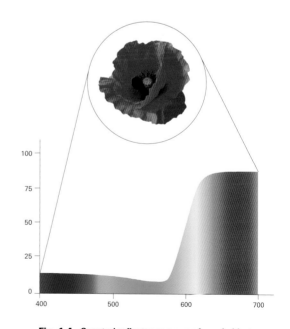

Fig. 1.4 Spectral reflectance curve of a red object

Physiology of the eye

The eye is spherical, slightly flattened from front to back. It consists of an outer white membrane called the **sclera**. The front portion of this membrane, which is transparent, is the **cornea**, through which light penetrates. [Fig. 1.5]

On the inner surface of the sclera is the **choroid**, a membrane with a system of blood vessels that irrigate the eye. The choroid's dark pigments eliminate light reflections so that the eye acts as a darkroom. The front part of the choroid is equipped with ciliary muscles that hold the **lens** in place and allow it to focus, terminating in the **iris**. The lens has a circular opening, the **pupil**, which regulates the amount of light that reaches the retina.

The **retina** is a delicate membrane that covers the inner side of the eye cavity and contains receptor cells. Immediately opposite the pupil is the **macula lutea** with its central **fovea**, a small, oval depression that is the most sensitive part of the retina. The fovea is where we have the greatest visual acuity, or ability to distinguish colors. In contrast, the point where the optic nerve joins the retina is known as the **blind spot** because it lacks photoreceptors.[5]

In the retina are two types of photosensitive cells: **cones** and **rods**. The cones are specialized for color vision, while the rods are specialized for the perception of lightness but not color (hue). [Fig. 1.6]

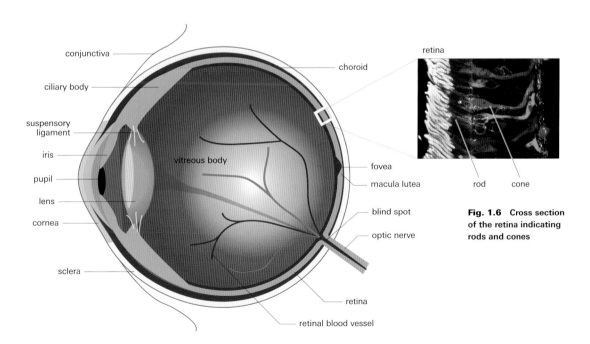

Fig. 1.6 Cross section of the retina indicating rods and cones

Fig. 1.5 Anatomy of the human eye

Rods react to low levels of radiant energy, providing **scotopic** (night) vision. The maximum spectral sensitivity of rods occurs at wavelengths that correspond to green (λ = 507 nm). This is why green lights seem a little bit clearer at night. Cones require a higher level of radiant energy to excite them, so they are involved in **photopic** (daylight) and **mesopic** (medium-light) vision but not in scotopic vision. The cones are particularly sensitive to the wavelengths corresponding to yellow (λ = 555 nm).[6]

Rods and cones are distributed unequally across the retina. The fovea, for example, contains only cones, which explains the heightened visual acuity of that area as well as the extension-contrast phenomenon—that is, that a color seems more saturated if its area is smaller and it is placed in the center of our visual campus. As we move away from the fovea, the number of cones decreases, while the number of rods increases. In the periphery of the visual field, color accuracy is low; the rods briefly capture movement, and a conditional reflex draws our gaze toward potential threats to focus and build up an accurate image in the center of our vision.

Young-Helmholtz theory

In about 1860 Thomas Young proposed the theory later developed by Hermann von Helmholtz: there are three different types of cones, each particularly sensitive to short (S), medium (M), or long (L) wavelengths, corresponding to blue, green, and red radiant energy, respectively. Every perceptible color is the result of the addition of stimuli to these three groups of receptors. Therefore, at a physiological level, we perceive color as the mixing of the stimuli of the three primary color lights, roughly equivalent to red, green, and blue (RGB) in different proportions. [Fig. 1.7]

Deficiencies in color vision

Some people suffer from glitches in any one type of cone in the retina (**dichromats**) or all three (**abnormal trichromats**). Although they are commonly known as "color blind," dichromats can be any of three types, depending on the type of cone affected: protanope (L-Red cones altered), deuteranope (M-Green cones), and tritanope (S-Blue cones).[7]

Ishihara's Test for Color Blindness and the **Farnsworth-Munsell 100 Hue Color Vision Test** are common examinations for color blindness (see Activity 1). There are exceptional cases of absolute color blindness or colorless vision (**achromatopsia**), as well as **tetrachromatia**: exceptional color vision resulting from having four different types of cones instead of three.[8]

Fig. 1.7 Spectral sensitivity curves of the cones specialized in short wavelengths/blues (S), mid wavelengths/greens (M) and long wavelengths/reds (L)

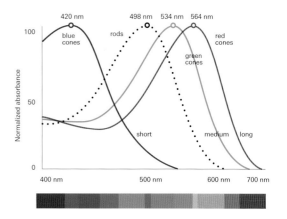

Standard observers

The Commission Internationale de l'Eclairage (International Commission on Illumination, or CIE) is the institution responsible for international recommendations for photometry and colorimetry. In 1931 the CIE standardized color management systems by specifying the light sources (illuminants), the observers, and the methodology to be used to find values for describing color in order to remove the subjective component that is part of any visual assessment.

The characterization of the human visual system was developed using psychophysical color-matching experiments to obtain the well-known **color matching functions**, or **standard observers**. The standard observers represent the color vision of the majority of people under specified observation conditions.

The CIE defined two different standard observers. The Standard Observer 2° (CIE 1931) specifies the color stimuli in a visual campus less than 4 degrees from the position of the observer, and the Standard Observer 10° (CIE 1964) for color stimuli more than 4 degrees from the observer. [Fig. 1.8] To give an idea of the size of each visual field, with a viewing distance of 19 3/4 in. (50 cm), the field corresponding to 2° would be a circle with a diameter of 2/3 in. (1.7 cm), while the field corresponding to 10° would be a circle with a diameter of 3 1/2 in. (8.8 cm). The distinction between these two observers is rooted in the heterogeneous structure of the human retina, in which the photoreceptors (rods and cones) are not evenly distributed: cones are concentrated around the foveal region, as mentioned previously.

So for small colored objects, the observer CIE 1931 (2°) is used, and for large colored objects, the CIE 1964 (10°) is used. Their color-matching functions are designated as [x (λ), y (λ), z (λ)] and [x_{10} (λ), y_{10} (λ), z_{10} (λ)], respectively. They represent the sensitivity of the human eye and provide the **tristimulus values** of a color (see section 2.3). [Fig. 1.9]

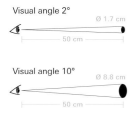

Fig. 1.8 Visual angles for the CIE Standard Observers

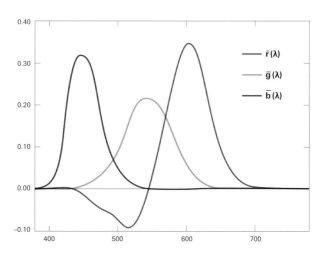

Fig. 1.9 Color matching functions corresponding to Standard Observers CIE XYZ 1931 (2°)

Standard illuminant or light source

Using physical measures, it is possible to characterize light sources by their **spectral power distribution**, E(A), for each of the wavelengths of the visible spectrum.

Illuminants with standardized spectral distributions are known as **standard illuminants**. Some of the most common are Illuminant A (incandescent), Illuminant C (direct sunlight), Illuminant D (indirect sunlight), and Illuminant F2 (white fluorescent light). The names in the daylight series start with a capital letter *D* followed by two numbers that indicate the approximate color temperature. D65 is the standard illuminant for color recognition in outdoor architecture (similar to natural lighting conditions on a cloudy day), with a color temperature of 6,500 K (see section 1.5). [Fig. 1.10] [Table 1.1]

Table 1.1
CIE Standard Illuminants

Name	Description
A	Incandescent filament light
B	Daylight at sunset
C	Direct light outside (without UV)
D	Outside indirect lighting (with UV)
E	Theoretical equal-energy illuminant used to calculate color (similar to D50)
F	Fluorescent
D50	Average lighting at midday in western Europe (standard for graphic arts)
D65	Average lighting at midday in western Europe (including UV, standard for architecture and photography)

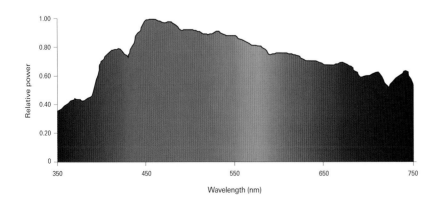

Fig. 1.10 Spectral potency distribution E(A) for the standard illuminant D65

1.2
Variables that perceptually describe color:
hue, value, and saturation

Hue, or tint or tone, corresponds to the dominant wavelength of the physical stimulus—namely, the color attribute that distinguishes a yellow from an orange or green.[9] **Value**, or clarity or lightness, indicates how light or dark the color is. It depends on the amount of radiant energy of the stimulus as well as the retinal nerve structure. Often, the term *lightness* is confused with brightness.[10] **Saturation**, or chroma, is the intensity of the perceived color. It ranges from gray (minimum saturation) to the maximum purity that can be achieved for the same hue (maximum saturation). We commonly use the word *vivid* to describe a saturated color. [Fig. 1.11]

Fig. 1.11 Variables to describe color: hue, value, and saturation

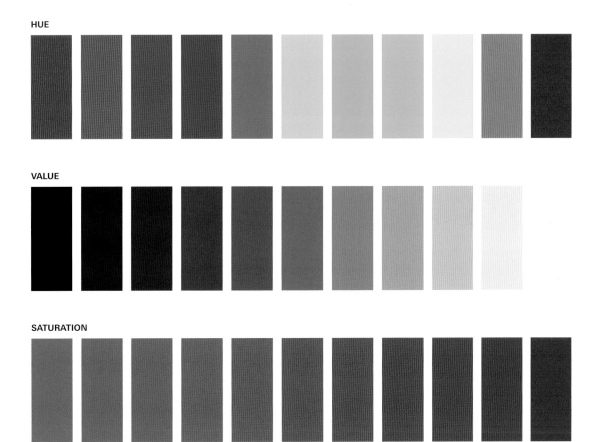

HUE

VALUE

SATURATION

1.3
Primary, secondary, and tertiary colors

Primary colors

The **primary**, or fundamental, colors are the three colors that can be mixed to obtain all the remaining colors of the visible spectrum. The primary colors of light are red, green, and blue (RGB), and combining them is called **additive mixing**. If the three primary **color-lights** overlap, the result is white light. We can say that we are "adding light to light"—that is, adding radiant energy at different wavelengths to rebuild a complete light beam containing energy throughout the whole visible spectrum. A beam of light that is broken down into the separate colors of the rainbow when passed through a prism (dispersion) is recomposed by adding lights.

The **primary material colors** (pigments and paints) are cyan, magenta, and yellow (CMY), and combining them is called **subtractive mixing**.[11] Mixing the three primary **color-pigments** results in black. A cyan surface absorbs more or less all the radiant energy reaching it except within the range of short wavelengths (S); yellow absorbs all but the medium wavelengths (M); and red absorbs all but the long wavelengths (L). When all three primary color-pigments are mixed, a surface appears black, as it absorbs all the visible light it receives. [Fig. 1.12]

While these three primary colors (cyan, magenta, and yellow) are used in printing systems, artists have traditionally used red-vermilion, blue-ultramarine, and yellow as the primary colors. [Fig. 1.13] These three primary colors form the basis of the history of painting in the West. As noted by professor Ángela García Codoñer:

> A magenta falls far short of the expressive possibilities and warmth of a red vermilion,
> not to mention the depth and gravity of the dark background of ultramarine blue.[12]

Fig. 1.12 Primary and secondary colors for additive mixing (lights) and subtractive mixing (pigments)

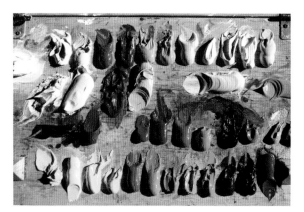

Fig. 1.13 Subtractive primary colors (cyan and magenta) are not typically used in painting; these are more typical pigments:
1. lemon yellow
2. cadmium yellow
3. vermilion red
4. carmine red

Fig. 1.14
Color wheel based on Johannes Itten's color theory

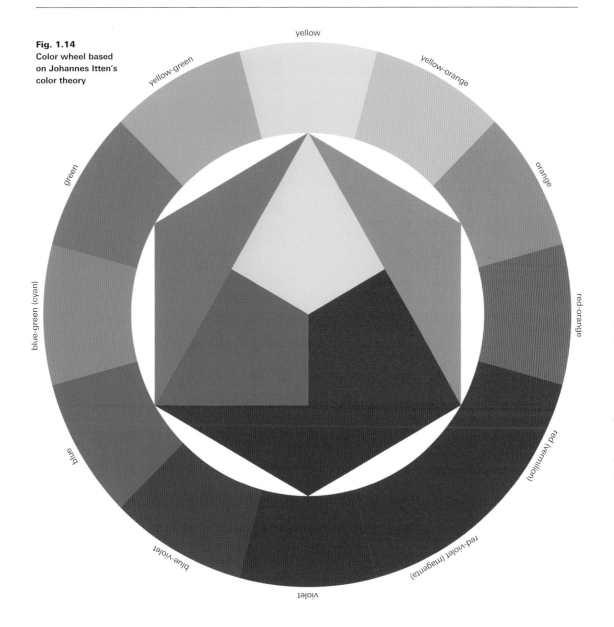

Swiss painter Johannes Itten built a very useful **color wheel** in 1961, using subtractive color mixing based on the red, blue, and yellow primary colors (which he had taught in the first year of the degree course in architecture at the Bauhaus design school in Germany).[13] A color wheel is a two-dimensional representation of the primary and secondary colors at maximum saturation levels. [Fig. 1.14]

Secondary colors

Secondary colors (orange, green, and violet in color-pigments) come from mixing two primary colors. A secondary color's shade will be closer to one or the other of its primary colors, depending on the proportion of each. For example, adding more red than yellow produces a reddish orange secondary color.

Tertiary colors

Tertiary colors contain a mix of all three primary colors in different proportions and correspond to a range of brown and gray colors. They generally lack lightness and saturation. [Fig. 1.15] Within these ranges of tertiary colors are the earth tones: reddish earth colors are obtained by mixing violet and orange, yellowish earth colors by mixing orange and green, and greenish earth colors by mixing green and violet.

1.4
Warm and cool colors

Warm colors are those close to red (yellowish green, yellow, yellowish orange, orange, reddish orange, red, reddish purple), and cool colors are close to blue on the color wheel (purple, bluish purple, blue, bluish green, green). There are transition zones in the areas of greens and purples where hues can belong to both groups. [Figs. 1.16, 1.17]

When mixing paint, it is worth noting that the red, blue, and yellow primary colors can produce very different results depending on whether the pigment used is warmer or cooler. Thus, red-vermilion, which is warm, provides a very good range of oranges but not violets and at best a range of uncertain browns. For violets, it is best to use a red-carmine, which is slightly cool, and lemon yellow is much cooler than the warm cadmium yellow or yellow-gold.

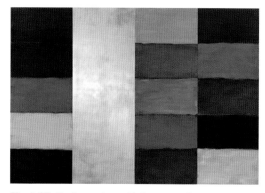

Fig. 1.15 Tertiary colors with low saturation: Sean Scully, *Landbar*, 2009, oil on aluminum, 110 × 160 in. (279 × 406 cm)

Fig. 1.16 Composition in cool hues: Claude Monet, *Wheatstack*, 1890–91

Fig. 1.17 Composition in warm hues: Claude Monet, *Wheatstack*, 1891

1.5
Color temperature of light sources

The concept of a color being warm or cool is different from the **color temperature** of a light source. The latter refers to the chromatic appearance of an illuminant.

Color temperature is measured in Kelvin degrees (K). It refers to the temperature to which a theoretical body, known as the **black body**, would need to be heated to emit light with a similar color appearance. Lower color temperatures mean yellowish lights or warm hues (less than 3.500 K is considered warm lighting); a higher color temperature means bluish lights or cool hues (more than 4.500 K is considered cool lighting).[14] In the technical specifications of lamps, **correlated color temperature** (CCT) indicates color temperature, providing a measure for color appearance (see section 6.2). [Table 1.2]

Table 1.2
Color temperature, warmth, and camera setting for lighting sources

Typical lighting source	Temperature (K)	Warmth	Camera setting
Candles, oil lamps	1,000		
Very early dawn, tungsten lamps	2,000		
Incandescent lamps	2,500		
Study light (continuous), "photo floods"	3,000		
Magnesium lamps (obsolete)	4,000		
Daylight, electronic flash	5,000		
Midday sunlight	5,500		
Very sunny day with clear sky	6,000		
Slightly cloudy sky	7,000		
Foggy sky	8,000		
Wide shadows on a sunny day	9,000		
Very foggy sky	10,000		
Blue sky without sun	11,000		
Wide shadows in the mountains or a very clear day	20,000		

1.6
Complementary colors

Complementary colors appear opposite each other on Itten's color wheel. The complement of each primary color is made by mixing the other two primary colors. [Fig. 1.21] [Table 1.3]

There are contradictory advantages to pairing complementary colors. On the one hand, juxtaposing two complementary colors increases their saturation and forces them to compete. This effect might feel uncomfortable during long viewing times, particularly with red/green pairs. On the other hand, complementary colors are necessary for balance in composition, particularly when an almost monochromatic hue family dominates a design; a complementary color brings harmony to the vision.

Each pair of complementary colors has its own characteristics. Yellow/violet compositions contain not only a complementary hue contrast but also a very pronounced light/dark contrast, while red/green pairings seem to have the same value. Therefore, to avoid visual fatigue, when they are juxtaposed, it is best not to use them in equal proportions (see section 4.2). A composition pairing red-orange and blue is complementary and also expresses the strongest degree of warm/cool contrast. [Figs. 1.18, 1.19]

Table 1.3
Complementary colors

Primary	Complementary
red	green (blue + yellow)
blue	orange (red + yellow)
yellow	violet (blue + red)

Fig. 1.18 Main pairs of complementary colors

Fig. 1.19
Complementary color contrasts of orange-blue and red-green emphasize their saturation: Henri Matisse, *The Dance*, 1909, oil on canvas, 103 3/8 × 154 in. (260 × 391 cm)

Activity 1
Color Vision and Color Discrimination

Color-vision deficiencies

For a typical observer, three primary colors (suitably chosen) are necessary and sufficient to match (**metamerize**) the visual effect produced by any wavelength of the visible spectrum. This principle of **trichromacy** holds true for any observer with standard color vision. But one out of every 12 males and one out of every 255 females is affected by some form of color deficiency. Some observers require the three primary colors but employ them in different quantities than those of a standard observer when color matching. The name given to these observers is **anomalous trichromats**. If the observer requires only two primary colors to match any wavelength of the visible spectrum, they are known as **dichromats**. And lastly, **monochromats** can do the same task using a single primary color, simply by adjusting the intensity. These variations are related to the presence or absence of the three different specialized cones in the retina.

Two further types of functional criteria are used to classify inherited color-vision disorders. The first of these is qualitative, with the prefixes *prot-*, *deuter-*, and *trit-*, indicating the type of mix-up the observer tends to make. The second is quantitative and refers to the degree or severity of the disorder, from mild to severe.

Both protanomalies and deuteranomalies affect the red/green axis of color perception, whereas the tritanomalies affect the yellow/blue axis. Daltonism, named after the English scientist John Dalton (1766–1844), refers to inherited color-vision disorders that affect the red/green mechanism, including protanomaly and deuteranomaly, regardless of their severity. Protanopes, protanomalies, deuteranopes, and deuteranomalies are the four types of Daltonism. There are also rare cases of achromatopsia, or total color blindness.

1   Check if you have visual deficiencies using **Ishihara's Test for Color Blindness** with twenty-four plates.

The Ishihara test helps to identify dichromatism (Daltonism). It presents compositions made up of twenty-four circles of varying color and size. Within each is a number that is visible for those with standard vision but invisible or difficult to see for those who are protanopes or deuteranopes. [Fig. 1.20] Note that online videos and images are just a visual approximation of Ishihara's reliable printed plates.

(See page 232 for answers to the plates above.)

Fig. 1.20 Examples of Ishihara plates for testing for color blindness, developed by Shinobu Ishihara, 1917–59

Ishihara's color vision test:
http://www.dfisica.ubi.pt/~hgil/p.v.2/Ishihara
/Ishihara.24.Plate.TEST.Book.pdf

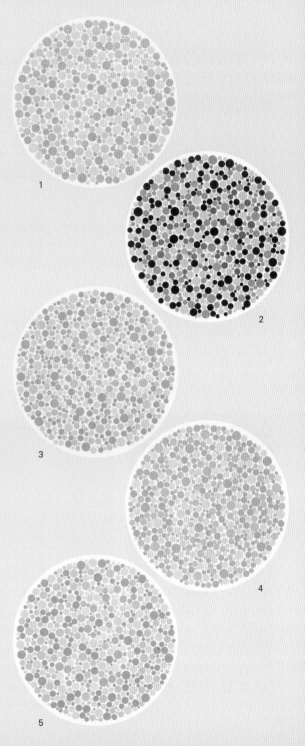

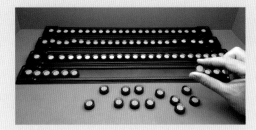

**Fig. 1.21 Farnsworth-Munsell
100 Hue Color Vision Test**

 http://xritephoto.com/cool-tools

2 Test your ability to distinguish among colors and your degree of color-vision deficiency using the **Farnsworth-Munsell 100 Hue Color Vision Test** (FM 100 Hue Test).

This test measures the visual assessment capacity of individuals and is widely used in jobs where accurate color control is needed. The test consists of four rows with twenty-three physical color swatches covering the full range of the Munsell color scale (see section 2.4). The observer orders the swatches from one hue to another under controlled lighting; a daylight-balanced light or an equivalent D65 in a viewing booth is necessary. The original FM-100 Hue Test includes user-friendly scoring software with graphs and charts that provide an at-a-glance determination of the observer's color-vision capability. [Fig. 1.21]

There is an approximate online version of this test hosted by X-Rite, the company that merchandises the original, physical FM-100 Hue Test. Note that the results of this online version are not reliable.

3 How would the colors of a building appear to an observer with a color deficiency?

There are many situations in which we want to be particularly careful with the colors of our designs, given that these can determine the accurate perception or legibility of spaces, typefaces, et cetera.

Open any color image in Adobe Photoshop CS software and select **View > Proof Adjustments > Daltonism** to view how it would be seen by a dichromat with protanope or deuteranope color deficiencies. [Fig. 1.22]

**Fig. 1.22 Comparison
of how observers with
normal and deficient color
vision would perceive
the same building:
Jean Nouvel, Agbar Tower,
Barcelona, 2005**

Metameric Colors

Two colors are said to be metameres when they are perceived as the same under certain lighting conditions but different under others because they have different spectral reflectance curves. [Fig. 1.23]

What are the colors of this dress? On February 26, 2015, a user of the social networking service Tumblr raised an unusual polemic on the internet as people strongly disagreed over whether the colors of a dress in a posted photograph were black and blue or white and gold. Some people reported being able to see both colors at different times or even to be able to swap the colors of the dress at will. #Thedress began trending on Twitter, along with related hashtags, and in the first week after the image surfaced, more than ten million tweets mentioned the dress.[15]

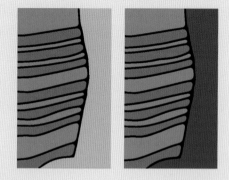

Fig. 1.23 What are the colors of this dress? Depending on lighting conditions, colors seem to shift from blue and black to white and gold. The proper standard illuminant for color recognition is D65, similar to sunlight conditions on a cloudy day.

1   In a viewing booth such as the CAC 60 VeriVide, check the perceptual stability of target colors selected from the Natural Color System atlas (see section 2.4) by changing the illuminant (D65, TL84, UV). Try to find a pair of metameres. [Fig. 1.24] For reference, see the study by Eduardo Cordero et al. that shows which samples of the NCS atlas are perceptually more unstable under changes in illuminant.[16] [Table 1.4]

Fig. 1.24 Spectral
reflectance graph for two
metameric colors

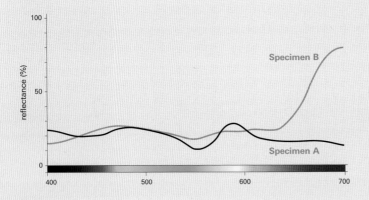

**Standard Illuminant D65
(Daylight)**

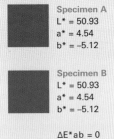

Specimen A
L* = 50.93
a* = 4.54
b* = –5.12

Specimen B
L* = 50.93
a* = 4.54
b* = –5.12

ΔE*ab = 0

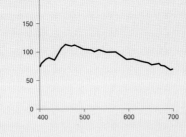

**Standard Illuminant A
(Incandescent)**

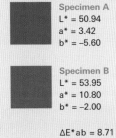

Specimen A
L* = 50.94
a* = 3.42
b* = –5.60

Specimen B
L* = 53.95
a* = 10.80
b* = –2.00

ΔE*ab = 8.71

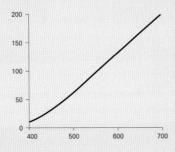

**Table 1.4
The ten most stable
and unstable colors
from NCS Color Atlas
under changed illu-
mination, according
to CIECAM02-UCS
formula**

Most Stable Colors	
NCS Notation	CIECAM02-UCS Dif.
S 9000-N	17.91
S 8505-R80B	19.43
S 8505-B20G	19.43
S 8502-G	19.77
S 8500-N	19.80
S 8502-R	19.85
S 8505-Y80R	19.90
S 8502-B	19.94
S 8505-B80G	20.03
S 8505-R20B	20.03

Most Unstable Colors	
NCS Notation	CIECAM02-UCS Dif.
S 0580-Y	42.01
S 0575-G90Y	41.39
S 0575-G70Y	41.22
S 0575-G60Y	41.05
S 0580-Y10R	40.94
S 0570-G80Y	40.92
S 0570-G70Y	40.87
S 0570-G90Y	40.66
S 1080-Y	40.61
S 1075-G70Y	40.46

Activity 3

Test: Color Basics

1 What we call **visible light** or the **visible spectrum** is only a small segment of the gamut of electromagnetic radiation. For humans this range spans the wavelengths (λ) between approximately 390 and 750 nm. These colors are…
a the subtractive primary colors: cyan, magenta, and yellow.
b the additive primary colors: red, green, and blue.
c the colors of the rainbow, which we call violet, blue, cyan, green, yellow, orange, and red.
d the full range of colors we can see, which are reduced to 360 (750–390).

2 Which of the following sentences is true?
a Color is a stable characteristic of an object.
b Color is independent of an illuminant.
c All people perceive the same colors.
d Color depends on light, object, and observer.

3 When visible light strikes an object…
a a part is refracted, a part dispersed, and a part sublimated.
b a part is reflected, a part is absorbed, and a part can be transmitted.
c all of it is reflected, absorbed, or transmitted.
d all of it is reflected.

4 If I see a green object, it is because…
a the object reflects the intermediate wavelengths (M), which are those corresponding to green, and absorbs all other wavelengths of electromagnetic radiation (S and L).
b the object absorbs electromagnetic radiation corresponding to the intermediate wavelengths (M), which are those corresponding to green, and reflects the short wavelengths (S) and long wavelengths (L), corresponding to blue and red.
c the object reflects the wavelengths corresponding to yellow and blue electromagnetic radiation.
d the object reflects the wavelengths corresponding to green (M) and red (L) electromagnetic radiation.

5 The additive primary colors, or color-lights, are…
a red, blue, and yellow.
b cyan, magenta, and yellow.
c red, green, and blue.
d The statement is incorrect: the additive primary colors are color-pigments.

6 The subtractive primary colors, or color-pigments, are…
a red, blue, and yellow.
b cyan, magenta, and yellow.
c red, blue, and green.
d The statement is incorrect: the subtractive primary colors are color-lights.

7 If I illuminate a white surface with green- and red-colored lights, I will see…
a yellow.
b brown.
c cyan.
d blue.

8 If I mix yellow and cyan pigments, I will see…
a green, under green-light illumination.
b something approximating brown, under red-light illumination.
c green, under white-light illumination.
d All of the above.

9 Colors perceived as the same under certain lighting conditions but which seem different in others are called…
a complementary.
b dissimilar.
c metameres.
d nonconforming.

10 With regard to the specialized cells in the retinal vision…
a the rods, involved in night vision, are most highly concentrated around the fovea.
b both cones and rods are equally distributed in the retina.
c cells that are specialized to identify colors are called "rods."
d according to the Young-Helmholtz theory, cones are specialized in the vision of short wavelengths (S-blue), medium (M-green), and long (L-red).

(See page 232 for answers.)

2 Naming Colors

The need for a rational method of sorting colors and accurately communicating their characteristics has led to the development of a number of different color notation systems.

In the fields of physics and optics, the most important color notation systems have been established by the Commission Internationale de l'Éclairage (International Commission on Illumination, or CIE) and define what may be called **color spaces**. Architects and other designers and artists typically work with color notation systems based on the three psychometric (perceptual) variables: hue, saturation, and value, with color swatches organized in order in a **color atlas**. The various systems describe any color with three attributes; it is therefore possible to plot the colors in three dimensions and obtain a **color solid**. The geometry of this solid depends on the colors selected as primary colors, their location in the color wheel, and their progression. A color notation system that works with primary color-lights (and therefore with additive color mixing) is different from one that works with primary color-pigments (subtractive color mixing).

2.1
RGB: additive mixing and color-light

RGB is an acronym of the three primary colors of light: red, green, and blue, which approximate the primary colors of color perception according to retinal level or the trichromatic theory of Young-Helmholtz (see section 1.1).

Fig. 2.1 Distribution geometry of the three primary lighting colors (RGB) in different displays (clockwise from top left): CRT television, CRT computer monitor, OLPC XO-1 LCD screen, and a LCD of a laptop monitor Lenovo X61

RGB is a suitable color space for images meant to be viewed on-screen (web pages, et cetera), where for each cell there are three phosphors corresponding to each of these three primary colors. Their values depend on the color depth of the image. [Fig. 2.1]

Color depth of an image / bits per pixel

Color depth is the number of bits of information that are used to record the color of a single pixel in a digital image. When referring to a pixel, the concept can be defined as bits per pixel (bpp); when referring to a color component, bits per channel (bpc). A bit depth n implies 2^n possible intensity values.

In a monochromatic image, just one channel describes each pixel; therefore, an 8-bit image contains 256 possible shades of gray. Color images in RGB have three channels to describe each pixel that correlate to each of the three primary color-lights: red, green, and blue. This format of 24-bit RGB (8 bits per channel) is the most common color depth for digital devices and is called True Color because of its similarity to what humans perceive. In 32-bit images, three channels are used to describe the color, and a fourth alpha channel is added to set the opacity of the pixel. This color space is called RGBA. [Table 2.1]

Table 2.1
Number of colors in an image based on the number of bits

Image Bits	Number of colors
8 bits (per pixel) = 8 bits × 1 channel	2^8 = 256 (gray scale)
24 bits (per pixel) = 8 bits × 3 channels	2^{24} = 256 × 256 × 256 = 16.7 million (True Color)
32 bits (per pixel) = 8 bits × 4 channels	2^{32} = 256 × 256 × 256 × 256 = 4,294.9 million (RGBA)

Hexadecimal color coding

Nine digits are used to indicate the color of a pixel in RGB coding: three for R, three for G, and three for B, each with a value between 0 and 255. Hexadecimal color coding makes it easier to express a particular RGB color in HTML and JavaScript, using six digits instead of nine. This system expresses the different intensities of the primary RGB colors with a combination of numbers and letters. In addition to the numbers from 0 to 9, six letters are used, each representing a numerical value: a = 10, b = 11, c = 12, d = 13, e = 14, and f = 15. The following formula expresses the correspondence between hexadecimal and decimal numbers:

decimal notation = (16 × 1st digit of hex. notation) + 2nd digit of hex. notation[1]

2.2
CMYK: subtractive mixing and color-pigment

CMYK corresponds to the initials of the three primary colors
for subtractive mixing (cyan, magenta, and yellow), to which a
black ink (K) is added. It is the standard color notation for offset
printing and therefore for the realm of printed paper. [Fig. 2.2]
A color is described using the dithering percentage of each
of these primary tints and is expressed either as a percentage
or with a value from 0 to 1.

2.3
CIE color spaces: XYZ, xyY, Lab, LCh

The CIE is responsible for international recommendations
for photometry and colorimetry; since 1931 it has developed
standards for color systems based on light source, observer,
and descriptive methodology.

CIE XYZ (1931)

The values X, Y, and Z, known as **tristimulus** color values, represent amounts
of a certain primary color that produce the color we want to specify using
additive mixing.

From a practical perspective, the devices known as spectrophotometers
provide us with these values directly. While the CIE tristimulus values (X, Y, Z)
accurately describe the color of an object, they give no clue about its visual
appearance. Only the color value Y represents the luminance of the color,
which directly relates to its perceived brightness or amount of light. Tristimulus
values for any color are obtained by multiplying:

1 The data of a standard CIE illuminant
   (the amount of light in every wavelength emitted by the illuminant)
2 The values of the spectral reflectance curve of the object
   (the amount of reflected light in each wavelength)
3 The color-matching function of the standard observer used
   (the human sensitivity in every wavelength).

In short, we can specify the color using three numbers, XYZ, where the
computation of three factors are involved: light source, object, and human
response.

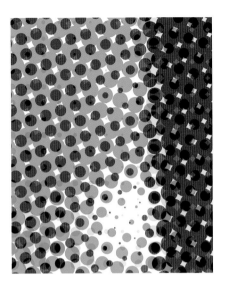

Fig. 2.2 Distribution
geometry of the three
primary pigment colors
(CMY) in a printed work

Fig. 2.3 CIE xyY (1931)
Chromaticity Diagram

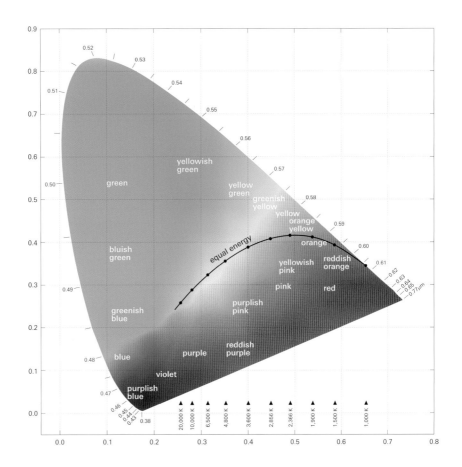

CIE xyY (1931) chromaticity diagram

The CIE defined other expressions (called **chromaticity coordinates**) that give information about the perceived hue, saturation, and brightness of a color. The values x and y refer to the chromaticity of the color (hue and saturation), while Y describes its brightness. Plotting the x and y coordinates of all the spectral colors on a graph creates a curve similar in shape to a tongue—what is known as the CIE chromaticity diagram. [Fig. 2.3]

The main drawback of this system is that it does not describe a visually uniform space. The numerical distance between any two colors' coordinates in the diagram is not a reliable measure of their difference in appearance. In other words, two pairs of colors with the same geometric distance might have perceptual differences of different magnitudes, depending on the area of the chromaticity diagram in which they are located.

MacAdam ellipses

MacAdam ellipses (or ellipsoids of discrimination) are those regions of the chromaticity diagram in which the human eye cannot distinguish surrounding colors from the color in its center. American physicist and color scientist David MacAdam obtained these ellipses in 1931 using twenty-five color patterns that observers had to match with other colors, given specific lighting conditions. [Fig. 2.4] The dimensions of these ellipsoids vary; they are larger in green areas than in red or blue. Therefore, our color discrimination is less accurate in green (M) wavelengths.

Over time, CIE has proposed other, more uniform color spaces, such as the CIE Lab color space.

CIE Lab (1976)

The color spaces initially defined by the CIE did not easily correspond to human perception. As mentioned previously, the distance between two colors plotted in the chromaticity diagram (x, y), for instance, is not equal to a similar perceptual difference in real stimuli, so they

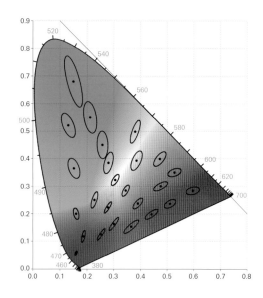

Fig. 2.4 MacAdam ellipses on the chromaticity diagram

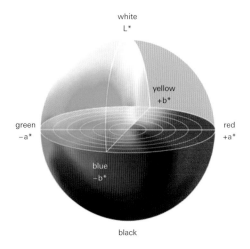

Fig. 2.5 CIE Lab color space

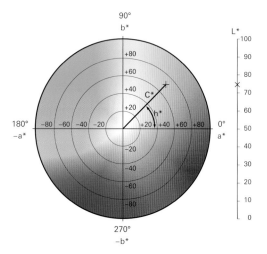

Fig. 2.6 CIE Lab color wheel showing the LCh coordinates

are not visually uniform. The perceptual dissimilarity between two colors plotted in the chromaticity diagram is uneven. To address this, the CIE proposed in 1976 the space CIE Lab, which is more similar to visual perception. In CIE Lab, the perceptual difference between two colors can be easily calculated by measuring the geometric distance between them. CIE Lab is a Euclidian, uniform color space and is widely used as a standard. Later formulas have improved on CIE Lab's evaluation of color difference, such as the DIN99 formula and the CIEDE2000, but these systems are based on calculations that are not as simple as Euclidian distance.[2]

CIE Lab is a three-dimensional space, where the L* coordinate represents lightness by a value of 0 for black and 100 for white; coordinates a* and b* represent chromaticity. [Fig. 2.5] The coordinate a* indicates the red(+) / green(–) content, while b* indicates the yellow(+) / blue(–) content. The range of values for a* and b* will depend on the specific implementation of Lab color, with 0 corresponding to the gray or achromatic colors. [Fig. 2.6]

Despite the regular, spherical shape of the CIE Lab space, if we represent the visible colors in CIE Lab, those usual for a standard observer under specific lighting (i.e., illuminant D50), an irregular solid is drawn, representing the **Lab gamut** for real colors. This solid is obtained mathematically by transforming the tristimulus values *XYZ* through a formula described by the CIE.

In image-editing programs such as Adobe Photoshop, L* values cover the range [0, 100], but the range for coding components a*, b* is restricted to [–128, 127] in 8-bit integer encoding. Therefore, not all visible Lab colors can be encoded using this scheme. [Fig. 2.7] Even when 16-bit values are used instead of 8-bit, the extra bits are used to make finer divisions between values rather than to extend the range of values. In addition, much of the available encoding space—about two-thirds of it—is wasted because these Lab values can never occur in real vision.[3]

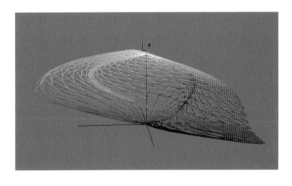

Fig. 2.7 Visible colors gamut represented in CIE Lab color space

CIE LCh (1976)

CIE LCh is similar to the CIE Lab color space. While CIE Lab uses Cartesian coordinates to locate the colors, the CIE LCh uses polar coordinates. The L* [0, 100] component defines the lightness; C* [0, 100] specifies the chroma, which is the distance from the center of the sphere to the target color; and h* [0, 359] indicates the color hue, measured as an angle in decimal degrees. CIE LCh offers an advantage over CIE Lab, as it is easily correlated with other perceptual color notation systems based on painted plates, such as the Munsell Color Scale.[4]

2.4
Color atlases: NCS, Munsell, Pantone, RAL

A color atlas is a collection of physical samples made from a consistent material and organized in a specific sequence. Color atlases are used in architecture and design offices because they are handy references for color combinations, as the visual difference between two adjacent samples of an atlas is always perceptually the same.[5] Nevertheless, they have three major drawbacks:

Fig. 2.8 NCS Natural Color System color wheel, indicating the hue R90B

1   Printed atlases fade over time.
2   They must always be viewed under the same lighting condition to avoid metamerism.
3   They have a limited number of examples, and sometimes it is impossible to find an exact match to the color sought.

Some of the most important color atlases for architecture are NCS in Europe and Munsell in the United States. Pantone is also widely used but more common in graphic arts.

NCS Natural Color System

The NCS Natural Color System was developed in Sweden in 1979 and currently consists of about fifteen hundred to two thousand color samples. The geometry of the NCS color solid is a double inverted cone, where colors are ordered according to three attributes: **hue, blackness,** and **chromaticness**.[6]

NCS is based on the color opponent hypothesis of the German psychologist Ewald Hering (1834–1918) and was developed by the Swedish scientific researchers Anders Hård and Lars Sivik in the 1980s. According to Hering, our perception of color is organized around three pairs of opposed colors: green/red, yellow/blue, and black/white. Therefore, it is impossible for us to perceive, for example, a greenish red or a yellowish blue, as these color pairs are located at opposite positions within the NCS color solid. [Fig. 2.8]

A color in NCS can be written as, for example, S 4030-R90B. The *S* refers to a standard NCS color contained in the atlas. The first four digits describe the **NCS nuance** of a color, with the first

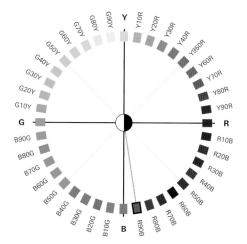

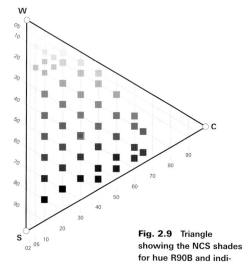

Fig. 2.9 Triangle showing the NCS shades for hue R90B and indicating the position of color NCS S4030-R90B

two (40) representing the blackness of the color and the second two (30) its chromaticness. The code after the dash (R90B) identifies the hue. [Fig. 2.9]

The **NCS hue scale** is circular and is organized around four basic or elementary colors: yellow (Y), red (R), blue (B), green (G). A color R90B is composed of 10 percent red and 90 percent blue.

The **NCS blackness scale** relates to the amount of black, ranging between two extremes: 0 (minimum blackness) and 100 (maximum blackness). The **NCS whiteness** is not specified in NCS, but may be obtained using the following formula:

whiteness = 100 − (blackness + chromaticness)

The whiteness of the color NCS S 4030-R90B is 30 percent. *Blackness* and *whiteness* are specific terms used in the NCS atlas and are slightly different from the terms *lightness* and *darkness* used in other color notation systems.[7] Blackness and whiteness express the visual similarity to the elementary black and white, and the lack of vividness or distance of a color from the ideal pure chromatic hue.[8]

The **NCS chromaticness scale** expresses how strong the color is, ranging between two extremes: 0 (minimum chromaticness or gray) and 100 (maximum chromaticness). It approximately but not exactly correlates to the perceptual **saturation** of a color.[9]

Munsell Book of Color

Albert H. Munsell (1858–1918) designed his own color atlas at the beginning of the twentieth century, using physical painted targets that were displayed according to their perceptual difference. Thus, this color system is not based on the physical attributes of color but on the perceptual ones, with three variables: **hue, value,** and **chroma** [H, V, C]. An example of Munsell color notation is 5YR 5/8.[10]

The hue scale is circular and is divided into five main colors (clockwise): red (R), yellow (Y), green (G), blue (B), and purple (P). The Munsell atlas consists of forty different hue color charts or **hue families**. Intermediate hues use the initials of the two nearest main colors; for example, oranges are denoted YR (mixture of yellow and red). [Fig. 2.10]

The **value scale** indicates the brightness of a color, or the amount of light of a sample; it ranges from 1 (minimum whiteness) to 9 (maximum whiteness). [Fig. 2.11]

The **chroma scale** refers to the saturation of the samples. Achromatic samples (grays) are located near the vertical axis of the color solid, while the most chromatic ones are at the edge, with values ranging from 0 (gray) to 26 (maximum saturation).

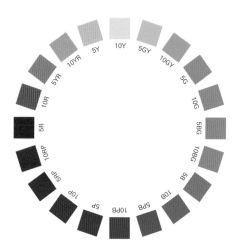

Fig. 2.10
Munsell color circle

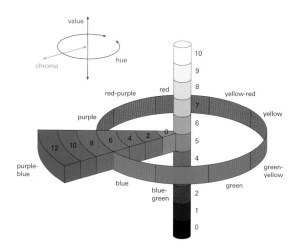

Fig. 2.11
Munsell color system

When Munsell colors are arranged in three dimensions, they form an irregular solid. [Fig. 2.12] Achromatic colors are arranged on the vertical or **neutral axis**, with a range of grays from black at the bottom to white at the top. The bigger the distance from the neutral axis, the higher the chroma of a color. This distance varies for color **values** and **hue** families, and so the solid is irregular. This is because humans perceive the different hues to inherently have different chroma and value, and the Munsell system relies on visual perception.

The Pantone Color Language

The Pantone Color Language supports the textile, apparel, beauty, interiors, and architectural and industrial design industries, encompassing over ten thousand color standards across multiple materials, including printing inks, textiles, plastics, pigments, and coatings. The Pantone Matching System (PMS) gives designers around the world a common language to promote accurate and consistent specification and production of spot color for print and packaging design.[11]

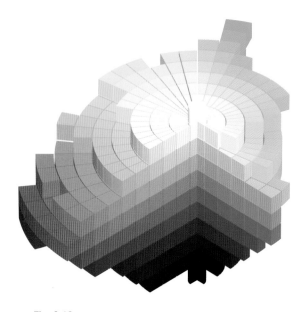

Fig. 2.12
Munsell color solid

RAL color atlas

The RAL system was defined by the Deutsches Institut für und Kennzeichnung Gütesicherung in Germany in 1927. Its initials are an acronym for the German words meaning "Quality Assurance Association." Its use in industry is widespread, particularly by metal manufacturers. [Table 2.2]

Table 2.2
Ranges of colors in RAL notation

Range	Range Name	First	Last	No.
RAL 1xxx	Yellow	RAL 1000 Green Beige	RAL 1037 Sun Yellow	40
RAL 2xxx	Orange	RAL 2000 Yellow Orange	RAL 2013 Pearl Orange	14
RAL 3xxx	Red	RAL 3000 Fire Red	RAL 3033 Pearl Pink	34
RAL 4xxx	Violet	RAL 4001 Red Purple	RAL 4012 Pearl Black Berry	12
RAL 5xxx	Blue	RAL 5000 Violet Blue	RAL 5026 Pearl Night Blue	25
RAL 6xxx	Green	RAL 6000 Patina Green	RAL 6038 Luminous Green	36
RAL 7xxx	Gray	RAL 7000 Squirrel Gray	RAL 7048 Pearl Mouse Gray	38
RAL 8xxx	Brown	RAL 8000 Green Brown	RAL 8029 Pearl Copper	20
RAL 9xxx	White/Black	RAL 9001 Cream	RAL 9023 Pearl Dark Gray	14

2.5
Conversion among color systems

The swatches of most color atlases are translated into digital color-light notations on their respective websites, but RGB, sRGB, and digital Lab color spaces depend on the digital visualization device used and might not be consistent. Although they can be used for rough visualization, there might be a significant perceptual difference from the physical painted atlas.

- NCS Navigator translates NCS into RGB, HEX, and Lab;[12] an NCS translation key into Munsell also exists.[13]
- Pantone is translated into RGB, HEX, and CMYK in the color libraries of Photoshop and some web pages.[14]
- RAL is provided in Munsell and other color spaces.[15]
- Munsell color tables are available for HVC, XYZ, Lab, and RGB.[16]

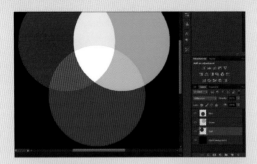

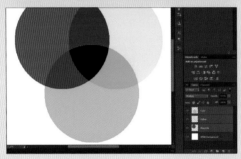

Figs. 2.13 and 2.14 Layers panel in
Adobe Photoshop CS with color layers
prepared for additive pigment mixing (top)
and subtractive light mixing (bottom)

Activity 4

Additive and Subtractive Color Mixing

1   Practice with the primary color-lights and their mixtures
    (additive mixing) and primary color-pigments and their
    mixtures (subtractive mixing) using one of the following
    software programs:

    • Adobe Photoshop CS. To experiment with additive/color-
      light (RGB) mixing, select Difference mode for layers
      [Fig. 2.13], while for subtractive/color-pigment mixing,
      select Multiply mode. [Fig. 2.14] These options can be found
      in the Layers window.
    • The Trycolors Mixer application teaches subtractive mixing
      using colors in hexadecimal notation.

 http://trycolors.com/

2   Do shadows have colors? What happens with cast shadows
    when objects are lit with primary RGB lights?

    • View the work of the light artist Yves Charnay, *Les Couleurs
      de l'esprit,* at the Saxe-Anhalt Parliament Building in
      Magdeburg, Germany (2003). [Fig. 2.15]
    • See the effect of the colored shadows cast by the iridescent
      glass fins on the Ohio State Chiller Plant, Columbus, Ohio,
      by Ross Barney Architects (2010). [Figs. 2.16, 2.17]

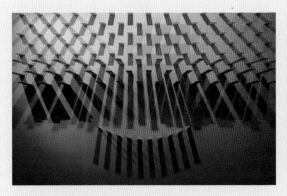
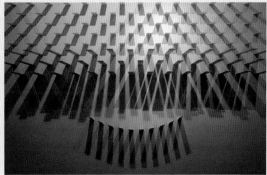

Fig. 2.15   Yves Charnay, *Les Couleurs de l'esprit*,
Saxony-Anhalt Parliament Building, Magdeburg,
Germany, 2003

http://www.yvescharnay.com/18-les
-couleurs-de-lesprit.html

Figs. 2.16 and 2.17   Effects of colored shadows
produced by iridescent glass. Ross Barney Architects,
Ohio State Chiller Plant, Columbus, Ohio, 2010

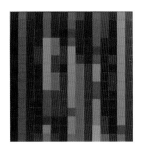 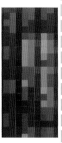  

Fig. 3.1 Color shifts as a result of the Purkinje effect before sunset (☼), at 8:35 p.m., and after sunset (☽), at 9:25 p.m.

3 Color and Perception

Color is a fugitive and unstable phenomenon. Depending on the conditions of perception, a color's hue, saturation, value, or sense of distance from the observer can shift. In this chapter, we will see how color perception is influenced by the lighting source, the area, the distance to the observer, the length of the stimulus, the colors seen before (successive contrast), or the colors surrounding (simultaneous contrast).

3.1
Color interaction

Interaction of Color by Josef Albers (1963) is one of the most influential books on color theory applied to architecture and design. In his color classes at the Bauhaus design school and later at Black Mountain College in the United States, Albers taught his students that color always deceives, as it is never perceived as it really is physically.[1] The appearance of color is influenced by numerous factors, including lighting conditions, the area of the colored surface, viewing distance, duration of viewing, and the presence of adjacent colors.

Lighting conditions
If lighting conditions change, our perception of color changes (see chapter 1). In fact, before noon, during the last hours of sunlight, and after sunset, reds darken, blues appear brighter, and whites appear more bluish. [Fig. 3.1] This

phenomenon is called the Purkinje effect, named after the Czech physiologist Jan Evangelista Purkinje (1787–1869): in low lighting conditions, our vision is more sensitive to low electromagnetic wavelengths (violet and blue).

Color area

If we expand the surface of a color, it tends to change, losing saturation and gaining value. This can be explained by the fact that a large area occupies a wide retinal area beyond the fovea, where the proportion of rods and cones changes, as does color sensitivity (see section 1.1). [Fig. 3.2]

Fig. 3.2
The smaller the target color is, the more saturated and darker it seems.

The phenomenon called **irradiation** also occurs: a light-colored figure on a dark background appears bigger than a dark figure on a light background. The brightest colors are more stimulating for the photosensitive cells in the retina and cause a diffuse perception of the contours of the figure, making it seem slightly bigger.[2] British architect Will Alsop might be referring to the color irradiation phenomenon when he answers with tongue in cheek the difficult question of why architects wear black: "Fat architects wear black because it makes them look thin."[3]

Viewing distance

The Swedish architect Karin Fridell Anter studied the perennial problem of colors that look different when painted on a large facade from how they appear on a color chart. She observed some constants in the shift between **nominal color** (that is, how the color of a painted facade visually compares with an NCS color atlas at a short distance) and **perceived color** (how that same color appears at a certain distance, compared to an NCS atlas). [Figs. 3.3, 3.4]

Perceived colors tend to have less blackness and more chromaticness than nominal color. From a distance, whitish colors seem even more white but keep the same chromaticness. In contrast, darker colors seem to increase their chromaticness but keep their whiteness when viewed from a distance.

In addition, colors observed from a distance seem to move slightly toward blue (somewhere between the NCS hues B and R70B): purple and green shift to blue, red shifts to purple, yellow shifts to green, and oranges shift to either yellow or red, with a breaking point positioned somewhere between the NCS hues Y35R and Y60R.[4]

Similar studies conducted in colored rooms comparing small patches of color with wall-size colors also found differences. Large areas of color in a room are perceived as being lighter and more saturated than small areas, independent of the light source. The shift in the hue is less evident.[5]

Duration of viewing

The perception of a color depends on how long it is observed. There is a shift in color from its appearance at first sight to how it appears after long observation to the afterimage remaining once the color stimuli has stopped (see section 3.2).

Adjacent colors

The perception of a color depends on those colors that surround it, causing slight changes to its three perceptive variables: hue, saturation, and value, as occurs in simulta-neous color contrast phenomena (see section 3.3).

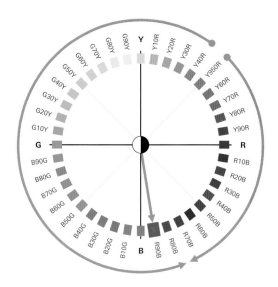

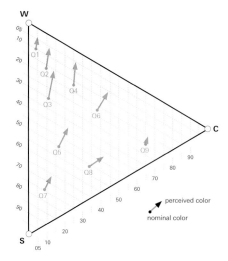

Figs. 3.3 and 3.4
Usual shift of NCS hue, blackness, and chromaticness between nominal and perceived colors in facades

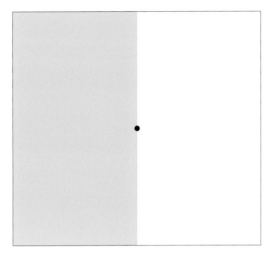
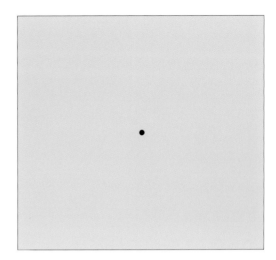

Fig. 3.5 Look at the black spot in the first square for about twenty seconds, then suddenly switch your gaze to the second one. The second figure seems not to be homogeneous in color; the right side of the square will appear slightly more saturated for a while.

3.2
Successive color contrasts (influence of time)

Our visual system perceives changes in stimuli more easily than lengthy uniform stimuli. Color sensations are most vivid when a light stimulus first strikes the eye and then disappears, rather than when the stimulus is constant or drawn out. [Fig. 3.5]

Negative afterimage

From a physiological perspective, the visual system has a medium level of nervous activity (or frequency of discharge) when it is at ease. When light reaches the eye, it reacts with an increase in this frequency, and we perceive a specific color. But while this stimulus is maintained, the frequency returns to normal values and color seems less saturated. During the first seconds after the stimulus stops, as the eye returns to its resting level of nervous activity, a compensatory opposite response is produced, decreasing the frequency of discharge to below the mean so that we perceive the color located immediately opposite in the color wheel, its complementary color. [Fig. 3.6]

This phenomenon is known as the **successive contrast** of colors, and the ghost image that remains when the stimulus stops is known as a **negative afterimage**. This phenomenon has been observed since ancient times by thinkers such as Aristotle, Leonardo da Vinci, Sir Isaac Newton, Johann Wolfgang von Goethe, Arthur Schopenhauer, and Charles Darwin.

When we look at an environment or a picture, successive contrast is not usually apparent, because our gaze is not fixed for a long time on one specific

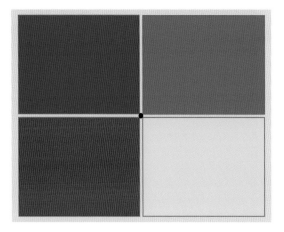
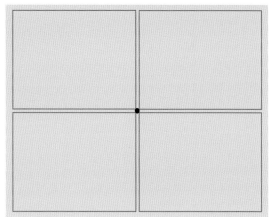

area but moves quickly from one color to another. We perceive afterimages when we gaze intensely for an extended period at colored surfaces (see Activity 7.1).

Positive afterimage

When we are exposed in a dark room to an intense red light that suddenly disappears, our eye not only perceives spots in the complementary blue-green but also in red. This residual presence of the original color once the stimulus has been taken away is called **perseverance** or **positive afterimage**.[6] This phenomenon has been used in marketing to sell a product without showing an explicit written message (see Activity 7).

3.3
Simultaneous contrasts

In about 1840 French chemist Michel-Eugène Chevreul (1786–1889) discovered the phenomenon he termed **simultaneous contrast**, or reciprocal contrast, also based on the principle of complementarity between colors. In addition to the successive image that appears after a period of observation, a complementary color image may appear in areas immediately adjacent to the stimulus during observation. This phenomenon, **chromatic induction**, is explained by the physiological process of lateral inhibition: when a retinal area is stimulated by the light of a spot color, the adjacent areas are somehow inhibited, resulting in an opposite impression. The effects of simultaneous contrast can be summarized as follows: when a part of the retina is stimulated, adjacent parts tend not only to decrease the perception of color but also to cause the perception of the complementary color.

Fig. 3.6 Look at the black spot in the left-hand figure for about twenty seconds, then suddenly look at the one to the right. You will observe an afterimage with the complementary colors (a negative afterimage).

Fig. 3.7 The same outline of a rectangle drawn over four different colored backgrounds appears to change color because of simultaneous contrast.

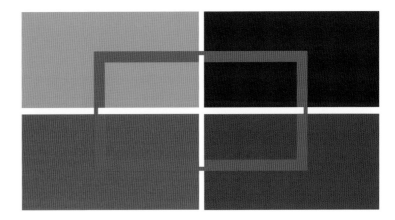

Fig. 3.8 Simultaneous contrast refers to shifts not only in hue and saturation but also in value. The four smaller gray rectangles all have the same value but appear to vary depending on the darkness of the background.

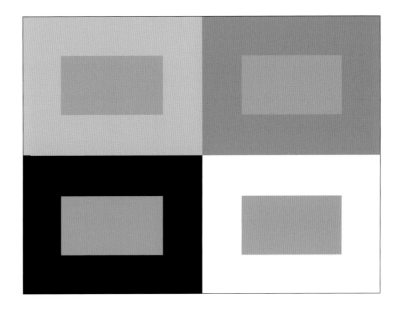

Fig. 3.9 The same green seems slightly yellowish on a blue background and bluish on a yellow background. It also appears to differ in value.

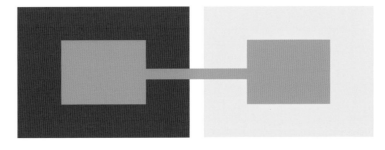

When two colors are close to each other, their perceptual variables (hue, value, and chroma) will shift to emphasize the maximum difference between both—that is, the same color will seem more saturated on a grayish background and duller on a saturated background (**chroma shift**). [Fig. 3.7] The same gray will seem clearer on a black background and darker on a white one; similarly, pale colors seem darker on white backgrounds and even clearer on black ones (**value shift**), and a green will seem yellowish on a blue background and bluish on a yellow one (**hue shift**). [Figs. 3.8, 3.9]

Not all color hues have the same ability to excite the retina. Red fatigues it the most, and blue the least.[7] Experiments have demonstrated that this secondary excitement in the area surrounding the directly stimulated one is maximized at certain distances but decreases when the relationship between interacting areas is changed; indeed, when there are alternating bands of different color, the opposite of simultaneous contrast occurs—namely, **leveling**, in which the two colors tend to look similar to each other and less contrasting, a phenomenon known as the **Bezold Effect**, named after the German physicist Wilhelm von Bezold (1837–1907).

When two complementary colors (opposite in hue) contrast with each other, each one undergoes an increase of intensity (saturation and value). This occurs because the eye superimposes the respective complementary color over each. This heightening of colors can produce remarkable color effects, as when we see a gray hue shift when placed on different backgrounds:

* On a red background, gray appears green-gray.
* On an orange background, gray appears bluish-gray.
* On a yellow background, gray appears violet-gray.
* On a blue background, gray seems orange-gray.
* On a violet background, gray seems yellow-gray.

Simultaneous contrast occurs between adjacent colors, accentuating the differences between them and underlining their margins in between; this occurs with contrasts not only of hue but also of value and saturation.

3.4
Color kinetics: advancing and receding colors

In a painting, a colored surface may appear to be closer or farther away from the picture plane, a phenomenon known as **color kinetics**. This can be used to give a two-dimensional canvas the illusion of depth. [Figs. 3.10, 3.11]

Josef Albers is a key figure in the study of the interaction of colors and their kinetic capacity. Experimenting with colored cards, Albers showed that each color corresponds to a certain depth and that by juxtaposing it with other colors,

Fig. 3.10 The red circle looks like it is on top of the blue background, but the blue circle appears to be a hole in the red surface.

Fig. 3.11 Blue gives an illusion of distance to the wall. Rupprecht Geiger, color design for Joseph-von-Fraunhofer-Schule, Munich, 1973. The school is named for the Bavarian physicist and optical lens manufacturer (1782–1826).

a sensation of varying depth can be achieved. [Fig. 3.12] Albers also worked with the **illusion of transparency** that happens when two colored papers are placed together and a third paper of a specific color is placed at their intersection; we may perceive that one of the papers overlaps the other and is transparent or translucent.[8]

In general, dull and bluish colors tend to recede from the viewer, while more saturated and reddish colors tend to advance. This phenomenon is well known and has been employed by painters throughout history. It is reminiscent of sfumato (also known as **aerial perspective**), a technique used by Leonardo da Vinci that blurs background colors to give a paler and more bluish look. Certainly, this color shift toward bluish, clearer, and less saturated colors to provide the effect of increased distance is similar to our experience of color when observing nature.[9] Professor Lois Swirnoff, a disciple of Albers, offers that "color hue is inherently spatial and each of the colors of the spectrum has its own spatial depth."[10]

Considering the influence of value in color kinetics, the psychologist Susanne Liebmann demonstrated in 1927 that when two colors with different hues but the same value are placed at different distances, they appear to occupy the same spatial plane under certain observation conditions. This phenomenon is called the **Liebmann effect**. Psychologists William Ittelson and F. P. Kilpatrick showed that when two spotlights with different levels of brightness are seen in the dark, they appear as two lights with the same brightness, positioned at different distances; the brighter the light is, the closer it seems.

In terms of value, pale colors are perceived as farther away than dark ones under daylight lighting conditions, but in the dark, pale colors appear to be closer to the observer.

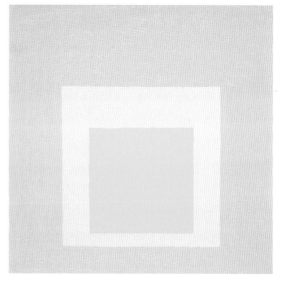

Fig. 3.12 Clockwise from top left: Josef Albers, *Study for Homage to the Square (Autumn Scent / Smell)*, 1966, oil on Masonite, 16 × 16 in. (40.6 × 40.6 cm); *Homage to the Square: Guarded*, 1952, oil on Masonite, 24 × 24 in. (60.9 × 60.9 cm); *Homage to the Square: Lone Light*, 1962, oil on Masonite, 18 × 18 in. (45.7 × 45.7 cm)

Activity 5
Interaction of Color

Three colors appear as two. One color appears as two, or three colors appear as four. [Fig. 3.13]

One and the same color, placed equally on 2 grounds of different colors, is to lose its identity entirely, and not only appear as 2 colors but repeat at the same time the colors of the adjacent grounds. As a result, one of the 3 colors seems to disappear in our perception. The question: What color will act in these two ways?
—Josef Albers, "Reversed Grounds, Plates VI-1 through 4," from *Interaction of Color*[11]

1   Find a color for the *X*'s that, when placed against two different backgrounds, is perceived as two distinct colors, each matching the opposite background. This works best if you gaze at the center of the plate from some distance.
    In Adobe Photoshop, use an existing color library, such as Pantone Solid Uncoated. Albers preferred working with color papers rather than pigments and paint, so we invite you not to use the Color Mixer. You can load this color library in "Swatches > Pantone Solid Uncoated."
    Note: You can also perform this activity in the Interaction of Color app produced by Yale University in 2013, working with Plate VI-3a.

Fig. 3.13 Three colors appear as two

Activity 6
Color Kinetics in 3-D

In his painting series *Homages to the Square* (1950–76), Josef Albers showed that each color corresponds to a certain sense of depth. In general, low-saturated, bluish colors tend to distance the viewer, while reddish, more saturated colors tend to bring them closer. This effect is produced not only in 2-D but also in 3-D.

1   Build a physical model in the shape of a 9.8 in. (25 cm) cube, containing four concentric frames arranged so that you can look through each to observe the farthest surface. Experience how colors advance and recede by displaying canvases of different colors on the various surfaces. [Figs. 3.14] Keep the closest two frames in low-saturated, light, bluish colors and the farthest in darker, saturated, reddish colors. The sense of depth will decrease. Do the opposite to observe the depth increasing.

2   Imagine that your model is a temporary pavilion placed in an open area. Shoot some photographs and create a photomontage that mimics the expected results. Include

Fig. 3.14 Exercise by Leon Gehse for Graphic and Chromatic Design course in master's program in architecture, Escuela Técnica Superior de Arquitectura, Universitat Politècnica de València, Spain, 2014–15

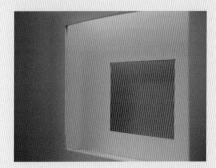

people interacting with your pavilion to give an idea of the scale of the construction, placing them at various distances. [Fig. 3.19]

3   Look for real examples of architecture with similar color kinetic phenomena. Compare the effects with those of your model. [Fig. 3.16]

4   View the image below right. [Fig. 3.17] Which building appears to be in the foreground? (The one on the left side is in the foreground, while the one on the right side is in the background.) Consider the color kinetic rules to explain why this photograph is so confusing.

Fig. 3.15 Exercise by Leon Gehse for Graphic and Chromatic Design

Fig. 3.16 Neutelings Riedijk Architects, the Netherlands Institute for Sound and Vision, Hilversum, 2006

Fig. 3.17 Which building appears to be in the foreground in this photograph?

Activity 7
Consecutive Contrast or Afterimages

Afterimages in architecture
Yasutaka Yoshimura architects, Red-Light Yokohama,
Kanagawa, Japan (2010) [Figs. 3.18, 3.19]
    This restaurant is located in the former red-light district
of Yokohama, Japan. As a nod to the neighborhood's past,
the restaurant has been divided into two rooms, one painted
white, the other green. If a visitor stays for a while in the
green room and then moves to the white one, for a moment
it appears red, the complementary color of green, because of
consecutive contrast.

Figs. 3.18 and 3.19
Yasutaka Yoshimura
Architects, Red-Light
Yokohama, Kanagawa,
Japan, 2010

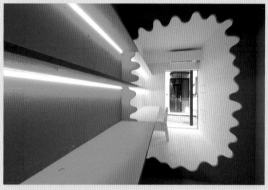

Afterimages in advertising
BMW cinema ad by Serviceplan Advertising Agency,
Executive Creative Director Matthias Harbeck, Munich, 2012
    Carmaker BMW conceived a cinema ad for its motorcycle
division that doesn't contain a directly visible logo, instead
relying on a positive afterimage.

 The ad, with an explanation of the effect and the reaction
of viewers, can be viewed at https://youtu.be/wGJd1IbzZrE.

Fig. 3.20   Jasper Johns,
Flag, 1969, lithograph,
17 1/8 × 25 7/8 in.
(43.5 × 65.8 cm)

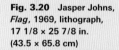

Afterimages in painting
American pop artist Jasper Johns used negative afterimages
in some canvases from his series of American flag paintings.
[Fig. 3.20]

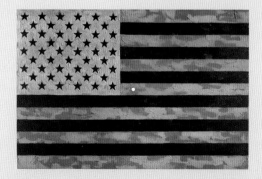

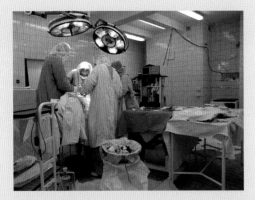

Fig. 3.21 Hospital operating room

1   Operating rooms in hospitals are usually painted in greens or blues. [Fig. 3.21] Some people might find pseudopsychological reasons for this, but there is a more powerful functional reason, and it involves afterimages. What is it?
(See page 232 for answer.)

Activity 8
Simultaneous Contrast

1   Look through the window in this green office in MVRDV architects' headquarters in Rotterdam and compare with the same view as seen with the office painted in red. [Figs. 3.22, 3.23] Because of simultaneous contrast perception, the colors outside the window appear different. Describe this change. Which color would you select for a room to enhance the view of a green landscape?

Figs. 3.22 and 3.23
The view of a landscape through a window might be enhanced by changing the color of the interior. Photomontage based on MVRDV's colors for its new offices in Rotterdam, the Netherlands, 2016

4 Combining Colors

Combining colors for an architect is similar to combining sounds for a musician. Colors and sounds each have rules that guide composers to find beautiful or pleasurable solutions. Color theorists since the nineteenth century have contributed to a grammar of color; in recent years, these rules have been translated into easy-to-use apps that provide handy ways to combine colors. These laws may be useful as a starting point in architectural design, but, as with music, once they are understood and embraced, breaking the rules may also produce pleasing results.

Fig. 4.1 If we display equal parts red and its opposite, blue-green, at their maximum chroma, we would get not a perfectly balanced composition but one in which red predominates. From T. M. Cleland, *A Grammar of Color*, 1921

4.1
Color harmonies

The literature of color includes a plethora of theories and studies attempting to link color with aesthetic response; these have led to sometimes contradictory research findings.

The architect Zena O'Connor correctly points out that the variations and contradictions among theories can be explained by the epistemological differences among the initial assumptions made in each study. She considers three main opposing paradigms for color and harmony research: positivism, postpositivism, and constructivism.[1] We will briefly examine these paradigms, following O'Connor's work.[2]

Positivism is the oldest model and is most evident in the writings of the most influential theorists of color. Sir Isaac Newton, for example, suggested that color harmonies are based on the proportional arrangements of colors in a rational manner, similar to the mathematical foundations of any musical composition.[3] Some current researchers continue to work on the relationship between color and music from the perspective of the physical phenomena.[4]

Under the positivist paradigm, reality can be apprehended, quantified, and broken down atomistically. Therefore, positivists tend to be associated with the doctrines of reductionism and determinism, arguing that aspects of reality can be studied while isolated from both time and context. This led some theorists to take an interest in reducing the phenomenon of color in a more simplistic way. The weakness of these color models is their inability to represent all the colors that we can perceive or to study color harmonies isolated from any context. Some theorists who applied the principle of Occam's razor,[5] attempting to obtain simple formulas and principles to predict the relationship between color and aesthetic response, were Michel-Eugène Chevreul (1839), Johannes Itten (1962), Albert H. Munsell (1921), Friedrich Wilhelm Ostwald (1916), and, more recently, Ming-Chuen Chuang and Li-Chen Ou (2001), as well as Ou with M. Ronnier Luo, Andrée Woodcock, and Angela Wright (2004).[6] [Figs. 4.1, 4.2, 4.3, 4.4] Their theories also reveal a deterministic approach that posits a strong causal relationship between color and aesthetic response.

Fig. 4.2
Colors with the same hue, with equal distance among them and centered in a medium chroma and value. Adapted from Cleland, *A Grammar of Color*

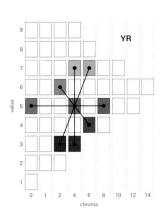

Fig. 4.3
Opposite hues with the same value and different chroma, with areas inversely proportional to chroma. Adapted from Cleland, *A Grammar of Color*

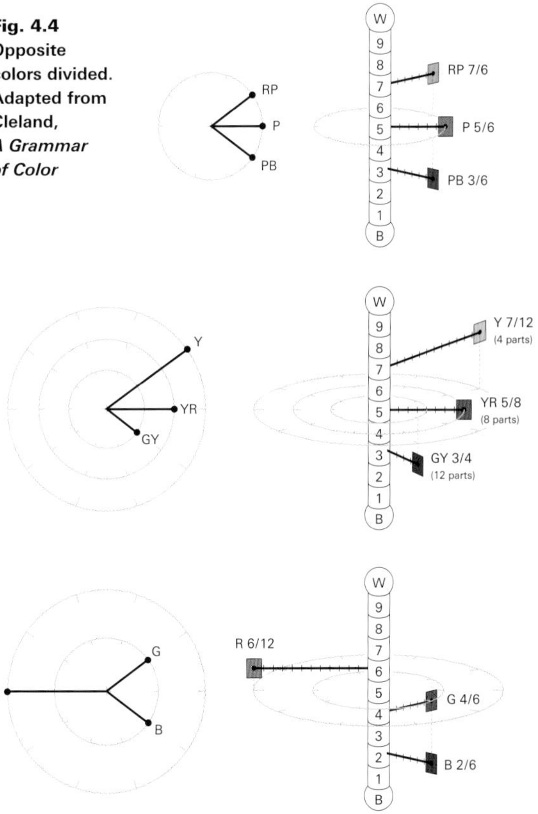

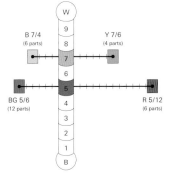

Fig. 4.4
Opposite colors divided. Adapted from Cleland, *A Grammar of Color*

Under the postpositivist paradigm that evolved from positivism, transferring the results of a study to other situations or contexts is not considered appropriate. Its proponents argue that reality is complex and it can be only partially comprehended.[7] This paradigm emerged in response to criticism directed at positivism: namely, the lack of consideration of contextual and subjective factors in its experiments.

The constructivist paradigm maintains that reality is "the result of multiple and intangible mental constructions...often shared among individuals and even among cultures."[8] While a number of individual constructs in a particular domain may achieve a general consensus, under the constructivist paradigm, this level of consensus is always open to revision, review, and reinterpretation. Aspects of the constructivist paradigm are evident in many current theories, as they contain notions or ideas that are constructs or inventions of human intelligence, such as "gestalt color," "color harmonies," "color ranges," "complementary colors," and "primary colors."

Taking into consideration the epistemological shortcomings seen in the three main paradigms, and with an awareness of the inability of any theory to adequately address such a complex phenomenon as color harmony, it is nonetheless possible to describe three major groups of color harmony theories, mainly based in the positivistic approach. They must not be considered universal and deterministic rules, but rather a possible starting point for any color composition, particularly for those architects who have a mental block when standing in front of a blank piece of paper. In fact, the latest easy-to-use color applications continue to rely on the classical positivistic rules, which might be considered the **grammar** of color combinations.[9]

Fig. 4.5
Color harmonies, from Johannes Itten: (1) Light-dark composition in black, white, and grays; (2) same composition in blue; (3) colors of equal brilliance (value); (4) colors of equal darkness; (5, 6, 7, 8) luminous yellow, orange, red, or blue are placed in the center of a checkered pattern of twenty-five squares. The four corners are neutral gray in the same brilliance (value) as the pure color. Graded mixtures of gray with the pure color produce intermediate shades of low saturation.

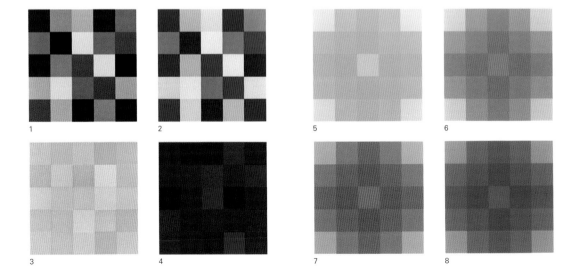

1   2   5   6

3   4   7   8

Color combinations based on similarities of colors

A first grammar rule could be that color harmony is achieved by combining color samples that have any of the three perceptual variables in common: hue, saturation, or value.[10]

The German chemist Friedrich Wilhelm Ostwald worked on color theory during the period from 1916 to 1936 and published his own color atlas. Within his system, colors are ordered by their hue, black/white content, and chromaticness, with the same hue colors drawn in triangles and turning around the color wheel to build up the figure of a double inverted cone. His color solid is similar to the NCS Natural Color System (see section 2.4). Ostwald considered twelve principles of harmony based on his system. The first five are rooted in the similarity of color attributes and the rest in the contrast:[11]

1 Harmony with grays
2 Harmonies with the same hue and white content
3 Harmonies with the same hue and black content
4 Harmonies with the same hue and chromaticness
5 Harmonies with the same hue or monochromatic
6 Harmonies in circles with the same chromaticness but different hue
7 Complementary hue pairs in circles with the same chromaticness
8 Complementary hue pairs with different chromaticness but the same blackness or whiteness
9 Noncomplementary pairs with the same chromaticness
10 Harmonies with two and three colors
11 Harmonies with many colors but the same hue
12 The annular star, drawing a circle with its center in the vertical gray axis[12]

Johannes Itten also suggested a link between aesthetic response and analogous colors in 1961. For him, color combinations commonly considered harmonic are combinations of colors without strong contrasts.[13] Color harmonies based on similarity have been widely accepted due to Itten's influence.[14] [Fig. 4.5]

More recently, Swedish scientific researchers Anders Hård and Lars Sivik (2001) demonstrated, using an empirical approach, that there is a link between similar colors (analogous in hue or value) and positive aesthetic responses.[15] [Figs. 4.6, 4.7]

Color combinations based on contrasts

Other theorists have described contrasting colors as harmonic, including German writer and scientist Johann Wolfgang von Goethe (1749–1832), who believed that harmonic colors were those that represented the entire color wheel. For these theorists, harmony lies in the balance between colors, understood in terms of the polarity of opposing forces.

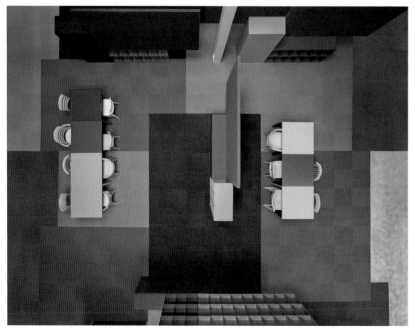

Figs. 4.6 and 4.7
Color composition in blue hues. VMX Architects and i29 Interior Architects, Social Workplace Combiwerk, Delft, the Netherlands, 2011

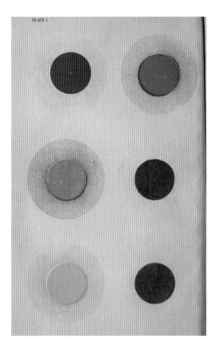

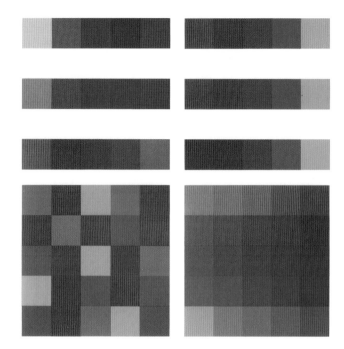

Fig. 4.8 Chromatic induction effect in the contour of the figure as a consequence of simultaneous contrast. From Michel-Eugène Chevreul, *De la loi du contraste simultané des couleurs et de l'assortiment des objets colorés*, 1839

Fig. 4.9 Complementary contrast, from Johannes Itten: (top) Bands mixing six complementary pairs; (bottom left) composition combining the complementary pair red/green and mixtures of the two; (bottom right) mixture square of two complementary pairs, orange/blue and red-orange/blue-green

The experiments of French chemist Michel-Eugène Chevreul (1839) marked a turning point in art history, establishing strong ties between color harmonies and contrasts of complementary colors (see section 1.6). [Fig. 4.8] Chevreul's *Principles of Harmony and Contrast of Colors and Their Application to the Arts* is considered to be one of the most influential handbooks of the nineteenth century.[16] [Fig. 4.9] Postimpressionist painters such as Paul Signac (1863–1944) and Georges Seurat (1859–1891) based their work on research by Chevreul and on phenomena such as simultaneous contrast (see section 3.3). [Figs. 4.10] Starting from the premise that color is mixed in the eye and not in the palette (as the earlier impressionists had maintained), and taking into account the theory of contrasts between complementary colors, the two painters perfected a technique known as **pointillism**, which consisted of applying dots of color to the canvas so they blended together when seen from a distance.[17]

As mentioned previously, Ostwald described principles of color harmonies that rely on the balance between colors with complementary hues. In general terms, those colors that are equidistant from the neutral gray axis with its center in a neutral gray are considered harmonious.

In the same period, to explain how to use the Munsell color system, artist Thomas Maitland Cleland (1880–1964) established nine principles of color

Fig. 4.10 Georges Seurat, *La Parade du Cirque*, 1887–88, oil on canvas, 39 1/4 × 59 in. (100 × 150 cm) with detail

harmonies in the publication *A Grammar of Color* in 1921.[18] All nine are based on the Munsell system, which describes any color with three perceptual variables: hue, value, and chroma (see section 2.4). In general terms, Cleland considered that a color combination is harmonious if it is balanced, meaning that the gravity center of all the colors plotted in the Munsell solid has to match a neutral gray, called N5. He also believed that it is possible to balance colors with different chroma using inverse surface proportions—for example, six parts of B 7/4 with four parts of YR 7/6 (see Figs. 4.2, 4.3, 4.4).[19]

Itten described seven kinds of color contrast, giving examples of renowned painters who used each in their canvases:

1   Contrast of hue: Henri Matisse, Piet Mondrian, Wassily Kandinsky
2   Light–dark contrast: Eugène Delacroix, Francisco de Zurbarán, Pablo Picasso
3   Cool–warm contrast: Claude Monet, Camille Pissarro, Seurat
4   Complementary contrast: Piero della Francesca, Jan van Eyck, Paul Cézanne
5   Simultaneous contrast: El Greco, Vincent van Gogh
6   Contrast of saturation: Matisse
7   Contrast of extension: Pieter Bruegel the Elder[20]

Color harmonies: an unpredictable phenomenon
Some architects, such as Will Alsop, believe that any random colors viewed together produce a pleasant sensation and thus are harmonious.[21] [Fig. 4.11] This simplicity contradicts the somewhat more complex rules of grammar

Fig. 4.11 The random distribution of colors in a marketplace always feels pleasant: Willy Müller, Flower Market in MercaBarna, Barcelona, 2008

mentioned earlier but attests to the difficulty of the problem. While there are many different approaches to color combinations, aesthetic responses to color are complex—not only hard to describe but also hard to predict or quantify.

There is little consensus in available literature regarding the concept of color harmony. Reality is essentially holistic and is therefore much more than the sum of independent parts—parts that maybe should not be studied and explained in isolation and with rules that sometimes might be ineffective.[22] As the Portuguese architect Fernando Távora explained to his students, "In architecture, the opposite is also true."[23]

4.2
Law of surface proportion

When one color has a bigger area than another, it tends to dominate the composition, but it is possible to reach a balance by increasing the visual potency (saturation and value) of the smaller color so that no one color stands out. The German philosopher Arthur Schopenhauer (1788–1860) developed a rule to balance the fundamental colors primary (yellow, blue, red) and secondary (orange, green, violet) according to their capability to "activate the retina" and drafted, in line with Goethe's theories, proportions for them.[24] [Table 4.1]

To determine that rule, Schopenhauer used a **Newton's disc,** which is a physical disc painted with different colors that merge together by optical mixing when it spins. [Fig. 4.12] If the complementary colors are placed in a Newton's

Table 4.1 Capability to "activate the retina" for colors in their highest saturation, according to Arthur Schopenhauer. It is approximately related to their perceived value.

Yellow	9
Orange	8
Red	6
Green	6
Blue	4
Violet	3

Table 4.2
Proportions for complementary colors to be balanced. These ratios are inverse to their perceptual value, or capability to "activate the retina," according to Schopenhauer.

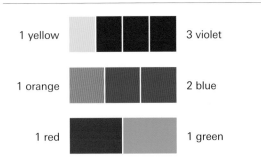

1 yellow	3 violet
1 orange	2 blue
1 red	1 green

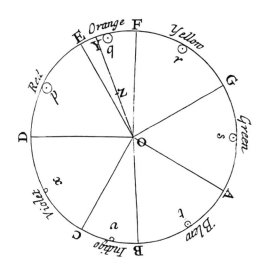

disc in inverse proportion to their capability to activate the retina, a medium gray is perceived, so some area ratios may be deduced between complementary colors. [Table 4.2] Itten refers to these same harmonious areas when talking about the contrast of extension.[25] This provides, of course, only a rough guide to ensuring that color compositions of complementary colors are harmonious, but it is a useful starting point.

The equilibrium areas described assure that no color will dominate the composition, particularly those with higher saturation. This is why it was recommended to display Munsell colors in inverse proportions to their chroma, as mentioned previously.

Le Corbusier suggested, in a short note describing the paint for his Maison du Brésil (1958), that the proportion of color in an architectural composition should be one-half white and one-half polychromy, including a maximum of 15 percent "vivid colors."[26]

Fig. 4.12 Newton's disc. A disc with segments representing the colors of the rainbow, when rotated at a high speed, will appear to be a single white-gray color as a consequence of optical mixing. Newton assigned the relative areas of the colors by analogy to the musical scale.

4.3
Applications to facilitate color decision-making

There are many applications that assist architects with combining colors, based more or less on the theories of harmony and contrast briefly described earlier in this chapter. The following are some websites and software that might come in handy.[27] Note that colors displayed on-screen often are available exclusively in RGB or CMYK notation but would need to be translated into a standard color notation such as NCS or Munsell to be rendered in architecture.

Fig. 4.13 Fragment of the NCS Navigator Tool showing the color notation of a target color alongside others with the same hue and different nuances

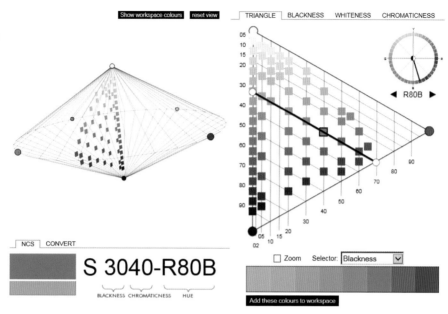

NCS Navigator

This interactive NCS-notation color palette provides sets containing a combination of two to five colors based on criteria for harmony: the same blackness/ whiteness, the same chromaticness, the same hue, the same nuance (blackness and chromaticness), et cetera. [Fig. 4.13]

 http://ncscolour.com/design/work-digitally-with-ncs/colouring-to-a-new-level/

ColorPicker

ColorPicker generates a custom color palette by allowing users to browse an interactive color space that suggests color combinations based on various harmony criteria.

 http://www.colorpicker.com/

Adobe Color CC

Like ColorPicker, Adobe Color CC generates a custom color palette by allowing users to browse an interactive color space that suggests color combinations based on various harmony criteria. It can be added to Adobe Photoshop as an extension, allowing other users' palettes to be accessed through Photoshop's Color window.

 https://color.adobe.com/

Coolors

An app available for iOS, Adobe add-on, or Chrome extension, Coolors generates a fast color scheme starting with a color combination suggested by the application.

 https://coolors.co/

COLOURLovers

Users can vote and comment on color combinations suggested by members (colors are given in RGB and hexadecimal notation). These combinations can be applied to different geometric patterns, which can be edited and used to customize, for example, users' personal Twitter frames. Additional useful applications can be found under Tools:

- *Color of the Year.* Users nominate and vote for the color of the year.
- *Seamless Studio.* Generates a geometric pattern to be colored.
- *Photocopa.* Suggests color combinations based on an uploaded photograph, providing individual color palettes based on different criteria: light, neutral, like, random, dark, and light colors.
- *Copaso.* Generates a custom palette of colors by browsing different color spaces in RGB, CMYK, HSV, or hexadecimal. Provides combinations of colors based on similarity or contrast criteria, roughly in line with Munsell's principles.

 www.colourlovers.com/

Blendoku 2

Designed as a game for mobile devices, this user-friendly entertainment helps develop visual acuity and provides many color-combination possibilities. [Fig. 4.14]

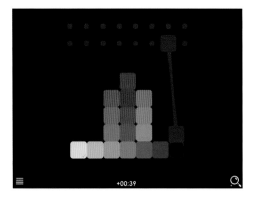

Fig. 4.14
Blendoku 2
app interface

Activity 9
Color Harmonies

Fig. 4.15 Rendering of Mansilla + Tuñón Architects' MUSAC, Museo de Art Contemporáneo de Castilla y León, Spain, 2004, showing the final color palette of the facades

Fig. 4.16 Detail of the color palette for the facade of MUSAC

The architects based the thirty-seven colors of the main building's entrance facade on the stained-glass windows of the city's cathedral, in particular on one called "the Falconer," dating from the thirteenth century. A photograph of the window was pixelated and the colors identified. [Figs. 4.15, 4.16]

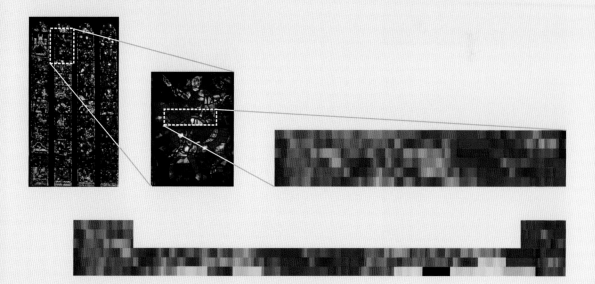

1   Choose a famous painting whose color appeals to you.
It could be in any pictorial style. List the title, artist, date,
dimensions, and pictorial movement it belongs to.

Fig. 4.17 Exercise by Eliska
Rimalova for the Color and
Interior Design Architecture
course in master's program
in advanced architecture,
Escuela Técnica Superior
de Arquitectura, Universitat
Politècnica de València,
Spain, 2015–16, based on
Gustav Klimt, *Danaë*, 1907,
oil on canvas, 30 1/4 ×
32 5/8 in. (77 × 83 cm)

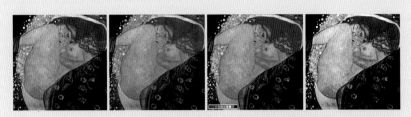

2   Transform the painting using Photoshop and answer the
following questions: [Fig. 4.17]

A   Convert the image to gray scale, using "Image >
Adjustments > Black & White," which provides good
control over the conversion. How are the darkest and
the lightest parts of the composition distributed?
Are there important value contrasts? Is it a composition
with high- or low-value colors?

B   Identify the hue families and assess the number of
colors present. Convert the picture to indexed color
using "File > Save for Web & Devices." This will allow
you to choose the number of colors for the final image
as well as the reduction criteria. How are the main hues
distributed in the painting? Are there complementary
color families? Are there cool/warm color contrasts?
Is there monochromy?

C   Find and identify the most and least saturated areas of
color. Saturation can be evaluated by exaggerating the
contrast of the image using "Image > Adjustments >
Brightness/Contrast."

Fig. 4.18 Original colors

3   Modify some of the most significant colors of the picture
(color accents, dominant colors, et cetera) to transform the
color harmony of the original painting. [Figs. 4.18, 4.19]

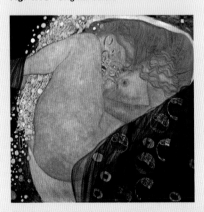

Fig. 4.19 Without color accents

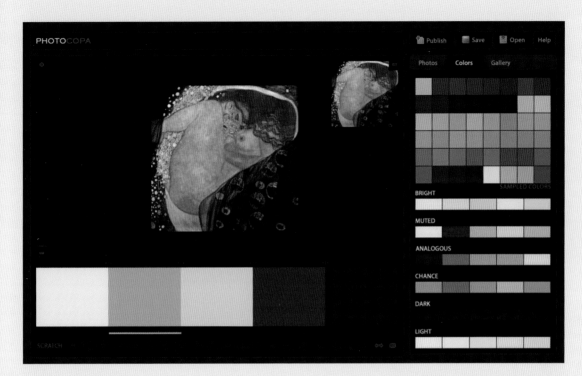

PHOTOCOPA

Fig. 4.20   Color palette in Photocopa

Fig. 4.21   Abstract composition by Rimalova based on *Danaë*

4   Create your own color palette using the colors of the painting. [Fig. 4.20] Use the tool Photocopa, available online at COLOURLovers. You will need to register to upload an image.

www.colourlovers.com

5   Make your own abstract composition based on the colors of the original painting, using the same surface proportions. [Fig. 4.21]

6   From the above analysis, answer the following questions:

A   Does the painting have a color combination criterion? What is it? Is there any similarity in hue, saturation, and value among colors? Is there any contrast of hue, saturation, and value?
B   Is there a dominant color or area in the painting? Why?
C   How are the masses of colors in the composition organized? Is it there a geometric distribution, symmetry/asymmetry, rhythm, balance of surfaces, et cetera?
D   Do you think the color harmony criterion of the picture is consistent with the artistic movement it belongs to?

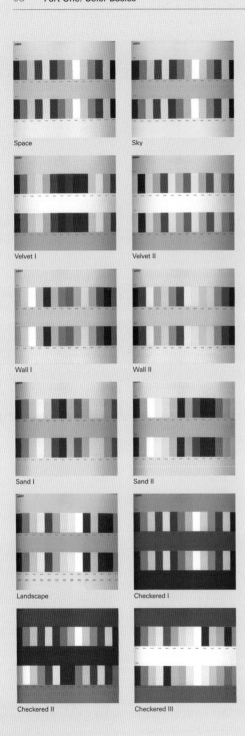

Space

Sky

Velvet I

Velvet II

Wall I

Wall II

Sand I

Sand II

Landscape

Checkered I

Checkered II

Checkered III

Activity 10

Le Corbusier's Color Combinations for Salubra Claviers (1931)

In 1931 the Salubra wallpaper manufacturer in Basel, Switzerland, commissioned Le Corbusier to compile an architectural color chart; a second version was completed in 1959. The first was arranged in a series of personal color combinations, following Le Corbusier's own preferences, called "keyboards," as they were similar in organization to the keys of a piano. In 1997 these color charts were republished with a previously unpublished text by Le Corbusier, *Polychromie Architecturale*, which dates to late 1931 through early 1932—without a doubt the most important document for understanding color in the designs of the Swiss architect. [Fig. 4.22]

I have researched the color combinations selected by Le Corbusier in his keyboards by analyzing their positions in the solid NCS. This allows us to understand the characteristics of the colors selected (hue, blackness, and chromaticness) as well as their combination criteria. [Fig. 4.23] The extensive presence of earthy hues and the absence of certain other colors, such as yellows, violets, black, and white, are notable. I have demonstrated graphically, by a navigable three-dimensional model and with statistical support, some principles of Le Corbusier's color preferences: the combination of colors with equal chromaticness, the search for contrast in blackness, and his frequent strategy of contrasting cool colors with warm ones but not complementary colors. I have also discussed other compositional criteria held by Le Corbusier in the use of color in his Purist architecture; these criteria are related to the position and extension of colored surfaces, the connotations associated with different hues, and the use of plain colors, among other considerations.[28]

1   Refer to the Salubra color keyboards to determine Le Corbusier's most preferred color combinations, in groups of two, three, and four colors. Use the app ColorArch, which is available for free at the Google Play Store.

Fig. 4.22 All of Le Corbusier's 1931 color keyboards for Salubra

Watch a demo of ColorArch at
https://youtu.be/EHq-ib3UsAo.

Fig. 4.23 All of the Salubra
color pairs, showing the number
of combinations and the geometric space for same NCS hue
pairs and complementary
color pairs, Juan Serra, 2016

2   Choose the color combination suggested by Le Corbusier
that you like the most and write its notation in NCS.
Use the figure below or download the app ColorArch.
[Fig. 4.23]
    The application allows you to browse the color space
NCS and to observe the spatial position of each of the
thirty-two Salubra colors. Users can select any of the color
combinations with one to four samples and determine
if combination criteria exist based on the similarity or
contrast of the colors' hue, blackness, or chromaticness.
The recurrence of each pair of two colors from the total of
1,248 pairs in the keyboards is also shown, giving an
idea of Le Corbusier's interest in that color combination,
based on how frequently it appeared throughout the
Salubra charts.

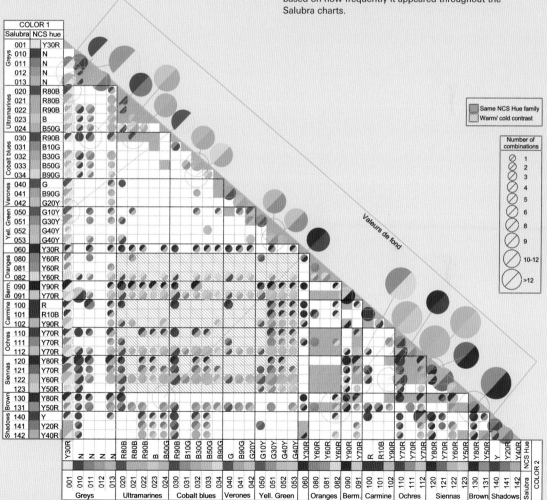

Part Two

Color for the Architectural Project

5 Choosing the Color That Fits the Form

This chapter addresses how color can be used to strengthen the formal concept of a building. Color can be a strategic tool to reinforce a building's dialogue with the surrounding cityscape or landscape. It can also modify the perception of the building's volumes and spaces in many ways, regarding its geometry, dimensions, visual weight, or texture—all of which contribute to a sense of the hierarchy of different elements. Finally, color can indicate the compositional order of a building, giving information about its function, structure, modulation, and so on.[1]

5.1
Color and landscape integration

The visibility of a building in its environment is governed by the laws of figure and ground, which have been studied by many psychologists, notably Edgar Rubin (1886–1951) in Denmark and Rudolf Arnheim (1904–2007) in Germany. We tend to see a building as a figure cut out from surrounding surfaces or backgrounds, an effect enhanced by several factors: its smaller size, its closed silhouette, its position at the base of the landscape composition, the simplicity of its shape and symmetry, its convexity versus concavity, and, of course, its color.

Color can help to visually distinguish an object from its background. The hue, saturation, and value of color can help or hinder this effect, which ranges between two extremes: mimicry, when figure and background are indistinguishable, and singularity, when both reach maximum levels of contrast.

Fig. 5.1 Friedrich-Ernst von Garnier, ThyssenKrupp AG Feuerbeschichtungsanlage FBA 8, Dortmund, Germany, 2003

Fig. 5.2 MVRDV, Studio Thonik, or the Orange House, Amsterdam, 1998–2001

Fig. 5.3 Alberto Campo Baeza, Guerrero House, Zahora, Spain, 2005

Mimicry

Mimicry in architecture is used to lessen the impact of anything that is visually unpleasant or out of scale with a building's environment [Fig. 5.1]. Sometimes architects want a building to disappear and the environmental qualities of the landscape to prevail.

Singularity

Other times, color is used to highlight and accentuate architecture located within a relatively sedate setting. It is common practice in run-down areas to draw attention to certain buildings and thus detract from areas of little visual interest. The challenge is to enhance the cityscape by working individually, without falling into the trap of those buildings described by the Spanish architecture critic Josep Maria Montaner as "autistic monads, which are completely disconnected from the environment."[2]

These color arrangements are currently in vogue and are often used for propaganda, advertising, or branding. Sometimes, singularity is achieved with very saturated colors, which can be extremely controversial and can truly turn a building into an advertisement, as the Dutch architects of MVRDV described their project Studio Thonik (2001): "It was amazing that the color of one house could lead to such a fuss. The design worked! The building got the attention the client wanted."[3] [Fig. 5.2] Not only saturated colors are used to singularize; white also can be used for this purpose, as it represents the purity of abstract-minimalist architecture objects. [Fig. 5.3]

The use of color to single out one's own home dates back to the origins of human civilization. Mediterranean villagers painted the facades of their buildings in different colors so that fishermen would be able to recognize their homes from the sea; despite the singularity of each property, the village was produced in a chromatic context that resulted in a harmonic set.[4] This strategy has been transferred to large housing developments, where color has been used to link inhabitants with architecture in settings such as the massive housing developments in Berlin (Berliner Siedlungen) by Bruno Taut after

World War I (for example, Siedlungen Onkel Toms Hütte in Zehlendorf, Germany) and in numerous examples of social housing dwellings built during the 1970s (for example, those designed by Tomás Taveira in Lisbon).

Intermediate positions

Between mimicry and singularity lie intermediate positions in which architecture establishes a dialectical relationship with the environment, entailing neither a color submission nor a color imposition. It is characteristic of contemporary architecture to take into account the environment but not to be contextual.

The German architect Louisa Hutton similarly stated, "I do not think that there is necessarily a contradiction between a strong presence and working with the context." To which her architectural partner Matthias Sauerbruch added, "The buildings that we have built do stand out as individual objects, but they have been generated in response to observations of the immediate reality that we find at a particular location."[5] This is the case with Sauerbruch Hutton's GSW Headquarters Building in Berlin (1999), where the architects "chose a family of reds for the west facade because it is a group of colors that has a noticeable contrast to the sky, which in Berlin is usually gray. But, in fact, it also does blend with one aspect of the surroundings, namely the brick and terracotta of the roofs," as Hutton explained.[6] [Fig. 5.4]

An exemplary case of colored architecture— exemplary in the sense of the attention paid to the natural landscape—is the small settlement in Longyearbyen, Norway, near the North Pole. [Fig. 5.5] As the inhabitants live with three months of total darkness and three months of midnight sun, the color consultant Grete Smedal posed the question "Should one attempt to hide the manmade structure within this setting or would a clear contrast be more appropriate?" Because it would be impossible to mimic the environment's changing conditions throughout the course of the year, "the decision was made to enter into a dialogue with nature. In other words, to let the manmade structures define themselves with their own characteristic color scale—inspired from, but not imitating, the natural colors."[7] The town's buildings form an artificially colored landscape that does not smother the exceptional natural environment but rather communicates with it.

Fig. 5.4
Sauerbruch Hutton,
GSW Headquarters,
Berlin, 1999

Fig. 5.5
Grete Smedal,
Longyearbyen Project,
Longeyearbyen,
Norway, 1981

5.2
Color and shape

Integration/disintegration

Different elementary components of form can be unified by color (integration) or, conversely, colored to express or reinforce their autonomy (disintegration).

The law of similarity described by Gestalt principles states that our perception tends to group in a single object all those shapes with similar visual properties, such as color, whereas they are perceived as autonomous or independent if they possess unequal properties.[8] So the maximum chromatic integration is achieved with a monochrome scheme that strengthens the unitary aspect of architecture and prevents a more detailed description of its components. [Figs. 5.6, 5.7]

To disintegrate is to separate the various elements that form a whole and may advance through different stages of intensity until a total breakdown of the object is achieved—which is difficult to accomplish without a fragmentary formal composition. These two degrees of disintegration—separation and breakdown— are exemplified in the work of Le Corbusier and Gerrit Thomas Rietveld (1888– 1964), respectively.

At the Schröder House in Utrecht, the Netherlands (1924), Rietveld arranged color to break the enclosure of the space and dissolve the boundaries between interior and exterior (see Fig. 7.12). Color frees the components of the spatial box, which is not a closed prism but the encounter of independent planes and edges. Le Corbusier, in contrast, developed in his Maison La Roche-Jeanneret (1923–25) in Paris (see Fig. 7.7) a chromatic composition that aims to introduce tension but without breaking the spatial box: "The wall plane as a carrier of color may have certain autonomy, but it remains a component of an intact space."[9] (Le Corbusier in many other cases did use color disintegration to reinforce the architectural volume and not to break it, clearly distancing himself from neoplasticism.)

Ludwig Mies van der Rohe (1886–1969) also used disintegration, transforming walls and floor structures into separate planes by using color. His famous Farnsworth House in Plano, Illinois (1951), is a large white pavilion, abstract and isotropic; its wooden furniture is colored in different hues to distinguish these objects from the container prism. There are many other contemporary examples, such as Jean Nouvel's Culture and Congress Centre in Lucerne, Switzerland (2000), and MGM Arquitectos' Níjar Theater, Spain (2008).

Geometric distortion

Color distorts geometry when there is a discrepancy between the real shape of an object and the one that an observer perceives: straightness versus curvature of edges, flatness versus concavity versus convexity of planes, two-dimensionality versus three-dimensionality, et cetera. This distortion results from a conflict between the color scheme perceived and the one expected.

Figs. 5.6 and 5.7
Florentijn Hofman,
Beukelsdijk, Rotterdam,
the Netherlands, 2006

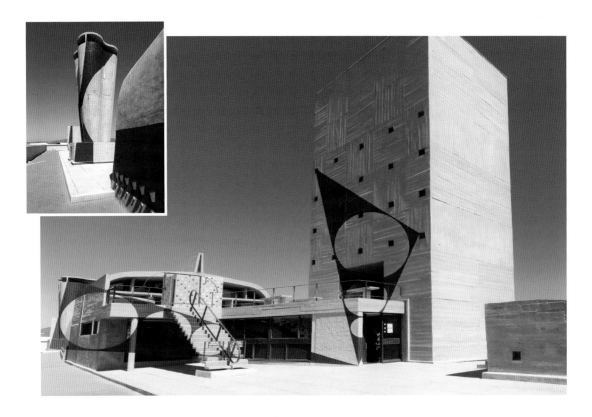

Figs. 5.8 and 5.9
Felice Varini, optical illusion on the roof of Le Corbusier's Unité d'Habitation, Marseille, France, 2016

Fig. 5.10
Boris Banozic with the students of the University of Applied Sciences, Darmstadt, Germany, *trillusion installation*, SaloneSatellite of Milan Design Week, 2012

One example of formal distortion is the anamorphic illusion, in which a two-dimensional painting unexpectedly appears when a building is viewed from a specific vantage point. The Italian artist Felice Varini is a renowned painter of anamorphisms (see Activity 19). [Figs. 5.8, 5.9]

Color distortion may be achieved through color value inconsistent with sunshades. Such is the case with Jorrit Tornquist's facade of the Depuratore Sud di Milano, Italy (2004), where color gradations make a smooth facade appear to undulate; here, color adds rhythm and movement to a homogeneous wall. On the chimney of the Termoutilizzatore in Brescia, Italy (1998), Tornquist used color to develop a similar dynamic, creating the illusion of a vertical prism that has been twisted.

Color patterns that are inconsistent with a form's underlying geometry or that are complex and difficult to apprehend also distort the perception of geometry. [Fig. 5.10] Josef Albers disciple Lois Swirnoff observed that "when the form of a surface is neither modular nor repeated, clues to form are very ambiguous. As a consequence, this model is radically altered in its appearance by light or by a shift in the observer's position."[10]

Dimensions of the building/space

Polychromy can cause space/volume contradictions between a building's real and perceived dimensions. Color interferes with the perception of an object's proportion (height, width, length); its size in relation to a reference (scale); and its separation from other objects (distance).

Color design manuals for architects often review these qualities, with pointers such as "A high ceiling and a wall that seem very distant, look respectively lower and closer if they are painted in a warm shade."[11] In addition, each color corresponds to a spatial distance from the observer. Le Corbusier noted, "Blue and its green combinations create space, give dimensions, make an atmosphere, distance the wall, make it imperceptible," whereas red and orange can "fix the wall, affirm its exact position, its dimension, its presence."[12]

This explains the color arrangement in Le Corbusier's Quartiers Modernes Frugès in Pessac, France (1924; see Fig. 7.9), where color imparts width to a small, rectangular-block courtyard: "We break the enclosure, by painting houses 'A' blue...; this barrier of houses then falls away toward the horizon. But in order for the outcome to be effective, we insist on anchoring the two lateral sides of the enclosure, to the left and to the right; we paint these B groups pure burnt Sienna earth (dark). The result is conclusive."[13]

Brightness of color is very important in the perception of a space's depth. Under gloomy conditions, brighter colors advance toward the observer, whereas under bright conditions, brighter colors recede. As Frank H. Mahnke, the former president of the International Association of Color Consultants (IACC), stated:

Lighting is one of the most important factors in our perception of openness in interior spaces. Light or pale colors recede and increase the apparent room size, as do cooler colors and smaller patterns. Dark or saturated hues protrude and decrease the apparent size of a room....A high illumination level will enlarge the appearance of volume, whereas a low illumination will diminish it.[14]

The American professor Mary C. Miller has demonstrated experimentally that the sense of depth in a room can be altered with the proper arrangement of white and black.[15] However, color is only one factor in the perception of depth, which involves many additional variables, such as overlapping, size, parallax, and visual focus.[16]

Visual weight

The visual weight of architecture is the observed sense of the force of attraction between a building and the earth. Color does not alter the real mass of the building but rather its feeling of lightness or heaviness. [Fig. 5.11] This sense

Fig. 5.11
Herzog & de Meuron,
Laban Center, London,
2002

is linked to a building's volume, its compactness, and its materials and is based on our own real experience with the physical weight of other objects. So a small body that is transparent, with many gaps, or a structure that is made from a material that we know to be light will be visually perceived as light.

Lightness is achieved by adjusting color to alter the perception of the three factors mentioned above:

1   Reducing the perception of size by fragmenting chromatically
2   Altering the perception of compactness by introducing chromatic confusion with the environment
3   Modifying the perception of materiality by interfering chromatically in the texture of the object

In Friedrich-Ernst von Garnier's industrial building for the shipyard of Stralsund, Germany (1999), the blues of the front facade reduce the visual weight of an architectural volume with huge dimensions in relation to the scale

Fig. 5.12
Friedrich-Ernst von Garnier, Stralsund shipyard, Stralsund, Germany, 1999

Fig. 5.13
Photomontage of Stralsund shipyard; depicting the building in red changes our perception of its mass.

of the town. In addition to mimicking the sky, the building's blue shades make its impressive mass appear lighter—especially if we imagine how it would look with reddish hues. [Figs. 5.12, 5.13]

Authors of color design manuals for architecture, such as Peter J. Hayten in the 1960s and Waldron Faulkner in the 1970s, often described color's capacity to alter the visual weight of objects. Faulkner stated that "elements in dark colors look heavy; those in light colors look light in weight. For this reason the color of tall structures is something graduated from dark at the bottom to light at the top."[17] Mahnke also posited that "darker colors appear heavier, whereas lighter and less saturated (pastel) tones seem less dense. If the hues are of the same value and intensity, the tendency is to perceive the warmer hues as heavier."[18] [Fig. 5.14]

In the late 1920s, Italian architect Piero Bottoni (1903–1973) referred in a very specific way to these phenomena. In his manifesto *Cromatismi architettonici*, he shows that, depending on its arrangement, a color gradation with different lightness (value) in ascending or descending order changes the apparent height of the centroid of a building.[19] If bright colors are located at the bottom of a facade, "it is easy to notice a sense of imbalance in the buildings of the street, and an anti-constructive consistency of the masses in the lower level." Bottoni relates the weight of the colors to Leonardo da Vinci's aerial perspective, which responds to the same principles:

> In general, the warm colors (red, orange) and earthy colors at their maximum intensity
> give a sense of mass-volume-color, higher than the one given by some cold colors
> (like green, or blue) and even light violet.... A red, black or earthy Sienna material resists
> better and is heavier than a light blue, gray, green olive, etc.[20]

Fig. 5.14 This translucent, orange textile skin seems lighter at night when it is backlit. Massimiliano and Doriana Fuksas, Zénith music hall, Strasbourg, France, 2007

Texture in architecture

Color may lend a different texture to building materials—an inexpensive resource that was commonly used in the past to emulate the finest materials. This technique fell out of favor because of Adolf Loos's manifesto *Ornament and Crime* (1906), in which Loos (1870–1933) calls for material truth. In consequence, color gradations were abandoned more or less consciously in favor of flat colors in later modern architecture. In fact, examples of contemporary buildings with colors that imitate specific materials are very scarce. One of these is the IADE Totobola Building in Lisbon (1984), by the Portuguese architect Tomás Taveira, in which the concrete is painted a metallic gray to mimic steel because of very exceptional circumstances that occurred during the execution of the building.

The expressionist painter Wassily Kandinsky pointed out that flat colors have inherent tactile qualities related to their synaesthetic potential:

Many colors have been described as rough or sticky, others as smooth and uniform, so that one feels inclined to stroke them (e.g., dark ultramarine, chromatic oxide green, and rose madder)....Some colors appear soft (rose madder), others hard (cobalt green, blue-green oxide), so that even fresh from the tube they seem to be dry.[21]

There are few contemporary buildings where the link between flat color and its intrinsic texture has been exploited consciously. However, an interest exists in producing colors with new textures incorporated. This was attested to by the Dutch architect Rem Koolhaas when he asked the more than thirty members of his firm, OMA, to choose their favorite color:

Only ten people chose a simple single color. Most imagined their colors as a treatment, a way to affect reality in a more subtle way than mere paint: not simply a layer of color but a more subtle conditioning, a layer that alters the state of the painted wall or object, a color that would interfere with the status of the painted object.[22]

Experimentation with novel textures incorporated into colored material has been a key feature in Swiss architecture during recent decades, with outstanding examples by Herzog & de Meuron. This is also the case with the color specialist Alain Bony's designs for Jean Nouvel's architecture, in which he uses different types of deterioration techniques to alter the walls' color and texture.

Although many contemporary buildings have textured finishes that do not match the actual construction material, these are usually based on a geometric

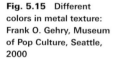

Fig. 5.15 Different colors in metal texture: Frank O. Gehry, Museum of Pop Culture, Seattle, 2000

pattern and not a naturalistic imitation of other
construction materials. In this sense, contemporary
color remains committed to the Loosian principle of
not simulating another material.[23] [Fig. 5.15]

5.3
How color describes architecture

When color is used as a strategy to describe architectural shape, it communicates some aspects of
the metric, the structural system, the logic of formal
operations used in the design, or the function,
among other elements.

Color and metrics

Color can provide information about the size of a
building and the proportional relationships among
its different parts. For example, Le Corbusier used
this strategy in the Pilgrim House in Notre Dame
du Haut, Ronchamp, France (1955), embellishing
the facade with a sequence of triangles of different
colors, which show the proportions that justify the
dimensions. [Fig. 5.16] Similarly, in Le Corbusier's
Heidi Weber Pavilion in Zurich, Switzerland (1965),
color identifies the structure's rectangular building
module, which has a two-to-one proportion.

Color and structural systems

When color highlights the structural system of an
architectural work, it tells us about its supporting method. A premodern example
is the Crystal Palace by Joseph Paxton (1803–1865), built for the International
Exhibition in London (1851) and colored by the Welsh architect Owen Jones
(1809–1874). This building epitomized an enlightened society that was confi-
dent in the progress of reason and science, and thus organized color in a
scientific way. Blue, yellow, and red were used to paint the cast-iron support
structure, following the elementary colors used by the French chemist Michel-
Eugène Chevreul in his representation of the *Cercle Chromatique*, which was
being exhibited at the same time in the French pavilion.[24]

Color arrangements that describe a structural system prevailed during the
modern period, thanks to the interest of architects in machine functionalism; this
strategy has provided a legacy for utopian designers from the 1960s through
the present.

Fig. 5.16
Le Corbusier, Pilgrim
House in Notre Dame
du Haut, Ronchamp,
France, 1955

Fig. 5.17
Sir Norman Foster,
Renault Centre,
Swindon, England,
1982

Fig. 5.18
MVRDV, Silodam
building, Amsterdam,
2002

The group of British architects Archigram renewed interest in industrial machinery as the emblem of a technological world that was to come. If Le Corbusier had been interested in the "machine for living," Archigram was mainly interested in the appearance of that machine. The Centre Georges Pompidou in Paris by Richard Rogers and Renzo Piano (1977) crystallizes this technological admiration and anticipates later High Tech architecture (see Activity 15). Rogers and other contemporary architects, such as Sir Norman Foster, continue to use color to express structural systems and introduce color accents to their buildings. [Fig. 5.17]

Color and architectural composition

Color can describe the formal operations of building design, expressing the process and highlighting composition mechanisms, such as the union, subtraction, juxtaposition, or hierarchy of components. Such is the case with MVRDV's residential building Silodam in Amsterdam (2002), where color defines the final volume of the building as the result of stacking a series of simple prisms, like a large container ship. [Fig. 5.18] The color of each piece also identifies different typologies of houses, offices, et cetera. This strategy is also developed in MVRDV's residential building Mirador in Madrid (2004). If the architects had

Fig. 5.19 MVRDV,
Mirador building,
Madrid, 2004

Fig. 5.20 Color helps
children to recognize
their classroom and
serves as a marker
of group identity for
the students. RCR
Arquitectes, Kindergarten
Els Colors, Manlleu,
Barcelona, 2006

resorted to monochromy, this building would have been perceived as simply
a large rectangular prism with a big hole rather than a collection of smaller parts
that combine to compose a bigger shape. [Fig. 5.19]

Color and architectural function

Modern architects, emancipated from the hierarchical composition systems of
classicism, expressed a new freedom by employing different formal devices.
One of these devices was the geometric pattern, an undifferentiated sequence,
homogeneous and isotropic, that arose as a logical consequence of prefabrication
and expressed the spirit of universality and democracy that underlay the modern
movement. Often in modular buildings, especially those for public use, architects
arranged color as a visual code to describe function and to allow users to find
their way around quickly. [Fig. 5.20] The Bauhaus building itself, in Dessau,
Germany, designed by Walter Gropius (1926), was subject to a functional color
scheme proposed by the German architect Hinnerk Scheper.

Sir Norman Foster asserts of his Commerzbank in Frankfurt, Germany (1997):

> *By color-coding the circulation cores in Per [Arnoldi]'s signature primaries of red, yellow,*
> *and blue, we were able to make the experience of navigating the building simple and*
> *pleasurable.... So you are guided from the lobby to your office by the simple experience*
> *of following your designated color.*[25]

Among the many outstanding examples of functional color composition is Terminal T4 at Adolfo Suárez Madrid-Barajas Airport, Spain, by Richard Rogers and Antonio Lamela (2005; see Fig. 8.9), where color indicates gate locations and permits travelers to visually estimate the distance to their gate. Another example is the chromatic intervention in Florentijn Hofman's Overschiesestraat in Schiedam, the Netherlands (2003), where the city's historic center has been revitalized by coloring the pavement of its main streets yellow.

At other times, colors express function by using conventional meanings, mostly recognized through context by any observer. Color can represent a corporation (the yellow of the Renault Centre by Foster in Swindon, England [1982]; see Fig. 5.17); a municipal service (the red and green of Sauerbruch Hutton's Fire and Police Station in Berlin [2004]) (see Activity 11); et cetera. In these contexts, color is coded according to the building's function and is difficult to misunderstand or interpret subjectively.

Color can also indicate the operation of building facilities, differentiating pipes for supplies, emergency systems, and so on (as with the Centre Pompidou; see Activity 15); this is a typical strategy for industrial architecture (for example, Jean-Philippe Lenclos's Solmer steel plant in Fos sur Mer, France [1974]). Color can even distinguish among "public spaces, gardens, and semiprivate spaces," as seen in color consultant Werner Spillmann's Kirchsteigfeld, a planned community in Potsdam, Germany (1997).[26] Color can represent the activities that take place inside the buildings, although not necessarily in a figurative manner [Fig. 5.21]; context remains crucial in interpreting the conventional meaning of color (see section 8.1).

Fig. 5.21 A sequence of saturated colors following the rainbow order gives joy and helps children to understand the function of the building, connecting the exterior facades with this central courtyard. RCR Arquitectes, Kindergarten El Petit Comte, Besalú, Girona, Spain, 2010

Activity 11
Analyzing a Project's Colors

Fig. 5.22 Sauerbruch Hutton, Fire and Police Station, Berlin, 2004

This project is an addition to a nineteenth-century building that contains a fire headquarters and a police station. The new prism-shaped structure was placed between a yard and the existing red-brick facades. The new facade's interesting backlit colored glass relates to the colors of the surroundings, the corporate colors of the services housed within, and a sense of weightlessness.[27] [Figs. 5.22, 5.23, 5.24]

Analyze the colors of the building. Try to understand the reasons for its color composition, avoiding as much as possible any psychological criteria. See that color can be used as a plastic strategy to reach some architectural goals.
    Use the checklist on the next page to help analyze the colors of any building.

 Find more examples of color analysis for architecture (in Spanish) at http://juaserl1.blogs.upv.es/juanserralluch /cuando-color-en-la-historia-de-la-arquitectura/color-en-la -arquitectura-contemporanea/.

Figs. 5.23 and 5.24
Sauerbruch Hutton, Fire
and Police Station, Berlin,
2004

Checklist for color analysis in architecture:

1   Color as a strategy for emphasizing shape

a   **In relation to context: mimicry/singularity**
Is a building's exterior color related to its environment?
Is there an intention to blend, camouflage, or even to
make the building disappear? Is there an intention to
outline the building and to singularize it? Is the building
in harmony with the environment while maintaining a
certain prominence?

b   **In relation to the geometry of the building:
integration/disintegration/distortion**
Does color help to unify the different parts of the
architectural composition? Does color suggest the
breakup or disintegration of the parts? Does color
introduce any confusion, distortion, or incompatibility
between its real geometry and the one perceived?

c   **In relation to dimensions**
Does color interact with the sense of width or height,
the proportions, or the scale of the architecture and
its spaces?

d   **In relation to visual weight**
Does color impart a sense of weightlessness to the
building? Does it make architecture lighter/heavier?
Does the building appear to be more emphatic as a
consequence of its color?

e   **Texture**
Does color add a new texture to the material? Does it
mimic any material different to that of the building?
Is there any geometric pattern play?

2   Color as a strategy for describing architecture

a   **Description of the function**
Is the color used as a code to define the use of the
architecture? Does color provide information about
routes, differentiate between public and private spaces,
give warnings about danger, et cetera?

b   **Description of the composition**
Does color give any clue about the composition of the
architecture? How has it been planned? What is its
metric? Its structural system?

3   Color used for its intrinsic value

Leaving aside other formal or functional questions,
can you determine any criteria for combining colors:
complementarity, cool/warm contrast, high/low
values? Can you identify rhythms, rules, gradations,
et cetera? Does color allude to any cultural references?

Activity 12
Architectural Color's Impact on the Urban Landscape

Certain buildings in the historic city center of Valencia are marked for demolition under local regulations because they are not in keeping with the aesthetic character of their surroundings, either because of excessive size, unsuitable facade elements, or other aesthetic considerations. These buildings will be replaced once they have come to the end of their useful life, which will not happen soon. We believe that it is meanwhile feasible to find simpler architectural solutions for those buildings whose facades overlook public spaces, working to improve their appearance and facilitate a certain degree of landscape integration. [Figs. 5.25, 5.26, 5.27, 5.28]

Figs. 5.25–5.28
Buildings in the city center of Valencia, Spain, with different proposals to improve their visual integration

We suggest three possible visual integration strategies: [Table 5.1]

Mimetic color arrangements, which are similar to the way in which animals camouflage themselves; these aim to make a building disappear by matching its color to its surroundings. See Roeland Otten, Transformatie Huisje, Rotterdam (2009). http://www.roelandotten.com

Harmonious color arrangements make a building congruent with its surroundings but not necessarily invisible, one example of which is the German artist Friedrich-Ernst von Garnier's Südzucker AG Mannheim/Ochsenfurt, Dresden (2005). It is noteworthy that British and American naval ships were painted in "dazzle," or disruptive camouflage, during the world wars as a kind of distraction. This type of painting was not intended to make the ships disappear but to transform observers' perception of their size, geometry, weight, or speed.

Contrasting color arrangements are a method of increasing the visual interest of the landscape. Architecture is not hidden but highlighted to increase the global cityscape's appeal, as seen in Boa Mistura Urban Art Group's Favela Vila Brasilândia, São Paulo, Brazil (2012; see Figs. 8.19, 8.20, 8.21). http://www.boamistura.com/

Another kind of contrasting integration is based more on an understanding of the character of the building than in any color-matching formula. Surrealist painters used this type of camouflage: the color of the object was not altered, but its meaning in context changed depending on the visual conditions of the surroundings.

Table 5.1
Integration strategies

Mimetic
Disappearance: colors camouflage the structure.

Cripsis of a praying mantis

Harmonious
Congruency: colors transform the perception of size, geometry, weight, rhythm, or other visual properties.

Passenger ship Zealandia in wartime dazzle paint, 1914

Contrasting
Discrepancy: contrasting colors offer a possible method of aesthetic integration.

Mae West's portrait room, Salvador Dalí Museum, Figueres, Spain

1   Find a building that has visual impact on an urban landscape and design a new facade to improve its integration. Decide if you will employ a mimetic, harmonious, or contrasting strategy.
     Review the possibilities for color to interfere with the visual properties of shapes (see sections 5.1 and 5.2). Look at von Garnier's industrial facilities in the landscape.

2   Experience in 4-D different architectural solutions for dwellings with visual impact in Valencia and describe your opinion about their landscape integration.
     Download my application LandArch: Evaluación del Impacto Visual. It is available for free in Google Play; users can observe the scenes on their personal devices or using Google Cardboard glasses.

View a demo video (in Spanish) at https://youtu.be/wY9hjar2dgs.

Activity 13
Architecture That Appears Integrated from a Distance,
Prominent from a Closer View

Fig. 5.29
Sauerbruch Hutton,
Museum Brandhorst,
Munich, 2009

This museum's compelling exterior skin is composed of vertical ceramic strips placed over other horizontal colored bars. From a distance, the colors blend into neutral earth tones that easily relate to the cityscape. From a closer vantage point,

the individual colors differentiate themselves and the lively, multicolored treatment of the facade reveals itself. The design provides two different solutions to the project's relationship to its environment, combining integration and singularity in a single treatment.[28] [Figs. 5.29, 5.30]

Fig. 5.30
Sauerbruch Hutton,
Museum Brandhorst,
Munich, 2009

1   Look for five to ten colors that blend into a single color when viewed
    from a distance, preferably a traditional color of your urban city center.
    [Fig. 5.31]

    a   Select one RGB color that the five to ten colors will blend into from
        the distance. In Photoshop, paint a blank image with that single color.

    b   In Photoshop apply "Filter > Pixelate > Color Halftone" to your image.
        It will be transformed into a grid of dots with primary colors, similar
        to a CMYK printed image. An alternative is to apply "Filter > Pixelate
        > pointillize," which creates an effect that resembles to a pointillist
        canvas. In both cases, the final image will still contain 256 colors per
        channel.

    c   Reduce the number of colors to the final amount that you would like
        to have on your facade (approximately five to ten), in "Image > Mode
        > Indexed Color." Choose the "Local (perceptual)" setting from the
        drop-down menu and enter the number of colors you want.

    d   Colors are indexed; you can find their notation in Lab, RGB, HSB, or
        CMYK in "Image > Mode > Color Table..." by clicking on each color.

    These five to ten colors can be translated to NCS or Pantone at
    http://www.e-paint.co.uk/Convert_RGB.asp.

    e   For the group of colors to blend into the initial single color from a
        distance, each needs to occupy approximately the same proportion of
        the facade.

    f   You can test the effect of viewing from a distance by mocking up a
        physical model using the selected colors.

2   Determine the approximate visual mixing of a group of colors when seen
    from a distance. Use the color palette of a real product.

    a   Find out the colors of the materials you want to use in RGB, Lab,
        HSB. The supplier can provide that information. Remember that these
        digital colors will always look different from physical ones. Choose a
        group of five to ten colors.

    b   In Photoshop, open a blank image and go to "Image > Mode >
        Indexed Color > Palette: custom." The color palette will open, and you
        can add the five to ten color notations manually by clicking on the
        gray grid. Now you have an image with a limited number of colors.

    c   Paint the blank image with the colors you have indexed, in the same
        proportion you want to render on the final facade.

    d   Apply "Filter > Blur > Average." You will see a digital approximation
        to the final color that you would see from a distance.

    e   You can test the effect of viewing from a distance by mocking up
        a physical model using the selected colors.

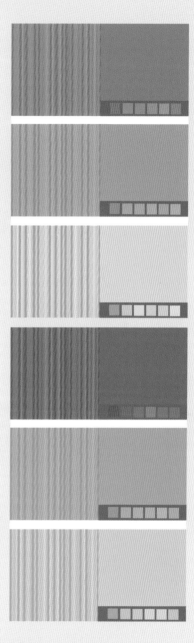

**Fig. 5.31 Color palettes that seem
to blend together when viewed from
a distance**

6 Visual Ergonomics

The disposition of colors in architecture can improve the performance of users. A good level of illumination, color rendering of lighting, and color contrast are necessary to help the visual legibility of a room so that observers can easily become oriented, recognize the room's different elements, and concentrate on tasks. These design considerations are particularly important for the visually impaired.

6.1
Visual ergonomics in the workplace

Vision is the primary sense that most individuals use to navigate the physical world. Consequently, workplaces need to be designed with a visual arrangement that is comfortable for workers. Even though workers' achievements are very much correlated with their overall abilities, good visual performance improves workers' ability to accomplish tasks and therefore to be productive.[1]
[Figs. 6.1, 6.2]

Several factors influence visual performance: the visual ability of an individual (see section 1.1), the visibility of the task, and psychosociological factors such as motivation, intelligence, stress, and so on. To establish efficient visual ergonomics, we must take into account both the worker's visual system and the visibility of the task.

A task that forces the visual system to its limits can cause general stress and eye fatigue and also increase the likelihood of mistakes or accidents. Therefore, workplaces should be adjusted in terms of minimum levels of illuminance and uniformity of glare rating, lighting, and color rendering index (see Appendix A).[2]

It has been experimentally demonstrated that color affects the level of fatigue experienced by the visual system; red hues accentuate fatigue, while blue ones

Figs. 6.1 and 6.2
The Bold Collective:
Ali McShane and Monika
Branagan, MEC 65 Berry
Street headquarters,
Sydney, 2012

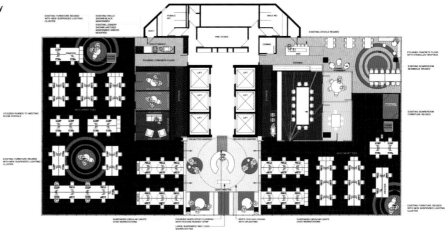

alleviate it. It has already been mentioned that the human eye is better adapted to deal with changing observation conditions than with a fixed color stimulus over a prolonged period of time. The larger the surface, the greater the fatigue, so it is especially important to understand a color's effects when choosing that color for a large area.[3]

6.2
Level of illumination, Correlated Color Temperature, and Color Rendering Index of lighting

It is common to associate visual performance with two basic variables: accuracy and speed. Good visual performance means that the task is performed without errors and in the shortest possible time. But how do visibility factors (size, distance, contrast, illumination, et cetera) affect visual performance? In 1945 the British researcher H. C. Weston created a basic framework for experiments measuring visual performance for various tasks. These results have been used to recommend levels of illumination in relation to the visual requirements of specific tasks.

Level of illumination
Weston's foundational research indicates that in order to improve visual performance, it is more effective to increase object sizes and color contrast than to increase only the illumination.[4] However, it is not always feasible to enlarge the size of the object of a task or to select more distinguishable colors, which means that the level of illumination must be controlled. To observe colors properly, a minimum level of illumination is needed, in the range of 300 lx to 1,000 lx.[5]

Correlated Color Temperature
Correlated Color Temperature (CCT) is a numerical measure of the chromatic appearance of an illumination source [Fig. 6.3], based on the light's similarity to the color of a theoretical body, called a "black body," heated to a certain temperature (see section 1.5). This is what lighting and color engineers call a **warm**, **neutral**, or **cool** appearance of lighting. The numeric value used to quantify it is called **color temperature** and indicates the chromatic aspect of the illuminant. Specific tones of lighting are recommended for various professional settings to improve their atmosphere of psychological comfort and to facilitate color discrimination.

   A color temperature value between 4,500 and 5,500 K (Kelvin degrees) is perceived as neutral: the illumination appears yellowish or bluish. A color temperature of 4,500 K or less seems more yellowish and reddish, which subliminally generates a psychological sensation of warmth and the (false) feeling of an ambient temperature increase. Finally, a color temperature of 5,500 K or higher

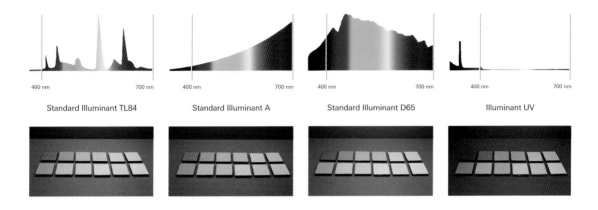

400 nm	700 nm	400 nm	700 nm

Standard Illuminant TL84   Standard Illuminant A   Standard Illuminant D65   Illuminant UV

Fig. 6.3
Color appearance
of different lights

indicates that the lighting is more bluish, giving the feeling of psychological cooling or an ambient temperature decrease.

Sunlight goes through several phases of color temperature or chromatic appearance during the day but is generally considered to be cold in appearance — over 6,500 K, with a high illumination level of 5,000 lx on asphalt on a sunny summer day. When color performance must be accurate, in industries such as textiles, printing, plastics, or paints, artificial lighting is always used as a simulator of daylight, aiming for a 6,500 K color temperature. In other activities, when color accuracy is not so crucial, other color temperatures can be used to generate psychologically warmer environments.

Color Rendering Index

The Color Rendering Index (CRI or Ra) is a colorimetric quality index for lighting.[6] The highest value on a qualitative scale from 0 to 100 is given to lighting that best simulates illuminant D65 in terms of matching the color appearance of eight target colors taken from the Munsell atlas (see Appendix A).

Street lighting, for example, is typically orange, which is not useful for good color discrimination. The color rendering value of conventional street lamps does not usually exceed 60. However, since these lamps minimize electricity consumption, city councils prioritize the reduction of costs over a more natural perception of the colors of streets and buildings. (This situation is changing with the increased use of LED lighting, which has a better CRI.)

Chromaticity in lighting must be coordinated with optimal lighting levels. For example, lighting levels for streetlamps (approximately 2,000 K) should not exceed 25 lx because if this level of illumination is exceeded, the feeling changes from comfortably warm to uncomfortably hot.

Likewise, for those professional activities where sophisticated color discrimination is required, cold lighting is recommended as well as a good simulation of daylight (approximately 6,500 K), if possible. This indicates that a comfortable illumination level should be greater than 500 lx, with an optimal range between 1,000 and 2,000 lx. If the level of illumination is too low for lighting with a cold appearance, the psychological sensation of cold is sharpened and feels uncomfortable. In brief, comfort in a cold-light environment requires increased illumination levels; in contrast, it is not appropriate to raise levels excessively in warm-light environments.

Gamut Area Index of Lamps

The Gamut Area Index of Lamps (GAI) is the area of the polygon defined by the chromaticity for each of eight target color samples defined by the International Commission on Illumination CIE, when illuminated by a source of light (see Appendix A).[7] [Fig. 6.4]

A higher GAI value is equivalent to greater saturation or vividness of the colors. CRI is a measure of how "natural" colors appear, while GAI is a measure of how saturated they look. High CRI and GAI values are ideal for good color observation; GAI values between 80 and 100 are recommended.

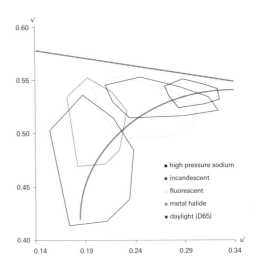

Fig. 6.4   Gamut areas of metal halide, high-pressure sodium, fluorescent, incandescent, and standard illuminants simulating daylight of 6,500 K. Based on Jean P. Freyssinier and Mark Rea, "A Two-metric Proposal to Specify the Color-Rendering Properties of Light Sources for Retail Lighting," *Tenth International Conference on Solid State Lighting, Proceedings of SPIE* **(San Diego, CA: SPIE, 2010): 7784.**

6.3
Color criteria for the visually impaired

The Spanish National Organization for the Blind (ONCE Foundation) makes the following recommendations for the design of architectural spaces and signage in buildings:[8]

Environments should provide chromatic contrast between backgrounds and shapes. Color schemes should be differentiated to facilitate spatial orientation and autonomous mobility, highlighting places of interest (such as information points, main rooms, and bathrooms), areas for caution (such as low ceilings or overhangs, stairs, ramps, and railings), windows, and other significant elements. [Figs. 6.5, 6.6]

- Use soft colors in interior rooms, highlighting details and areas with vivid colors.
- Indicate with color where floors end and walls begin and whether doors are open or closed.
- Create basic color codes referring to different elements and itineraries, based on security conditions, information, and evacuation procedures.

Table 6.5 source: Pablo Martín Andrade and Soledad Luengo Jusdado, *Accesibilidad para personas con ceguera y deficiencia visual* (Madrid: ONCE, 2003), 36–40.

Fig. 6.5
The Bold Collective,
Hollard Insurance Group,
Sydney, 2018

Fig. 6.6
The Bold Collective,
Third Horizon,
Sydney, 2016

**Table 6.5
Recommended
reflectance
percentage**

Ceilings	70–90%
Walls	40–60%
Floors	30–50%

Avoid reflections

- Use uniform and diffuse lighting. Light should come from many different directions, as this provides a greater ease of viewing, eliminating the shadows produced by a single light source and highlighting spatial structure. When diffuse lighting is used, lighting levels can be increased without provoking visual discomfort—the opposite of direct lighting, in which high luminance leads to high glare. Fluorescent and LED lights provide more diffuse lighting than incandescent ones.
- Modify the location of a light according to the surface onto which it shines, using less concentrated lamps and avoiding excessive illumination on surfaces with light colors. In those cases, it is better to choose matte or nonreflective finishes. See Table 6.5 for recommended reflectance percentages for surfaces.
- Choose matte rather than polished surface finishes; shiny ceilings, floors, walls, furniture, and fittings cause reflections and glare.
- Light sources should be located above the typical line of sight. Keep bulbs out of sight.
- Avoid using wall-fitted lights (other than uplights—those that are directed toward the ceiling) because they provide imbalanced lighting for the visually impaired and, at times, glare, although they can help with orientation if diffusing screens are used.
- Keep windows clean because dirty windows increase reflections.
- If exterior light sources are excessive and produce glare, due to either their intensity or the location, use colored glass or shutters to regulate the light.

Facilitating adaptation: photopic/scotopic

- In access areas, avoid excessive contrast in lighting between entrance halls and the outdoors (the so-called curtain effect). Offer transitional lighting; during the day, entryways should be well lit, and in the evening, entrance lights should be dimmed.
- The same is recommended for the rooms inside a building. Excessive changes of lighting between adjoining spaces such as corridors and rooms should be avoided; even if no glare is produced, shifts in lighting require constant eye adjustments, generating a feeling of insecurity. Provide a smooth transition in lighting levels in areas that are successively frequented (lobby, stairwells, elevators, offices, et cetera). The Canadian National Institute for the Blind (CNIB) recommends that the change in lighting from any one space to the next should not exceed 100 to 300 lx.
- Eyes are subject to fatigue when they are required to constantly adapt to different lighting levels. Take this into account when planning light distribution in different areas, following a ratio of 5 for core areas (work areas or highlighted areas) to 3 in subcore areas (those in close proximity to a core area) to 1 in peripheral areas (the rest of the room).

Size adjustment

For a visually impaired person with vision of about 10 percent, the minimum size for labels will depend on the distance from which they can be clearly read. [Table 6.6] It is important to be able to distinguish letters and figures from their backgrounds—especially for the elderly or people with visual impairments. Letters should be at least 1/4 in. (7 cm) high to be read from a distance of 19 11/16 in. (50 cm), and 2 13/16 in. (7 cm) high for distances of 16 5/8 ft. (5 m). Place the signs at a height between 35 and 69 in. (90 and 175 cm), with a maximum width of 24 in. (60 cm).[9]

Table 6.6
Size of a capital letter *E* for the visually impaired

Distance	Minimum size	Recommended size
≥ 5 m	7.0 cm	14 cm
4 m	5.6 cm	11 cm
3 m	4.2 cm	8.4 cm
2 m	2.8 cm	5.6 cm
1 m	1.4 cm	2.8 cm
0.5 m	0.7 cm	1.4 cm

Table 6.7
Color recommendations for signage for the visually impaired

Wall	Sign background	Lettering
gray	black	white / yellow
white / beige	black / garnet	white / yellow
red	white	black / green / blue
green	white	black / green / blue

Tables 6.6–6.8 source: Pablo Martín Andrade and Soledad Luengo Jusdado, *Accesibilidad para personas con ceguera y deficiencia visual* (Madrid: ONCE, 2003), 36–40.

Color contrast

Color should assist with orientation, providing enough contrast of both hue and value, because some people with visual impairments can neither differentiate nor identify color hues but are able to distinguish between different levels of value. Color can be used to locate and identify rooms or other elements (entrances, doors, et cetera). [Fig. 6.9]

- Colors used for signs, pictograms, doors, and so on should contrast with the background to facilitate visibility.
- For signs containing text, the CNIB recommends selecting colors for lettering based on that of the background wall (see Table 6.7). Letters should have sharp edges and saturated colors that contrast with the background of the sign; in turn, both should contrast with the wall or door on which they are placed.
- For posters that need to be read from a distance, high-value color lettering over a dark background will provide the greatest contrast and, generally, will be the most legible. [Table 6.8]
- For text that will be quickly read, choose an appropriately large point size with a clear resolution and plenty of spacing between the letters.
- Select colors for light switches, sockets, doorbells, et cetera that contrast with their backgrounds.
- Fittings such as doorknobs and door handles should contrast with the color of the door. Their positioning should remain constant in all rooms.

Fig. 6.7 The Bold Collective, Wunderman-Bienalto, Sydney, 2014

Table 6.8
Recommended color contrasts for the visually impaired

Detail	Background surface
black	yellow
green / red / blue / black	white
yellow	black
white	red / dark green / dark blue / black

7 Does Architecture Need to Be White?

Color has always been an essential visual attribute of architecture. Historians of modernity paid no particular attention to it, nor did many professionals and academics laboring under a false understanding of the modern tradition, but the fact remains that the architects of modernity (approximately between 1920 and 1960) used color in a very deliberate manner, at a time when psychology was striving to come to terms with the mechanisms of the perception of shape. Although the myth of the color white in modernity has been debunked, a somewhat discontinuous chromatic tradition remains to be reread; it bears remembering that there was not a single building by Le Corbusier in only white.

7.1
Purism, expressionism, and neoplasticism

Discussions of color composition in modern architecture have often been overly simplistic. In fact, it is a complex topic, given the variety of approaches and the uniqueness of their authors. [Fig. 7.1]

Three major architectural color-composition schemes arose in the first half of the twentieth century: Purism (Le Corbusier), expressionism (Bruno Taut), and neoplasticism (Gerrit Thomas Rietveld). Based on a study of all three, some noncategorical principles of color composition in modern architecture can be identified: (1) use a limited variety of hues, but not only white; (2) color should reinforce shape, but also transform it; and (3) the connotations of color go far beyond their aesthetic qualities.

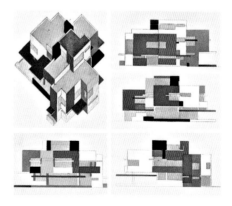

Fig. 7.1 Theo van Doesburg's design for a university hall, 1923

7.2
The myth of white in modern architecture

Architectural modernity became associated with certain fixed ideas about color, especially a predominant use of white, the use of flat and homogeneous colors (without variation of hue, value, or chroma), and the idea that color must be considered from the first design stage.[1] Generations of architects believed that "modern architecture should not contain any color except the white and gray of natural materials"[2] and that "in the search for the purity of form, color [must be] eradicated in order to avoid distortions."[3]

The belief that modern architecture used only the color white has become almost a mythical concept. This has been proved erroneous by numerous authors, but it persists in a notion of architectural purism and heroism. Historian and architecture critic Josep Maria Montaner has pointed out a historiography of the modern movement, the aim of which was to justify and legitimize the activities of avant-garde architects who were "splendidly isolated from everything that had gone before, as if they were mythical heroes battling against the enemy of academician decadence, legitimizing the values of a new moral order through education, regeneration and hygiene."[4]

International Style
In 1932 Philip Johnson (1906–2005) and Henry-Russell Hitchcock (1903–1987) published *The International Style: Architecture Since 1922* to accompany an exhibition at the Museum of Modern Art (MoMA), New York. The exhibition and book set the canonical foundations of a style that had not been previously identified as such. Johnson and Hitchcock, inspired by the iconological criticism of Swiss art historian Heinrich Wölfflin (1864–1945), focused on the appearance and language of the European modern movement rather than its socialist-utopian ideological background. They highlighted three essential principles of the new modern architecture: (1) its design as volume rather than as mass, (2) the principle of balance as opposed to classical symmetry, and (3) the lack of decoration.[5] Formal aspects such as the open plan, oblong windows, flat roofs, lack of ornamental features, and the use of steel, concrete, and glass for cladding appeared to be the inexorable stylistic dictates that any building must follow if it wished to be "modern."[6] [Fig. 7.2]

Considering that the MoMA exhibition contained a model of Le Corbusier's Villa Savoye and a caption in the catalog highlights the use of pink and blue on its roof, architect Mark Wigley is correct to point

Fig. 7.2
Photo of the exhibition *Modern Architecture: International Exhibition* at the Museum of Modern Art, New York, in 1932

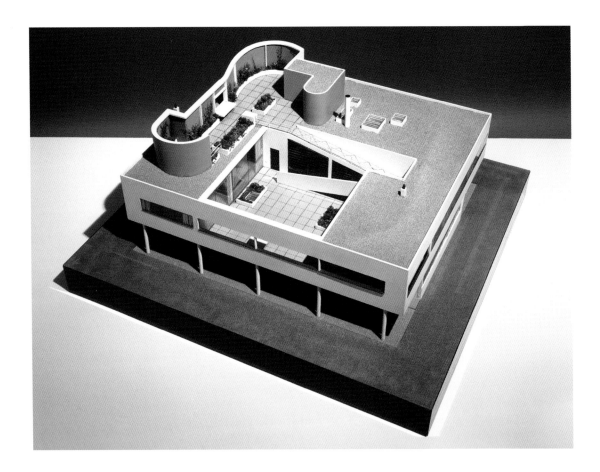

Fig. 7.3 Le Corbusier, model of the Villa Savoye exhibited in *Modern Architecture: International Exhibition* at the Museum of Modern Art, New York, in 1932, curated by Philip Johnson and Henry-Russell Hitchcock

Fig. 7.4 Le Corbusier, Villa Savoye, Poissy, near Paris, 1929. The ground floor of the Villa Savoye maintains its original green color, which mimics the surrounding greenery, but the curved walls on the roof were not restored to their original red and blue.

out that the only possible explanation for the success of white in modernism is a blindness toward color, resulting in it "being separated from the main architectural narrative."[7] [Figs. 7.3, 7.4]

This blindness is nurtured by both the hostility toward decoration of Adolf Loos and the defense of "material truth" by Victorian art critic John Ruskin (1819–1900). There are, however, other more far-reaching cultural reasons for what some people have described as a veritable case of chromophobia in Western thinking, fueled by such influential characters as Aristotle, Plato, and Goethe.[8]

Weissenhofsiedlung

The culmination of this opposition of white and colored architecture occurred with the opening of the Weissenhofsiedlung in Stuttgart, Germany (1927). [Fig. 7.5] The most renowned architects from the Deutscher Werkbund, which was a German association of artists, architects, designers, and industrialists, established in 1907, contributed model homes to this complex of twenty-one buildings, with Mies van der Rohe in charge of the master plan. The critic Tom Wolfe has noted with irony that all these dwellings display a common nonbourgeois "international style" because of their reductionist use of just white, beige, gray, and black.[9] Nevertheless, and despite the fact that *Weissen-hofsiedlung* can be translated as "settlement of white houses," only a third of the units were completely white.

Mies himself expressed his disapproval of color when the facades of his dwellings at the Weissenhofsiedlung took on a red cast from the light reflected

Fig. 7.5 Mies van der Rohe designed the master plan of the Weissenhofsiedlung, 1927; other renowned architects contributed designs for houses: Peter Behrens, Hans Poelzig, Bruno and Max Taut, and Hans Scharoun, among others.

off Bruno Taut's facades, painted in bright colors. Taut offered a sharp rejoinder to Mies: "If it seems out of place in the present state of the project, this may well mean, not that the colors have been wrongly used, but that the surrounding buildings are unfinished."[10]

In any case, the Weissenhofsiedlung went down in history as a settlement of white houses, which was used as leverage by anti-Semitic naysayers who gave the neighborhood the nickname "the new Jerusalem." Some authors argue that the link between modernity and white that occurred after the Second World War could partially be put down to the reaction to this aggravation—so much so that after 1945, white became synonymous with internationalization.[11]

Fig. 7.6 Richard Meier, Hartford Seminary, Hartford, Connecticut, 1978

Fig. 7.7 Le Corbusier, interior of the exhibition room, Maison La Roche-Jeanneret, Paris, 1925

The New York Five

Following the 1972 publication of the book *Five Architects*, the architects it profiled, Peter Eisenman (b. 1932), Michael Graves (1934–2015), Charles Gwathmey (1938–2009), John Hejduk (1929–2000), and Richard Meier (b. 1934), became known as the New York Five, or the "Whites," because of their pursuit of architectural purism and the use of white or natural materials, as well as their often categorical remarks, such as those of Meier:

> For me, white is the most wonderful color because within it you can see all the colors of the rainbow. For me, in fact, it is the color which in natural light, reflects and inten-sifies the perception of all of the shades of the rainbow.... It is against a white surface that one best appreciates the play of light and shadow, solids and voids.[12]

Meier's echo of Le Corbusier's well-known phrase "architecture, the masterly, correct, and magnificent play of masses brought together in light"[13] shows the influence that Le Corbusier's villas of the 1920s had on the Whites, although it also reflected the bias against color that had become commonplace among the architects of the late twentieth century. [Fig. 7.6]

7.3
Fewer hues, but not only white

In his early texts, Le Corbusier primarily warned architects of the dangers of color rather than promoting its use. The Swiss maestro refused

to let "the wall turn into a tapestry, and the architect into an upholsterer" but rather suggested "eliminating colors that can be qualified as nonarchitectural; better than that, research and select the colors than can be called eminently architectural, and restrict them so that we can tell ourselves: These are enough!"[14] And true to his word, he chose an abbreviated selection of thirty-two colors for the charts he created for the Salubra Wallpaper Company (1931; see Activity 10).

Bruno Taut, like Le Corbusier, distinguished between his vocations of painter and architect, prioritizing the latter: "The painter inside of me is subordinated to the architect. For me, painting can never be an end in itself."[15] He believed that certain colors are better suited to architecture, while others are best suited to painting. He generally rejected the secondary colors (oranges, violets, and greens) because he considered them somewhat gaudy for architecture and chose instead pure colors with different degrees of value, in line with the characteristics of spaces: "Above all, the purity of the chromatic composition has to prevail,

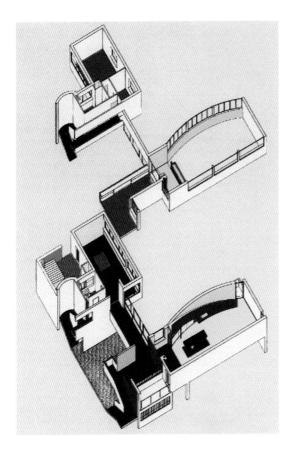

Fig. 7.8 Le Corbusier, axonometric drawing of Maison La Roche-Jeanneret, Paris, 1925

as the essential postulate, so that said purity of color and light is in line with the purity of the remaining elements of the construction, namely, space, mass, and style."[16]

Taut also warned of the dangers of variegated color: "Pure, intense colors are impressive, but incorrectly applied are much worse than no color at all. A combination of intense colors is not coloration, in the same way that a combination of loud noises is not a melody."[17]

But lest we be fooled, the German architect was a firm defender of bold color compositions, especially in urban areas, where he advised against "half measures." The "purity" of Taut's color is not in contradiction with high levels of creative liberty and is, of course, far removed from the strait-jacketing rationalism of Purist Le Corbusier or of the narrow range of colors favored by his neoplasticist colleagues.

Indeed, neoplastic architecture was characterized by a tonal range that included only the subtractive primary colors (red, yellow, and blue) and the neutral ones (white, black, and gray). Certain authors associated this essential color range with notions of primitivism, which encouraged other contemporary architects to resort to the use of white. Neoplasticists claimed a symbiosis between painting and architecture without favoring one or the other. Both need and complement each other, given that, in the words of artist Piet Mondrian (1872–1944), "By the unification of architecture, sculpture, and painting, a new plastic reality will be created. Painting and sculpture will not manifest themselves as separate objects, nor as 'mural art' which destroys architecture itself."[18] As the Dutch painter Bart van der Leck (1876–1958) affirmed, "If architects are looking for a painter who can supply the desired image, the modern painter is no less seeking an architect who can offer the appropriate conditions for the joint achievement of a true unity of plastic expression."[19]

7.4
Colors that not only reinforce shape but also transform it

In modern architecture, color is consonant with the composition of form and space, with shape determined by the conceptual idea. Le Corbusier therefore used color to bolster the geometry of the volumes of his architecture. That said, he also used color to introduce a certain tension into the "boxed space" and transform interior spaces to achieve the "elastic rectangle" of artist Fernand Leger.[20] The Swiss master himself stated, "To tell the truth, my house will only radiate white, in view of the fact that I have applied the effective powers of colors and color values at appropriate places."[21] [Figs. 7.7, 7.8]

Fig. 7.9
Gerrit Thomas Rietveld, Schröder House, Utrecht, the Netherlands, 1923

Gerrit Thomas Rietveld went even further and used color to express the breakdown of the architectural volume and the visual independence of each of the elements in his famous Schröder House. [Fig. 7.9] The house's component parts are physically and visually separated using color, which distinguishes and determines the identity of each individual one. In this sense, color reinforces the idea of the shape, expressing the dispersion of the architectural elements. Coloration was intrinsically linked to the concept of the form and contrasted with classic coloration, which was considered superfluous decoration that was added a posteriori.

We see, however, that modern architects did not always conceive the color during the design stage but sometimes after the fact. This was the case with the color intervention in urban areas overseen by Bruno Taut when he was named the Magdeburg councilor of public works. These color compositions were applied to preexisting facades, clearly transforming both their form and the interpretation of their classical composition.

Similarly, we are aware of at least two cases where Le Corbusier added polychromy once a building was completed: Unité d'Habitation residential housing in Marseille, France (1952), and Les Quartiers Modernes Frugès housing development in Pessac, France (1924). [Fig. 7.10] In other examples, such as the Swiss Pavilion at the International University Campus in Paris or the Villa Savoye, Le Corbusier even developed two different color interventions over the course of the buildings' lifespans (although in the Villa Savoye, the second intervention was never carried out). According to Le Corbusier, the proportion of the jambs and lintels of the concrete Unité dwellings were contrary to his wishes, so he used color to offset construction errors:

> During the busiest period of construction there was never a false step, not an ugly wall, not a blemish, not a dead space....With the exception of two liberties taken by a careless engineer...: windows outside the regulating proportion and cast concrete squares of a different module....Such off-hand behavior of numbers in the midst of the Modulor's harmonies was, to me, so distressing that, near exasperation, I hit upon the idea of exterior polychromy. But a polychromy so dazzling that the mind was forcibly detached from the dissonances, carried away in the irresistible torrent of major color sensations....But for these faults, the exterior of the Marseilles Unité might, perhaps, not have been multi-colored.[22]

In Pessac Le Corbusier used color on the facades of a building complex that, once built, appeared excessively compact. Color was used "to create distance between each home and the adjoining one, so that they were opened up, breaking away from the sense of crowding from the walls....Through color, we are able to create the optical illusion, and, inside us, we have a different perception of said elements."[23] Beyond these dimensional considerations, the architect addressed a simple, vital need, as the gray cement plaster had an "unbearable sadness," which required color to "give interest." The colors might well have been suggested by Monsieur Frugès himself when the developer had difficulty finding buyers for the houses, which were of a uniform style that differed greatly from that of the traditional homes of Bordeaux.[24]

It should not be a surprise that Le Corbusier provided colors for his designs a posteriori.[25] Purism maintains that the idea of form precedes that of color. As with cubism, the initial focus is on the form, in contrast to movements such as expressionism and fauvism that prioritized color. Wassily Kandinsky contrasted the artwork of Pablo Picasso with that of Henri Matisse: "If color seems to bulk him in his search for a pure artistic form, he throws it overboard and paints a picture in brown and white....In the pursuit of the same supreme end Matisse and Picasso stand side by side, Matisse representing color and Picasso form."[26]

For Le Corbusier, the essential element in architecture was the volumes of the design, followed by how light plays on the form, whereas for Taut the light (color) came first, and then the form. For Taut, the architect should "shape the appearance of light." Quoting the German architect Hans Poelzig (1869–1936), Taut states that "color is the starting point of a new style before form is refined."[27]

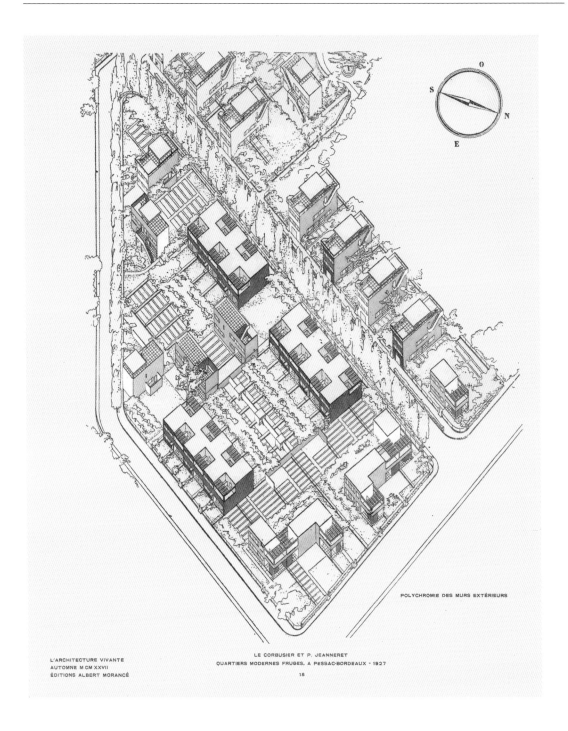

POLYCHROMIE DES MURS EXTÉRIEURS

LE CORBUSIER ET P. JEANNERET
QUARTIERS MODERNES FRUGES, A PESSAC-BORDEAUX · 1927

L'ARCHITECTURE VIVANTE
AUTOMNE M CM XXVII
ÉDITIONS ALBERT MORANCÉ

15

Fig. 7.10
Le Corbusier,
Les Quartiers
Modernes Frugès
in Pessac,
France, 1926

Whether advocating the addition of color in the initial stages or afterward, it is true that modern architects appear to remain faithful to a single principle: color always expands until it becomes an architectural element in its own right, and it does so without changes of hue, value, or saturation. This principle of "plain colors" is shared by Le Corbusier, Rietveld, and Taut. Even Johnson and Hitchcock suggest it as a criteria for modernism, believing that "it is also important that the surface remain a plane without convexities and concavities. Otherwise the effect becomes picturesque and the sense of equal tension in all directions is destroyed."[28]

To be more precise, at times there could be color variation within the same architectural element, although the demarcation between colors was abrupt, not gradual, drawing a clear line. For example, in the Aubette Cafe, the German architect Theo van Doesburg (1883–1931) worked with different colors on the same surface, but these were always separated by a black line; one can clearly see the start and the end of the colored surfaces. In modern architecture, colors either corresponded with the entire object or they built their own borders.

Nevertheless, amid the debate about modernity, the Italian architect Piero Bottoni suggested using color gradations instead of plain colors in his 1927 manifesto "Cromatismi architettonici." This theoretical paper was accompanied by a set of watercolor views of a street in which the buildings' luminosity of color varied vertically. He presented it as part of the third Monza International Decorative Art Festival, convinced that the "volumetric function of color has never been studied enough and, moreover, the 'mass-volume' power attributed by a color to a geometric solid plays an important role in the aesthetic balance and the perception of the 'resistant' values of any structure."[29]

But it was clear that the gradation of color violated the orthodoxy of "flat-constructive color" and opened the dangerous possibility of unjustifiable color — color that would deform rather than conform. Accordingly, it was inevitable that Bottoni would earn the disapproval of certain architects, including his compatriots.[30]

7.5
Colors with connotations that go beyond the purely aesthetic

If there were a single element common to all the architectural movements of modernity, it was the desire to serve as the motor of a social and cultural shift. This drive for change was manifested in opposition to the academic architecture of the nineteenth century, which was criticized both "for its lack of color by some architects, and for its use of color by others."[31] The use of crisp colors and color overload share a common aesthetic undercurrent of rejecting the past.

A number of authors have pointed out that Le Corbusier's penchant for white is better understood in terms of ideological concerns than visual ones. Le Corbusier's concerns were more culturally than socially based. In contrast to those of the German *Siedlungen*, the colors used at Pessac had no social motives but rather were employed in service of a "completely new and fundamentally rational polychrome."

Bruno Taut considered color compositions audacious, such as that of his own Glass Pavilion for the Deutscher Werkbund Exhibition in Cologne, Germany (1914), which augured the arrival of a new time. [Figs. 7.11, 7.12] Taut's design synthesized the utopian ideals advocated by Paul Scheerbart (1863–1915) in his manifesto "Glass Architecture" (1914), as well as the emergence of a new culture prophesized by architect Adolf Behne (1885–1948). According to Taut, color gives rise to shadows, which should be understood from not only a visual but also a metaphorical perspective: color is able to illuminate a new society and a new architecture. Color has moral and physical consequences that can be observed in the behavior of children, who prefer to play in brightly colored streets rather than gray ones.

The artistic convictions of the neoplasticists were also based on spiritual or even mystical substrata, influenced by the writings of Kandinsky, who spoke about the "inner need" of the artist, who may use "any form which his expression demands, for his inner impulse must find outward expression."[32] Even so, neoplasticism adopts a less committed social position than those of other movements, according to Dutch architect J. J. P. Oud (1890–1963):

> A healthy, broad, universal social architecture could never come from this, i.e. from so abstract an aesthetic.... My position is similar to that of the alchemists of the past, who did not find gold in their search for gold, but some other precious material.[33]

At the end of the 1920s, van Doesburg stated that "white is the color of modern times, the color which dissipates a whole era."[34] The neoplastic approach to color was not dogmatic, given that both primary colors and the color white could be the standard-bearers of the new culture.[35] [Figs. 7.13, 7.14, 7.15]

Independent of colors used, the common ethical awareness that led the different movements to reject academic art also made them avoid the use of color for decoration. To achieve this, they relied on a variety of mechanisms: imitation was abandoned in favor of "material truth"; figuration was replaced with abstraction; and overall, an intellectual attitude toward color was encouraged, to avoid arbitrary or capricious decisions.

Figs. 7.11 and 7.12
Exterior and interior of Bruno Taut's Glass Pavilion, Cologne, Germany, 1914

Fig. 7.13
Gerrit Thomas Rietveld, Vries Garages, Utrecht, the Netherlands, 1928

Figs. 7.14 and 7.15
Original building
and reconstruction.
J. J. P. Oud, Coffee de
Unie, Rotterdam, the
Netherlands, 1925

Fig. 7.16
Piet Mondrian,
*Composition II in Red,
Blue, and Yellow* (detail),
1930

The neoplastic group achieved this by depriving color of "any emotional content, understanding it as an abstract matter that can be organized according to rational principles."[36] They believed that cubism did not go far enough in its abstraction and were suspicious of expressionism, believing it to be excessively personal.[37] Members of the de Stijl movement were not interested in representing sensual experience or in "the stimulating effect of color on the nerves" or "the concentric effect" of Taut's color experiments in his Glass Pavilion,[38] but rather they imagined artists as scientists in their laboratory, intellectually examining form and color.[39] The neoplasticists aspired to a more universal and aesthetic culture, as expressed by Mondrian: [Fig. 7.16]

> *Gradually art is purifying its plastic means and thus bringing out the relationships between them. Thus, in our day two main tendencies appear: the one maintains the figuration, the other eliminates it. While the former employs more or less complicated and particular forms, the latter uses simple and neutral forms, or, ultimately, the free line and the pure color."[40]*

This distancing from nature was achieved by taking architecture back to its basics: lines and planes, in the case of the spatial box, and the primary hues, in the case of color. In other words, neoplasticists used the fundamental colors on which all the others rely—those to which the neoplatonic philosopher M. H. J. Schoenmaekers (1875–1944) gave a metaphysical sense: "Yellow is the movement of the ray (vertical)....Blue is the contrasting color to yellow (horizontal firmament)....Red is the mating of yellow and blue."[41]

Purism forewent decoration, searching instead for universal and invariable rules. "The work should not be accidental, exceptional, impressionistic, contestatory, picturesque, but on the contrary general, static, expressive of what is constant," stated Le Corbusier and his collaborator, the French painter Amédée Ozenfant, in their doctrine on Purism.[42] Purism advocated an "ultra-rationalist" theory that champions the intellectual dominance of color and achieves a formal cleansing.[43]

Le Corbusier sometimes used color to separate one architectural element from another so that each would appear to be autonomous, but very few times did his use of color reduce a volume to its component elements (lines and planes), as occurred with neoplasticism. Although somewhat paradoxical, when Le Corbusier broke up a volume through color, it facilitated the apprehension of the volume itself, extricating it from its secondary additions, as can be seen with Villa Savoye. Le Corbusier states that color enables one to put into order, prioritize, or unify the final space.[44]

Similarly, Taut went from early expressive compositions to the use of colors with a functional purpose during his final period. Describing his own house in Dahlewitz, outside Berlin (1927), he stated that "here, the pure aesthetic... is nothing more than the result of what was practical."[45] The architect ended by rationalizing the chromatic composition, proffering functional arguments to substantiate his formal decisions.

7.6
Conclusions: color in modern architecture

Upon a review of the three most significant color composition systems from the first half of the twentieth century (Purism, expressionism, and neoplasticism), three noncategorical principles of modern color emerge:

1   A limited variety of colors were used, but not only white. Having debunked the myth of all-white color, we see that the architects examined drew on a limited palette of architectural colors: Le Corbusier selected a considerable range of secondary colors (oranges and greens) and earth tones, Bruno Taut rejected secondary colors, and Gerrit Thomas Rietveld used exclusively primary colors with maximum saturation. They did so to avoid the "excess of color" of painted decoration and to refine the form.

2   Color not only reinforced shape, but also transformed it. Color in modern architecture was in keeping with the composition of spaces. It moved away from nineteenth-century color schemes added a posteriori, which did not always tie in with the ideation of the form. It has been shown that modern architects were not dogmatic in their approach to implementing color in their designs, with examples from Le Corbusier, who used it to transform an already constructed reality. It was common in modernity for color to cover a whole architectural element or to create its own limits; it did so without any variation in hue, value, or saturation. Neither is this principle of "plain colors" categorical, as Piero Bottoni pointed out the possibility of color gradations in the midst of modernity.

3   Color responded to moral concerns that transcended aesthetics. Color schemes, whether simple or gaudy, were selected to bring about a cultural break from the past: abandoning imitation and instead seeking to express "material truth"; foregoing figuration in favor of the essential and the abstract (neoplasticism, Purism); searching for universal rules to systematize color (Le Corbusier); addressing social and utopian concerns (expressionism); and, in general terms, imbuing color with intellectual significance.

Activity 14

Color in Modern Architecture and the Myth of White

1 Read the following texts. Is any information unexpected? Do you find any contradictions with your previous beliefs about color in modern architecture between 1920 and 1960?

2 Can you explain the main color tendencies in architecture during the modern movement? Choose a modern building and describe it as a case study.

3 Do you think that white has still a different status from other colors for architects?

4 Compare the text by Rem Koolhaas with the others. In his opinion, what's the logic of color in the future?

Le Corbusier, in _Journey to the East_ (1911)
You recognize these joys: to feel the generous belly of a vase, to caress its slender neck, and then to explore the subtleties of its contours. To thrust your hands into the deepest part of your pockets and, with eyes half-closed, to give way to the slow intoxication of the fantastic glazes, the burst of yellows, the velvet tones of the blues; to be involved in the animated fight between brutal black masses and victorious white elements.[46]

John Ruskin, in _The Seven Lamps of Architecture_ (1880)
The true colors of architecture are those of natural stone, and I would fain see these taken advantage of to the full. Every variety of hue, from pale yellow to purple, passing through orange, red, and brown, is entirely at our command; nearly every kind of green and gray is also attainable: and with these, and pure white, what harmonies might we not achieve?... This is the true and faithful way of building.[47]

Adolf Loos (1908)
I do not understand architects! They are always afraid of using strong colors beside each other.

I find that a meadow full of flowers is very beautiful, and yet every flower is a different color.

Colors can be used together in a room in exactly the same way as long as they are pure as the colors of a meadow of flowers. It is only the blended colors, the dirtied colors, that are not pretty.[48]

Rem Koolhaas, in _Colours_ (2001)
In a world where nothing is stable, the permanence of color is slightly naive; maybe it could change. In a world where nothing is what it seems, the directness of color seems simplistic— maybe it can create more complex effects....

It is only logical that, with the incredible sensorial onslaught that bombards us every day and the artificial intensities that we encounter in the virtual world, the nature of colour should change, no longer just a thin layer of change, but something that genuinely alters perception. In this sense, the future of colours is looking bright.[49]

Michiel Riedijk (2007)
How color is used and expressed in a building is decided by that building's material form. The distinction between structure and finish made by uncoupling the physical properties of interior and exterior allows color to be regarded as a separate design layer in the elevations, distinct from the material used.

This is both the beauty and the tragedy of using paint to color buildings. It can be painted over at any time. Thus, expressing the building and its cultural significance is left to the whims of the janitor. Paint as a color medium would appear to run counter to the architectural desire to express a design in enduring, permanent terms....It seems, therefore, that the color of the material itself is the only true means of expressing the architect's obsessions and desires.[50]

8 The Meaning of Color

If color in architecture in previous chapters has been addressed from a
grammatical point of view, highlighting its link with the formal conception of
the shape, in this chapter we will pay attention to its semantic characteristics.
Colors have meanings for the observer in specific contexts, and architects
can use color to codify specific information. These meanings can be cultural
and conventional or might rely on more unconscious psychological roots.
Much current research is being conducted to understand how human reactions
and activity performance might be influenced by color.

8.1
Color's meaning in context

Color has an inherent ability to transmit messages. It provides coded information
that we translate, consciously or unconsciously—at least, that is what evolution-
ary psychologists believe when they discuss why color occurs in nature and why
Homo sapiens evolved to perceive color in such a sophisticated way.

Colors attract attention, provide information, and convey emotion. Psychologists believe that humans still experience an ancient, unconscious response
to color, even though survival in our multicolored contemporary built environment
no longer depends on it.[1]

A color's meaning depends on its context. For example, the color red is used
in the animal world both to attract and to repel, so it can represent something
threatening, like an open mouth, as well as something attractive, like a woman's
red lips. Therefore, the context is essential to understand the meaning of red.[2]

Turning to our built surroundings, the architectural critic Dirk Meyhöfer
came to a similar conclusion after reviewing about seventy contemporary
colored buildings: "Color does not mean the same thing in every context; on the

contrary…to a specific color can be associated different meanings depending on the case assigned."[3]

The relationship between **signs** and their **significance** is studied in depth in semiotics. Semioticians such as the Italian scholar Umberto Eco have proposed that every cultural phenomenon may be studied as communication.[4] The Argentinean architect José Luis Caivano posits that from a semantic point of view, there are three types of color signs: **icon**, **index**, and **symbol**.[5]

Color is an icon when its significance is related to natural phenomena; for instance, the blue of the air-conditioning pipes on the Centre Georges Pompidou, Paris, draws on our common experience of the blue sky (see Activity 15). The use of red and blue to identify hot and cold water from a faucet is also an iconic meaning, as these colors are linked to our experience of fire and ice in nature.

Color is an index when its significance reflects the physical state of the colored element itself. For example, the green facade of the NEMO Science Museum in Amsterdam, designed by Renzo Piano (1997), is a result of the natural patination of the exterior's copper surface as it weathers; the color is an index of time's passage.

Color acts as a symbol when it has an arbitrary and conventional meaning that is understood in a particular cultural and physical context. For example, red can be useful to identify the emergency exits in a public building, as many cultures associate the color with danger. In another context, red might symbolize a famous trademark—and, by extension, speed and thrill—as when it represents Ferrari at the Ferrari World Abu Dhabi theme park in the United Arab Emirates (2010).

It is important to remember that these meanings are not universal and that they should not limit the creative freedom of architects. When the Danish artist Per Arnoldi was collaborating with British architect Sir Norman Foster on the color palette for the Reichstag Parliament in Berlin, he demonstrated that it is possible to free color from strict symbolic associations—for example, green with ecology-minded practices, black with fascism, red and blue with right- and left-wing political parties—and use it purely toward compositional ends, even in a parliamentary building.[6]

8.2
Color meanings codified by the architect

Colors are useful for formulating and understanding a message within a specific context; this narrative potential of color can help the viewer to understand an architectural space/object and some of its peculiarities. In architecture these codings usually relate to a building's function, metric, structural system, or the logic of formal operations used in the design, among other elements (see section 5.3).

Fig. 8.1 Color coding indicates vegetation in green and built area in red, linking the facades with their surroundings. Sauerbruch Hutton, Federal Environmental Agency, Dessau, Germany, 1998

Le Corbusier assigned universal meanings to some colors when he gave names to his twelve color keyboards for Salubra in 1931: sky (blue ranges), earth (brown ranges), landscape (green ranges), et cetera (see Activity 10). Thus, we can understand that when Le Corbusier chooses green to paint the parapets of the terrace in his own studio-apartment in Paris or in the houses at the Weissenhofsiedlung, he is stressing the idea of the "green roof," one of his five points for the new architecture. Color is meaningful as a reinforcement for an architectural principle.

Simple combinations of colors are often chosen to be easily distinguished and to be associated with a more or less conventional meaning. [Figs. 8.1, 8.2, 8.3] The architect must be aware of the color discrimination thresholds of each variable of perception (hue, value, and saturation), as well as the laws of contrast; Rudolf Arnheim asserts that "by itself, shape is a better means of identification than color not only because it offers many more kinds of qualitative difference, but also because the distinctive characteristics of shape are much more resistant to environmental variations."[7]

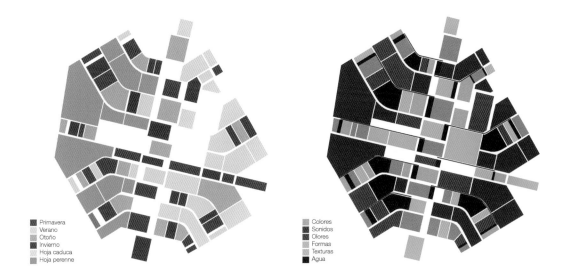

Primavera
Verano
Otoño
Invierno
Hoja caduca
Hoja perenne

Colores
Sonidos
Olores
Formas
Texturas
Agua

Fig. 8.2 Functional diagrams explaining program with visual color coding: Richard Rogers, competition for Valencia Parque Central, Spain

Fig. 8.3 Zaha Hadid, competition for Valencia Parque Central, Spain

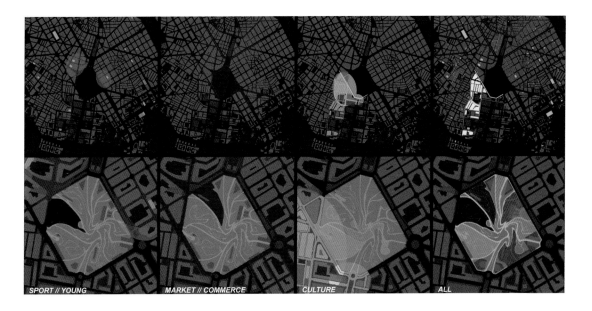

SPORT // YOUNG

MARKET // COMMERCE

CULTURE

ALL

Table 8.1
Meaning of colors in different Western cultures

	Anglo-Saxon Australia, New Zealand, UK, USA	Germanic Austria, Germany, Holland, Switzerland	Latin European Belgium, France, Italy, Spain	Nordic Denmark, Finland, Norway, Sweden	Slavic Russia, Poland, Czech Republic, Slovenia, Hungary, Romania	Hispanic American Argentina, Chile, Peru, Colombia, Mexico, Venezuela
white	happiness purity for brides					
blue	dependability high quality corporations trustworthiness masculinity[USA]	warmth femininity[Hol]		coldness masculinity[Swe]		
green	envy good taste adventure[USA] happiness		envy[Bel]			
yellow	warmth happiness purity[USA] jealousy[UK]	envy jealousy[Ger] envy[Hol]	infidelity[Fr] envy[It]		envy[Rus, Yug]	death[Mex]
red	masculinity[UK] fear anger envy jealousy love adventure[USA] danger defiance hostility strength excitement lust	fear anger bad luck, jealousy[Ger]	masculinity[Fr]	positivity[Den]	positivity[Rom] fear anger jealousy[Pol, Rus] envy[Pol]	positivity[Arg] anger envy jealousy[Mex]
purple	authority power progressiveness low cost[USA]				anger envy jealousy[Pol] envy[Rus]	death anger envy[Mex]
black	fear anger envy power luxury[USA] despondency ceremony	fear anger jealousy[Ger] despondency	fear anger despondency		fear anger envy[Pol, Rus] jealousy[Rus]	fear anger envy jealousy[Mex]

Table 8.2
Meaning of colors in different Eastern cultures

	Chinese China, Taiwan, Hong Kong	Japanese	South Korean	SE Asian ASEAN states	Near Eastern Iran, Pakistan, Turkey	Indian	West African Ghana, Niger, Nigeria, Senegal
white	purity mourning	mourning death	mourning death			mourning death	
blue	high quality	high quality sincerity trustworthiness	high quality sincerity trustworthiness	coldness evil[Malaysia]	death[Iran]	purity	
green	purity sincerity trustworthiness dependability	love happiness good taste adventure	purity adventure	danger disease[Malaysia]			
yellow	purity pleasantness progressiveness royalty authority	envy purity happiness good taste	happiness good taste dependability		envy[Turkey]		
red	happiness good luck love for brides	love anger jealousy	love adventure good taste			ambition desire	bad luck negativity[Nigeria]
purple	luxury love	sin fear luxury	expensive love				
black	power luxury high quality	fear power luxury dependability	power luxury			dullness stupidity	

8.3
Cultural and conventional color meanings

Shared color codes with special meanings exist within specific cultures, composing a kind of metalanguage. It is well known, for example, that white is associated with weddings, purity, and innocence in Western culture, while in Eastern countries it is associated with death.[8] The significance of color within a given culture should always be considered, while taking into account that its meaning also depends on context, the previous experiences of the individuals, the mood, and many other intangible aspects. [Tables 8.1, 8.2] In architecture, shared cultural meanings may carry less weight than associations with previous noteworthy buildings: again, context is essential. For example, it is unlikely that the red stucco plaster of the Sala de las Musas in Rafael Moneo's extension of Madrid's Museo del Prado (2007) will be understood to indicate "danger," "fire," or "warmth," despite those universal meanings in Western culture. Rather, it reproduces and recalls the well-known Pompeian red that appeared in the ruins of that Roman town, an apt association for a room that houses classical sculptures.

Moreover, cultural color meanings evolve over time. For example, in 1956 Austrian psychologist Hans Kreitler (1916–93) found that 86 percent of Jewish people did not like the color yellow because they associated it with the yellow patch that identified them during Nazism. In contrast, the blue of the Israeli flag was a sign of hope. When the experiment was repeated in 1960, 41 percent said they liked yellow and only 3 percent associated blue with hope.[9]

Colors also can take on a particular significance for a collective or professional sector. With humor, some have attempted to discover why architects always dress in black![10] Some architects are identified not only by the way they design and draw but also by an association with a particular color, as some of their most famous buildings have been developed around a personal color palette. Zaha Hadid's color brand roughly corresponded to her use of saturated colors on black backgrounds; minimalist architecture is identified with stark color schemes linked in the collective imagery with the myth of white in the modern movement (see chapter 7); and much Dutch architecture uses either highly saturated primary colors reminiscent of de Stijl or orange, the Dutch national color.

Color has been examined in great depth in the marketing of products, showing that consumers' associations of a color with a brand are much more important than their own color preferences when shopping and that color associations are sometimes difficult to change.[11] It is said that departing from the expected colors for a category of products can be risky, but this was not the case with Jean Nouvel's Life Marina apartments in Ibiza, Spain (2012), where the unusual colors of the balcony railings differ radically from the neutral color coding typical of high-end apartment buildings (such as Nouvel's Monad Terrace in South Beach, Miami [2015]).[12]

Tables 8.1–8.2 (previous spread) source: Cultural meanings of some colors collected from multiple sources, in Mubeen M. Aslam, "Are you selling the right colour? A cross-cultural review of colour as a marketing cue," in *Developments and Trends in Corporate and Marketing Communications: Plotting the Mindscape of the 21st Century: Proceedings of the 10th International Conference on Corporate and Marketing Communications*, ed. I. Papasolomou (Cyprus: Intercollege, Marketing Department, School of Business Administration, 2005), 1–14, http://ro.uow.edu.au/cgi/viewcontent.cgi?article=2092&context=commpapers.

Table 8.3 source: Naz Kaya and Melanie Crosby, "Color Associations with Different Building Types: An Experimental Study on American College Students," *Color Research & Application* 31, no. 1 (2006): 1–5.

8.4
Color psychology

The term *color psychology* generally refers to the range of **emotional**, **behavioral**, and **cognitive** associations linked with a specific color. [Table 8.3] According to researchers Xiao-Ping Gao and John H. Xin, emotional responses to color can be divided into two broad categories: **descriptive** responses (using terms such as *warm/cool*, *light/dark*, or *heavy/light*) and **evaluative** responses (which are related to color preference and are expressed in terms such as *like/dislike*, *good/bad*, *comfortable/uncomfortable*). Descriptive responses to color are considered more universal or intercultural, while evaluative ones are generally considered personal or cultural.[13]

Descriptive dimensions of colors

One of the most important tools for evaluating subjective meaning is the **semantic differential method** developed by Charles Osgood in 1957, consisting of a list of adjectives arranged on a scale, which subjects are asked to evaluate.[14] Osgood structured his scales according to three factors: evaluation, activity, and potency. Using this method, studies have been conducted in search of connections between color and meaning—and more specifically, among the three perceptual attributes of color (hue, saturation, and lightness) and meaning. Many of these studies confirm that lightness and saturation are the most significant factors that influence the meaning of color, with hue the least influential, except as related to the concepts warm/cool, which are closely linked to hue.[15]

However, subjects' personal characteristics, including age, gender, background, and previous experiences, can affect the interplay of color and emotion, as well as color preferences in architecture.[16] Men and women seem to

Table 8.3
Color preferences and emotional associations in residences, for American college students

Residence area	Preferred color	Emotional associations
bedroom	pink	warm, romantic, enjoyable
living room	light blue	calm, peaceful, modern, relaxing
dining area	light yellow	simple, classic, plain
children's room	pink	cheerful, striking
kitchen	off-white, green, blue, yellow	hygienic, pure
bathroom	off-white, green, blue, yellow	hygienic, pure
entrance/stair hall	light yellow	plain, simple

experience different responses to color saturation. Women report feeling greater depression, confusion, and anger in less saturated spaces, while men do so in more saturated ones.[17]

Moreover, contradictions exist between popular beliefs about color and scientific findings.[18] For example, red belongs to the longer wavelengths of the visible spectrum and therefore to those with lower wave energy, while blue falls at the opposite end of the visible spectrum, with short wavelengths and higher wave energy. This scientific condition contradicts the subjective impression that red signifies warmth and blue coolness, which is quite consistent across cultures. These contradictions increase when considering other popular meanings linked to red, such as its promotion of arousal, excitement, and stimulation. Some physiological measurements actually indicate that red reduces levels of arousal; for example, heart rates can be lower in red rooms than in blue ones.[19]

A useful study by the sociologist and psychologist Eva Heller involved two thousand German subjects. Respondents were asked to associate 13 sample

Table 8.4

Opposite colors from a psychological point of view, according to German respondents

Opposite colors	Symbolic contrast	Opposite colors	Symbolic contrast
red / blue	active / passive hot / cold high / low corporal / spiritual male / female	white / brown	clean / dirty noble / ignoble diaphanous / dense smart / fool
red / white	strong / weak full / empty passionate / insensitive	black / pink	strong / weak rude / delicate hard / soft insensitive / sensitive exact / diffuse big / small male / female
blue / brown	spiritual / earthly noble / ignoble ideal / real		
yellow / gray	bright / off flashy / low-key	silver / yellow	cold / warm imperceptible / striking metallic / immaterial
orange / white	colorful / colorless flashy / moderate	gold / gray	pure / impure expensive / cheap noble / everyday
violet / green	natural / artificial realistic / magical		

Table 8.4 source: Eva Heller, *Psicología del color: Cómo actúan los colores sobre los sentimientos y la razón* (Barcelona: Gustavo Gili, 2004).

colors with 160 different adjectives; Heller then created a "color chord" for some of these terms—that is, a color palette containing the most frequently chosen colors, in proportion to how often they were selected (see Activity 17). Although the study had its limitations (the small number of sample colors, the uniform nationality of respondents, and the limited statistical relevance of some findings), it provides a good starting point for a psychological approach to color design. Heller points out some psychologically opposed colors that have a symbolic contrast meaning and which are different from the complementary colors that have a visually contrasting appearance.[20] [Table 8.4]

Evaluative dimensions of color and color preference

The evaluative dimension of color involves those judgments that could be summarized as "like" or "dislike" or by answering the question "Which one do you prefer?" In short, the evaluative dimension of color relies on a global assessment to create a specific architectural environment. Using nine bipolar semantic scales based around existing studies of color emotion, Taiwanese researchers Mei-Yun Hsu and Li-Chen Ou concluded that the opposition "harmonious/disharmonious" has the highest correlation with "like/dislike."[21]

Some studies have begun with the question "What is your favorite color?" then have tried to match that preference for a specific color in isolation with the preference for that color in a particular product. Berkeley psychologists Stephen E. Palmer and Karen B. Schloss proposed the **ecological valence theory**, asserting that color preferences reflect people's cumulative emotional responses to environmental objects and to events or objects strongly associated with particular colors.[22] However, it is not clear that a direct correlation exists between a favorite color and specific architecture.

The few studies that have been conducted have, in fact, provided some evidence that color preferences depend on the type of object. For example, Emporia State University researchers Cooper B. Holmes and Jo Ann Buchanan conducted a study in which subjects were asked to write down their favorite color as well as the color they preferred for a number of named (not shown) items.[23] This demonstrated that stated favorite colors do coincide with color preference for some, but not all, objects. The most frequently mentioned favorite color for both males and females was blue; Holmes and Buchanan's data show that for some items (skirts, dresses, shirts, and slacks) the most frequently listed favorite color was also blue, but subjects listed this color infrequently, or not at all, as their favorite color for sofas, walls, carpets, or chairs.[24]

Experiments exploring color preference through eye-tracking technology show that when observing seven different categories of objects, "generally speaking, people [spend] longer time, and there are more fixations and fixation counts on their preferred colors."[25]

The German-born psychologist Hans Jürgen Eysenck carried out an investigation on color preferences that suggested the following order of general color preferences for fully saturated colors: blue, green, violet, orange, and yellow.[26] Although there were some limitations in the research, such as an unknown age range and unspecified color samples,[27] many different studies demonstrate blue to be the most preferred hue in isolation.[28]

Leaving aside hue, it seems that colors with maximum levels of saturation and value are the most preferred in isolation.[29] But we should also bear in mind that "human aesthetic evaluation of color seems to function at a holistic level—we can appreciate harmonious color schemes even when the individual colors used differ significantly from our personal favorites."[30] In this sense, Heller's color chords stand as a reasonable tool.

Color specialists are currently working to identify regional color trends by examining how people in different countries personalize their web applications.[31] For example, account information for over one million Twitter users was analyzed to determine color preferences; blues were found to be the most favored colors, with yellow the least preferred. Distinct differences were found between genders. Men preferred blues to a greater extent than women, and women preferred magentas to a much greater extent than men. Men preferred darker colors to a greater extent than women. These findings are consistent with previous research.[32]

The majority of color-preference studies, however, have not demonstrated a gender difference in children and adults. Some indicated that blue was preferred more by children than by adult females, although blue was the most preferred color (followed by red) for both genders. Some studies have shown that males consider the range of cool colors most pleasant, whereas females consider the range of warm colors most pleasant. Anya C. Hurlbert and Yazhu Ling, researchers in neuroscience at Newcastle University, found gender difference in color preferences using a rapid paired-comparison task.[33] The study found that "females prefer colors with 'reddish' contrast against the background, whereas males prefer the opposite." Gender differences in color preferences might be associated with neural components that underlie color encoding in the human visual system.[34]

8.5
Human reactions to color

Color is important in the configuration of habitable space and for activity performance, but that doesn't suggest that color rules directed at specific architecture according to its typology or function would be supported by any categorical psychological finding. Some authors have tried to specify colors for particular building activities, but that would be as simplistic as trying to dictate the color palette of a painting based on whether it is a portrait or a still life.[35]

Fortunately, some rough color strategies can be used to improve visual ergonomics (see chapter 6) or psychological comfort: the selection of appropriate lighting,[36] the use of color that supports the well-designed orientation of a building,[37] and a considered use of color variation.[38]

As Australian architect Zena O'Connor points out, many studies have demonstrated that light influences the human circadian rhythm and that changes in light-dark exposure can desynchronize the circadian cycle. This affects the ability to sleep and wake, and alters physiological and metabolic processes as well.[39] Furthermore, disruptions to the circadian rhythm may result in changes in mood and behavior, as evidenced by studies that focus on seasonal affective disorder (SAD).[40] Light seems to have an effect on the human neuroendocrine system and may also suppress melatonin and elevate cortisol production, both of which may have negative impacts.[41]

University of Sheffield researchers Bryan Lawson and Michael Phiri[42] showed that a certain degree of color variation in an architectural environment led to a 70 percent reduction in the recovery time of patients with mental illnesses in hospitals when compared to the use of a monochromatic color scheme, while researchers M. G. Shogan and L. L. Schumann[43] demonstrated a link between stress and lighting through an examination of the effects of lighting on preterm infants in an intensive care environment. Some authors further maintain that color can influence the mood[44] or reduce aggressive behavior[45] (see Activity 17.2).

Performance of activities seems to improve measurably in rooms with a chromatic scheme over those conducted in achromatic environments.[46] While reading and writing, people make more mistakes in white spaces than in colored ones,[47] despite the predominance of pale, neutral colors in most schools and offices.[48] Regarding color hue, some studies found no significant differences in the performance of typing tasks conducted in rooms with different colors, but errors seem to increase when the color changes, particularly from blue to red hues.[49] The difficulty of the task seems to have a bearing on the effects of color; this effect can be mitigated by the presence of decorative elements, such as photographs.[50] The speed at which children execute a task might be influenced by the presence of their favorite color.[51] Green spaces seem to be better than red ones for the performance of motor tasks, reducing tremor of the hand and motor inhibition.[52] However, psychological well-being does not always correlate with effective performance. For example, blue and yellow were judged by students to foster a positive mental state, even though they achieved better results in reading comprehension when surrounded by other hues.[53]

Activity 15
Color Meanings Codified by the Architect

Fig. 8.4 Richard Rogers and Renzo Piano, Centre Georges Pompidou, Paris, 1977

The color composition of the Centre Georges Pompidou reflects its mechanical workings. Its descriptive colors act as codes that identify its different parts and systems: blue for the air-conditioning ducts, green for water pipes, yellow for electrical lines, red for elevators, white for underground air ducts, et cetera. Richard Rogers strove to make objective color decisions based on three criteria: the aforementioned color coding, the durability of the colors against fading, and the scale of the building. Despite this rationality, Rogers admits that the colors were also personal and subjective and intended to inspire joy: "We have always consciously designed with color because of our interest in what Renzo and I call happy buildings—buildings that people react to."[54] [Fig. 8.4]

1   In the following projects, colors are linked with coded meanings. Sometimes colors are related to wayfinding; other times they represent the brand of the organization or bear other cultural connotations (see section 5.3). Try to determine the criteria for how color is used in each project. [Figs. 8.5, 8.6, 8.7, 8.8]

2   Choose an architectural project in which colors are given coded meanings and explain them.

Fig. 8.5 (top)
Norman Foster, Repsol petrol station, 2012

Figs. 8.6 and 8.7 (middle)   Jan Kaplicky and Andrea Morgante, Enzo Ferrari Museum, Modena, Italy, 2014

Fig. 8.8 (bottom)
Richard Rogers Partnership, Terminal T4 in Adolfo Suárez Madrid-Barajas Airport, Spain, 2005

Activity 16

Historical and Cultural Color Meanings

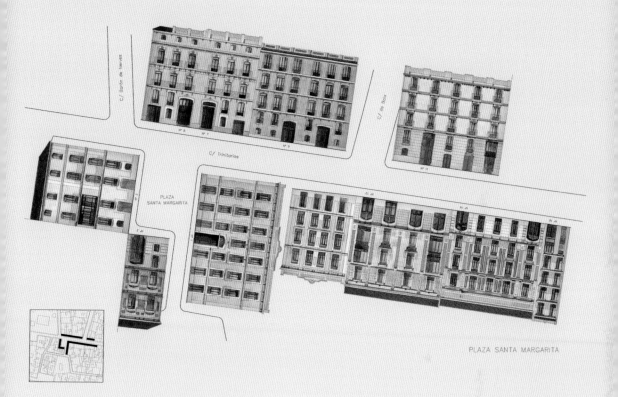

Fig. 8.9 A space dominated by residences: Santa Margarita Square, Valencia, Spain. Ángela García Codoñer et al., color research group of the Universitat Politècnica de València, color study, 1995–2012

The members of the color research group of the Universitat Politècnica de València, a team (including the author) with more than twenty years of experience in the recovery of the original colors in different historical city centers in Spain (Valencia, Ontinyent, Cartagena, San Mateo) and abroad (Havana, Lisbon, et cetera), have demonstrated that historical colors are the consequence of the dominant formal trends and available construction techniques in each period. [Fig. 8.9] Colors express the social and cultural factors behind a city's development, as well as the dominant aesthetic and technological influences through time. There exists a profound relationship between color and architectural typology. [Table 8.5] These features and meanings need to be understood and respected in architecture restoration.[55]

Table 8.5
Color characteristics for the different typologies in the historical city center of Valencia

Period	Types	Characteristics
Classicism 1a: Padre Tosca's Valencia (18th century)	Artisan Classical aristocratic Workers' houses	• Saturated colors • Background colors predominate • Moldings are few or absent • Only one or two colors used in each building
Classicism 1b: Academicist classicism (19th century)	Artisan buildings (types A, B, C) Classic residential Classic aristocratic Palaces	• Medium saturation • Background colors are saturated but to a lesser extent than in the 18th century • Abundance of formal classicist elements
Classicism 1c: Monuments	Special buildings	• Colors specific to each monument
The transition to eclecticism (19th century)	Eclectic residential Eclectic aristocratic	• Medium saturation • Light colors • Background color predominates but to a lesser extent than in the 18th century • Formal classicist and/or eclectic elements
Eclecticism and modernism (19th and 20th centuries)	Full eclecticism Neo-baroque eclecticism French-style eclecticism Classicist eclecticism modernist art nouveau Modernist medieval Modernist	• Polychromy • Medium saturation • Background color not predominant • Absence of a common chromatic structure for all buildings: solutions are particular to each
Historical exceptions (19th century)	Workers' houses Residential developments	• Medium-intensity chroma • Chromatic and graphic uniformity • Similar characteristics to 19th-century classical residential • Background color predominates but to a lesser extent than in the 18th century • Abundance of formal classicist elements
Modern movement (20th century)	Late eclecticism Rationalist—art deco	• Colors supplied by the materials • Few hues, mainly white • Low saturation • Colors with high value

Source: Angela Garcia Codoñer, Jorge Llopis Verdú, Ana Torres Barchino, Ramón Villaplana Guillén, and Juan Serra Lluch, "Colour as a Structural Variable of Historical Urban Form," Color Research and Application 34, no. 3 (2009): 253–65, https://doi.org/10.1002/col.20491.

Fig. 8.10
**Building typologies
in the historical city
center of Valencia:**
A. artisan
B. classicist
C. eclectic
D. modernist
E. late eclectic

1   Determine the typology corresponding to the building in the
    picture and describe the color with reference to that typology.
    [Fig. 8.10] (See page 232 for answers.)

2   Discuss the relationship between older and newer colors.

Activity 17

Evaluative Dimensions of Color (Emotional Meanings)

Although numerous studies have tried to link color and emotion, their findings have a limited usefulness for architecture design. The significance of color should always be considered with great caution, not only because it depends on culture but also because it depends on the context, as well as the previous experiences of observers; their gender, age, and mood; and many other emotional factors.

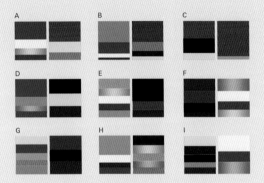

Fig. 8.11   Color studies by Eva Heller from *Psicología del color: Cómo actúan los colores sobre los sentimientos y la razón*, 2004

1   Try to match Eva Heller's color chords with their emotional meanings in order to experience the extent of color's evaluative dimensions.[56] (See page 232 for answers.)

Heller's study was conducted on two thousand German subjects, who were asked to choose among thirteen colors that were associated with emotions. A final color chord was developed for each emotion, composed of the four to six most significant colors in proportion to their recurrence. Note that the light gray represents a silver color and the light brown a golden one. Match these pairs of opposites with their corresponding color chords: [Fig. 8.11]

1   Falsehood/Truth
2   Ugliness/Beauty
3   Cold/Heat
4   Naturalness/Artificiality
5   Hate/Love
6   Kindness/Sullenness
7   Fidelity/Infidelity
8   Calm/Excitability
9   Courtesy/Rudeness

2   Watch the following videos and discuss the effectiveness of the following curious color experiments:

a   In 1979 psychologist Alexander Schauss convinced the director of a naval correctional institute in Seattle to paint some prisons in a color that was denominated Baker-Miller pink (RGB = 255,145,175). This color was supposed to lower blood pressure and reduce strength, and therefore reduce violent behavior. Similar experiments in Swiss jails by psychologist Daniela Späth have demonstrated a calming effect,[57] but other studies have failed to produce these results.[58] [Fig. 8.12]

(Despite the perception that pink is a girls' color, it is interesting to note that before 1950 in North America, pink was the color preferred for boys and blue for girls. This color and gender stereotype seems to have shifted after World War II.)[59]

Fig. 8.12   A 2006 study showed that the color pink was effective for calming prisoners in a Texas penitentiary.

 https://youtu.be/YWFOr557uzc

b   British Airways' "happiness blanket" measured fluctuations of neuronal activity with a blanket that changed color. When people were stressed, it was red; when they were relaxed, it turned blue. [Fig. 8.13]

Fig. 8.13   The "happiness blanket" by British Airways

 https://youtu.be/9oF0-28MOoU?t=1m41s

Activity 18
Color Meanings and Social Concerns in Photomosaics

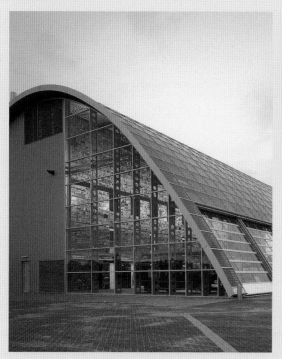 

Figs. 8.14 and 8.15
Philippe Samyn and
Partners, 373-Fire Station
Houten, Houten, the
Netherlands, 2000

Philippe Samyn describes this project:

In this socially problematic area of the city, it was asked of the 2,200 five-to-seven-year-old schoolboys and schoolgirls of the 22 schools of the city to represent the epic of the firemen on DIN A3–size panels. The 2,200 panels, changing color as a flame from dark blue at the bottom over green and yellow to orange at the top, were laid out on the main brick wall of the Fire Station, renamed "house of the firemen." It resulted into a magnificent hieroglyph-like composition protected by the glazed facade. The project gathered all the families of Houten, so that an emotional link was woven between the population and the building. In this way, the "house" is protected from the vandalism it was likely to suffer…[because] in each family, a little brother or a little sister's piece of artwork was integrated in the work.[60] [Figs. 8.14, 8.15]

Figs. 8.16 and 8.17
Joan Fontcuberta, *El mundo nace en*
cada beso **(The world is born in every**
kiss), photomosaic, Barcelona, 2014

Made from about four thousand photographs (chosen from six thousand images submitted by readers of the newspaper *El Periódico*), this mosaic was created to commemorate the tricentennial celebration of the newspaper's founding in 1714. *El Periódico* collected photographs about "Liberty Moments," which citizens submitted via Twitter, Instagram (#Momentsdellibertat), and email. [Figs. 8.16, 8.17]

1   Create a photomosaic. Imagine a building for which you would like to design a large-scale, colored mosaic by using smaller photos as tiles. Compose your mosaic with photographs whose meanings are related to the social community or the cultural values represented by the building.

The free application Foto-Mosaik-Edda is available at download.cnet.com/Foto-Mosaik-Edda/3000-2192 _4-75201.html.

This median wall [Fig. 8.18] is located in the Carmen neighborhood of the historic city center of Valencia, Spain. To its left is the Centre del Carme, the museum of contemporary culture, which previously was the Carmen convent, and beside it the church of Santa Cruz. Think of cultural references for this location: contemporary art, religious themes, ancient photographs of Valencia, or others to develop concepts for this median wall.

Fig. 8.18   A median wall in the historic
city center of Valencia, Spain

Color Meanings and Social Concerns in Anamorphism

Fig. 8.19 Boa Mistura Urban Art Group, *Light in the Alleyways*, Favela Vila Brasilândia, São Paulo, Brazil, 2012

Boa mistura (good mixture) is a Madrid-based team of young architects and designers with a strong interest in involving social communities in their urban actions. In a statement on their website, they describe their project within a Brazilian favela [Figs. 8.19, 8.20, 8.21]:

We had the opportunity to live in a favela with the Gonçalves family. During the first few days, we [recognized] the possible framework made by the narrow and winding passageways that connect the up and low urban areas, known as vielas. *The project aims to respond to this characteristic spatial complexity. By flattening the perspective, from a certain spot (anamorphism), the words* beleza, firmeza, love, doçura *and* orgulho *can be read and framed by a flat color, equally covering all the construction materials, democratizing the space. For us, these words are the best portrait of the* favela.[61]

Figs. 8.20 and 8.21 (opposite, top)
Boa Mistura Urban Art Group,
Light in the Alleyways, Favela Vila
Brasilândia, São Paulo, Brazil, 2012

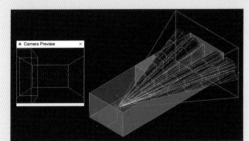

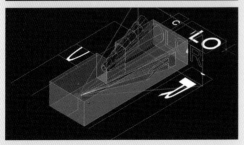

1   Make up your own **anamorphism** using typography
    to introduce a particular meaning into architecture.
    [Fig. 8.22, 8.23]
        Decide on the position of the observer, assuming an eye
    height of approximately 5 ft. 3 in. (1.6 m). To calculate the
    shape, size, and positions of the figures to be drawn on each
    2-D surface for the final rendering onsite, it may be useful
    to draw the space in 3-D and convert the letters to a solid
    figure, with the position of the eyes as a vertex (**solevation**).
    The intersection of the solevation and the surfaces determines
    the 2-D elevations.
        Keep in mind that you will need to make final in situ
    adjustments by placing an observer at the same vantage point
    you used for the camera in the 3-D model.

Figs. 8.22 and 8.23 Using Autodesk AutoCAD to
construct an anamorphism of the word *color.* Top: 3-D
model with a camera in the position of the observer.
The red figure is a solid solevation, with the letters as
a base and the camera as a vertex. Bottom: The intersection of the solevation and each surface in the room
provides the elevations to paint the letters on site.

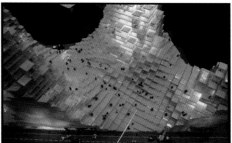

9 Trends in Color and Architecture

This chapter provides an overview of color tendencies in recent architecture, offering clues to understand how colors are evolving. The improvement of computer-aided design techniques as well as new colored building materials and light sources—together with a general overstimulation of contemporary perception—are at the root of contemporary color trends. The key idea can be summarized as "seeking color versatility." To a lesser extent, groups forecasting color tendencies in marketing can also be influential in setting trends in architecture.

9.1
Color tendencies

The artistic revolutionaries of the late nineteenth and early twentieth centuries considered architectural color trivial because of its seductive character. Color was dismissed along with other excesses of nineteenth-century bourgeois style, forming the foundation for how we understand architecture even today. The great architects of that time tried to rationalize color so that it might serve the new architecture, which was seen as a driving force for cultural change (see chapter 7). This established the myth, endorsed by later generations of architects continuing through the 1970s and 1980s, that any architecture with aspirations of being truly modern should use only the color white or materials in their natural finish.

This approach no longer predominates, and although some architects continue to employ restrained, minimalist finishes, color has made a spectacular return to much of contemporary international architecture. [Fig. 9.1]

Fig. 9.1 A very saturated, almost fluorescent green is featured in the pages of Bjarke Ingels's *Yes Is More: An Archicomic on Architectural Evolution*, 2009

Style trends in present-day architecture do not constitute rigid color codes. On the contrary, buildings are still envisaged as long lasting, and ever greater concern is being given to the dialogue between building and environment—which should translate into a more accurate understanding of color in our built surroundings, beyond the dictates of fashion.

Nevertheless, a common tendency emerges in noteworthy architects' remarks about color in their own designs: they pursue versatility—color that is meant to be dynamic rather than static. This versatility is achieved by a wide variety of means, including colors that change depending on the viewing angle, colored lights that modify a color scheme, color compositions that are difficult to perceive and therefore always appear to be different, and reflections, transparencies, and overlaid images that produce ambiguous and morphing results.

Contemporary architects experiment widely with building materials to achieve new finishes, which has exponentially increased the possibilities of color. Sometimes, however, color has been used rather too frivolously in architecture, particularly in urban city centers, where new buildings share the stage with old ones and should perhaps be designed with more attention to their surroundings. Some buildings make no attempt to blend in with local color, but rather aspire to global color: the intention is for them to stand out. Likewise, some architects have embraced color to create an image, a kind of facile and enticing brand. After the euphoria of recent years, we see, with some degree of bewilderment, what remains as the leftover confetti from a party, somewhat cheerful but also somewhat superficial. Color in architecture could be more ambitious.[1]

9.2
Bolder colors

Some architects, such as Rem Koolhaas, contend that the growing intensity of color in architecture mimics how we experience color through technology. The Dutch architect describes our contemporary experience as "overstimulated," saturated with the expanded virtual reality that technology provides:

We have increasingly been exposed to luminous color, as the virtual rapidly invaded our conscious experience—color on TV, video, computers, movies—all potentially "enhanced" and therefore more intense, more fantastic, more glamorous than any real color on real surfaces. Color, paint, coatings, in comparison somehow became matt and dull.[2]

Perhaps boundaries have become blurred, as we confuse reality with fiction—such is the effect of technology on our perception. If the unreal appears more attractive, we endeavor to make reality resemble the virtual, according to Koolhaas:

Color in the real world looks increasingly unreal, drained. Color in virtual space is luminous, therefore irresistible A surfeit of reality TV has made us into amateur guards monitoring a Junkuniverse.…Conceptually, each monitor, each TV screen is a substitute for a window; real life is inside, cyberspace has become the great outdoors.[3]

Zaha Hadid made a similar remark when expressing her predilection for digital rather than printed images, which appear "much nicer on the screen than when it is printed on to paper, because the screen gives you luminosity and the paper does not, unless you do it through a painting."[4] Hadid drew her artwork on a black background, like the black interface of CAD software, so that the colors appear to shine with their own light, as if we view them on a computer screen.

Phosphorescent colors in actual architecture—those that shine as if they were self-lit—are just a symptom of this preference for virtual colors; see, for example, the neon-yellow escalators in Koolhaas's Seattle Central Library (2004). [Fig. 9.2]

Fig. 9.2
Rem Koolhaas, interior escalator of the Seattle Central Library, 2004

9.3
Computer-aided abstract color compositions

Computers have enabled us to create color compositions for specific types of architecture as canvas, or "decorated sheds," to borrow to the terminology of the American architect Robert Venturi.[5] The notion of the pixel has made its way into the color composition process and has provided a new means of expression.

Pixelation is a process of abstracting and reducing an image to its core components, which software can do with great ease. Sometimes this process involves increasing the size of an image until it is reduced to a close-up of a few colors, which are then applied to a building. This increased-scale fragment corresponds to the broader whole of the image, but sometimes the observer is unaware of that whole.

Spanish architects Enric Miralles and Benedetta Tagliabue (EMBT) applied this technique for the roof of Barcelona's Santa Caterina Market (2005) by pixelating a color photograph of the products that are sold in the market and rendering the resulting image as a mosaic of roof tiles on an undulating canopy that provides ample protection for the merchants beneath. [Figs. 9.3, 9.4] It adds a new layer to the site, which in the past had served as a convent, then a square, then a market, among many other functions. The roof responds to the character of the building that it represents—namely, its return to being a market.

Spanish architects Emilio Tuñón and Luis Moreno Mansilla developed a similar color intervention outside MUSAC, the contemporary art museum of León,

Figs. 9.3 and 9.4
The Santa Caterina Market displays a poetic reinterpretation of the colors of a food stall through pixelation. Enric Miralles and Benedetta Tagliabue (EMBT), Santa Caterina Market, Barcelona, 2005

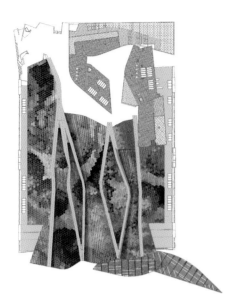

Spain (2004), where colored glass is a reference to the major Gothic stained glass windows of the city's cathedral (see Activity 9). The color scheme of Sauerbruch Hutton's pharmacological research facilities in Biberach, Germany (2002), also references an image: the microscopic structure of one of the drugs being synthesized by the laboratory.

In these three cases, the relationship between each building's color scheme and its purpose is not immediately obvious. It might be labeled "virtual color," as corresponding to a reality far removed from the building itself.

The pixel is not only the basic color unit but also an elementary and indivisible unit of information. Using this premise, the Spanish architect Eduardo Arroyo carried out an urban project for the Plaza El Desierto in Barakaldo, Spain (2002). [Figs. 9.5, 9.6] The surface was organized

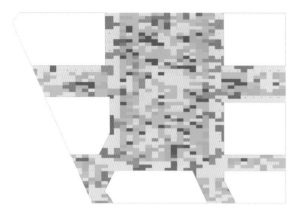 

around a random distribution of pixel-like squares composed of different
materials; these maintained the proportion of those materials found in the site
before this plaza was designed: grass, wood, stone, water, et cetera. Pixelation
was used as an open process, a compositional strategy to randomize a set
of materials without seeking a final figurative image.

On occasion, computers can be used to generate images that are so bold in
terms of color and form that they dominate a building's appearance, as is the
case with the MVRDV's Hagen Island dwellings in Ypenburg, The Hague (2003).
[Fig. 9.7] The extreme formal abstraction of the complex, whose artificiality
expresses the ideal concept of a detached house, appears to display—a little
more prosaically perhaps—the literal translation to a built environment of
a simple computer-generated rendering in a single color.

Figs. 9.5 and 9.6
NO.MAD, Plaza El Desierto,
Barakaldo, Spain, 2002

9.4
Changing colors and versatility:
transformation, fragmentation, and movement

During the first two decades of the twenty-first century, color has been a
useful resource to express **versatility**, the ability to adapt to different situations.
This versatility is based in different strategies:[6]

**(1) A transformation of color that changes
the building's visual aspect.**
This **transformation** may be achieved by including variable light sources, by
incorporating reflections, by using changeable materials, or by taking advantage
of the observer's limitations, among other techniques.

New artificial lighting systems can transform the colors of architecture;
many projects now feature neutral surfaces onto which changing colors are

Fig. 9.7 MVRDV,
Hagen Island dwellings
in Ypenburg, The Hague,
2003

projected, such as Herzog & de Meuron's Allianz Arena in Munich (2005) or
Tom Wright and Mark Major's Burj Al Arab Hotel in Dubai (1999). Reflective
materials, including glass, mirrors, and satin-finish surfaces, continuously shift in
appearance as the fugitive colors of an ever-changing reality are superimposed
on their surface. The French architect Jean Nouvel makes the most of these
effects. [Fig. 9.8] The reflection integrates the outside, the alien, and the building
becomes immaterial, as in the Vieux Port Pavilion in Marseille, France, by Foster
and Partners (2013).

Many new materials change their color in different situations, such as iridescent foils that make facades shimmer with all the colors of the rainbow, as seen
in UNStudio's La Defense offices in Almere, the Netherlands (2004). [Fig. 9.9]

Sometimes the visual limitations of observers create an appearance of
changing color, even when neither light conditions nor the object have changed.
Color compositions that are complex and difficult to apprehend can make a
building as a whole seem unstable. This effect can be observed in buildings that
use a large number of small colored fragments without any obvious order of
composition, such as Sauerbruch Hutton's Sedus high-bay warehouse in Dogern,
Germany (2003).

(2) Color that affects the sense of unity.

Color can alter a structure's unity and result in **fragmentation**. The architectural
project is understood as something diffuse and contradictory rather than as a
unitary object. Fragmented architecture usually involves complex color disposi-
tions that reinforce the idea of a hybrid reality. Color is doubly fragmented: it is

Fig. 9.8   Jean Nouvel,
Hotel Silken Puerta
América, Madrid, 2005

Fig. 9.9   UNStudio,
La Defense offices,
Almere, the Netherlands,
2004

disassociated from the structural aspect of the building (in the way that structure and finish are divorced in many High Tech buildings), while at the same time the breakdown, dispersion, or conflict among parts is emphasized (in fragmented composition systems such as deconstruction). Fragmentation often expresses notions of freedom from monolithic interpretations of reality.

(3) Color movement that suggests a change in position.
The interest in expressing **movement** in the arts has its roots in the early avant-garde period, but contemporary architects continue to investigate it, either with static colors that suggest movement or with colors that actually move. Movement in architecture has traditionally been understood in a musical sense: color suggests rhythm or can act as a cadenza that relieves the monotony of a stable composition, with the distribution of silences and accents providing visual punctuation.

At the T4 terminal of Adolfo Suárez Madrid-Barajas Airport by Richard Rogers and Antonio Lamela (2005), a rainbow color range gives the appearance of movement to a long and monotonous sequence of identical structural supports (see Activity 15).

In contemporary architecture and interiors, many colors do in fact move, thanks to new artificial lighting technologies, from simple changeable lighting schemes to media surfaces that contain dynamic text, graphics, or images. These media surfaces can leave the color design unfinished, open to interactions with observers. One example is the outer skin of the Graz Art Museum in Graz, Austria, designed by Peter Cook, Spacelab UK, and Colin Fournier (2003), which functions as a large screen. [Fig. 9.10]

Figs. 9.10 Peter Cook and Colin Fournier, Graz Art Museum, Graz, Austria, 2003

9.5
Sources: color and architecture

Some useful sources for color trends, color forecasting, and other issues specific to fashion and industrial design are the following:

- **The Color Marketing Group.** A private, international association founded in 1962 that meets every six months to examine color trends in different areas of design and anticipate color trends for the coming year.

   https://colormarketing.org/

- *MIX* **magazine.** Focuses on color and trends; published by Colour Hive, a London-based creative agency recognized internationally for its accurate color and trend forecasting.

   https://shop.colourhive.com/collections/mix-magazine

- **Pantone.** The Pantone Color Institute is a consulting service within Pantone that provides customized color standards, brand identity, and product color consulting, as well as trend forecasting initiatives, including the Pantone Color of the Year. [Fig. 9.11]

   https://www.pantone.com/pci

Fig. 9.11
Color of the Year 2018 by the Pantone Color Institute, Ultra Violet 18-3838

- **WGSN (World's Global Style Network).** Forecasts consumer tendencies in fashion and lifestyle for the following two years and provides a biannual color report for businesses and professionals in various fields. It invented its own color notation system, Coloro, based on Munsell's theories.

   https://www.wgsn.com/en/

- **Paint companies.** Behr, Sherwin-Williams, Benjamin Moore, Akzo Novel, and others release their own creative directors' picks for colors of the year.

Breaking the Color Code

Figs. 9.12–9.14
Emmanuelle Moureaux /
emmanuelle moureaux
architecture + design,
Sugamo Shinkin Bank,
Itabashi-ku, Tokyo, 2011

The design of this branch office reflects Sugamo
Shinkin Bank's slogan: "We take pleasure in serving
happy customers."[7] [Figs. 9.12, 9.13, 9.14]

 emmanuelle moureaux architecture + design,
http://www.emmanuellemoureaux.com/sugamo
-shinkin-bank-shimura

Fig. 9.15
Interior of the Sugamo
Shinkin Bank, Itabashi-ku,
Tokyo, 2011

Fig. 9.16
Auguste Charles Pugin,
*The Great Hall, Bank
of England (Microcosm
of London, plate 7)*,
London, 1808, hand-colored
etching and aquatint,
sheet: 9 3/4 × 11 1/2 in.
(24.7 × 29.2 cm)

1   Compare the color palette of Sugamo Shinkin
Bank with another more traditional bank
design. [Fig. 9.16] What is the significance
of each design? What do color and design
communicate about the values of each
corporation?

Activity 21
Monochromy with Bold Colors

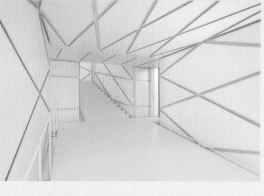

This project rehabilitated a Belgian sawmill as a cultural center for the digital arts. Architects introduced what they nicknamed "the thing," a kind of technological element with changing LED colors, containing a fluorescent yellow staircase. [Figs. 9.17, 9.18, 9.19]

Figs. 9.17–9.19
Langarita Navarro Arquitectos,
Media Lab Prado, Madrid, 2012

Figs. 9.20 and 9.21 Más que Espacio
Architects, exterior and interior of Doctor
Manzana shop, Valencia, Spain, 2013

Fig. 9.22 MVRDV, the Tribune,
TU Delft University of Technology,
the Netherlands, 2009

Figs. 9.23 and 9.24
Supermachine Studio,
Bangkok University
Student Activity Center,
Bangkok, 2003

1   Research the pictured projects, which use bold
colors. Why were these highly saturated colors
chosen? How do they relate to the buildings'
function and character? [Figs. 9.20, 9.21, 9.22,
9.23, 9.24]

10 Color in Proposals for Architectural Competitions

In this chapter we address the problem of displaying colors in proposals for architectural competitions. Color is a useful resource to seduce a jury, helping in the reading of the proposal and giving coherence and hierarchy to the whole project. On the other hand, if color is wrongly applied, it can complicate the understanding of the submission and diminish its quality. Some architects make a distinction between the full-color, two-dimensional ideas in their competition drawings and their final built architecture, which is far less colorful.

10.1
Color attracts attention

Researchers have demonstrated that yellow, when viewed on a black back-ground, is the most rapidly perceived color, which is why this combination is commonly used to indicate imminent danger. Then comes white, followed by red, green, and blue, the latter registering the slowest reaction times by observers.[1]

The CIE has shown how this is borne out by the physiology of the human eye; considering the spectral sensitivity curve of the photosensitive cells (cones), a standard observer registers the highest value for the color yellow with day-time or **photopic** vision (wavelength λ = 555 nm). With nighttime, or **scotopic** vision, the photosensitive cells (rods) register the greatest sensitivity with wavelengths corresponding to a greenish color (λ = 507 nm) (see section 1.1).

In general, the most saturated colors—those we call "vivid"—have the greatest capacity to grab our attention. In the author's research with the color group of the Universitat Politècnica de València, eye-tracking technology showed that: [Figs. 10.1, 10.2]

Fig. 10.1 Original image presented in an architectural competition. BG Studio Architects, intervention in the historical city center of Alcoy by M. Espí, Alcoy, Spain, 2009

Fig. 10.2 Map of the observer's gaze overlaid in color (the more reddish, the longer time observed).

- Among the three dimensions of color (hue, saturation, and value), contrasts in value influence observation the most.
- Color contrast is not the only factor in determining the areas that attract the greatest intensity of gaze, although it is directly related.
- The more luminous an object is in relation to its surroundings, the longer it attracts the gaze.
- The most observed zones are those that present the greatest fragmentation in small color areas. In general, for the same level of color contrast, those areas with smaller dimensions attract a more intense gaze.
- Color is important in attracting attention but is subordinate to the subject matter of the image; people and nature, in particular, draw human attention.[2]

10.2
Chromatic hierarchies:
dominant colors, subordinate colors, and accents

Color hierarchy is the structure conceived by the designer so that the different colors of a composition can be read in a particular order. This is not a conscious act by the observer (and not always by the designer, either) but rather completely intuitive. If colors are correctly structured, one's gaze is drawn to where the architect wants it. This is why a simple color scheme is effective for posters or panels for an architectural presentation, using three categories of colors:

1   Dominant colors: those that most predominate
2   Subordinate colors: accompanying colors that are used as the foundation or the background
3   Accents: more saturated or complementary colors that are used to a much lesser extent or to highlight particular aspects or details. They act as the counterpoint for the composition.

The overall appearance of a color composition can be substantially transformed simply by changing a color accent, without modifying the dominant and subordinate colors. [Fig. 10.3] This is true not only for two-dimensional compositions but also for architectural spaces. When Le Corbusier provided guidelines for applying color to architecture, he designated certain colors for large surface areas (dominant colors) and others for highlighting secondary architectural elements (color accents), with white acting as the foundational (subordinate) color.[3]

Color reverberation
For a color composition to appear unified and well organized, colors should repeat or recur in different areas. In the same way that a color reflected upon a surface tinges the objects around it, key colors of the composition should reappear as a kind of leitmotif for integrating the various elements.

10.3
Color and texture

Computer tools make it much easier to superimpose layers of images so that colors and textures change according to degrees of overlap or transparency. This relatively new phenomenon lends additional versatility to color (see section 9.4).

Be sure to take the textures of the printed surface into account. Colors printed onto paper with a matte or coarse-grain finish will appear less saturated than those on a glossy or photographic paper. Some architects have tried to develop a system to describe the effect of texture on perceived color, known as "cesia," referring to the "types of appearance produced by the different spatial distribution of light when reflected off

Fig. 10.3   Edgar G. H. Degas, *The Dance Class*, 1875, oil on canvas, 33 1/2 × 29 1/2 in. (85 × 75 cm), Musée d'Orsay, Paris. If we eliminate some color accents, our gaze as observers and the whole composition seem to be shifted. Top: Original canvas; bottom: without color accents

a surface." Attempts have been made to define these effects based on three variables: "permeability (or its opposite, opacity), darkness (or its opposite, luminosity) and diffusivity (or its opposite, regularity)."[4]

10.4
A digital return to the handmade

As electronic gadgets have evolved to be more user-friendly, the experience of using new technology has become increasingly similar to drawing. [Fig. 10.4] We have seen a return to the gesture and to traditional ways of drawing, albeit drawing that is tweaked and retouched using a computer. Incorporating the hand lends a certain romantic ambience to competition proposals, decreasing the need to add extremely detailed information (which is helpful if final building solutions have yet to be elaborated). A common strategy is the use of dawn lighting—with rays of sunlight providing a seductive warmth—or the ephemeral light of dusk, when streetlights are switched on and the sky is tinged with red.

Fig. 10.4 Some renderings apply digital colors to a hand drawing. Richard Rogers, competition for Valencia Parque Central, Spain, 2011

10.5
Color and legibility

Establish a color scheme that permits figures to be seen against background colors. This is essential to improve the reading of information and particularly important if the target audience is elderly or visually impaired (see section 6.3).

Aim to provide enough contrast between the colors of letters and backgrounds for legibility, but not so much so as to cause visual fatigue. Always establish contrast in value and chroma rather than just a contrast of hue; the latter does not provide well-defined edges between colors. [Fig. 10.5] For easy readability, avoid using complementary colors unless you establish a high level of value and saturation contrast, use an intermediate color, or introduce a contour line in black or white.

Color criteria for type

The Colour Contrast Check Tool allows users to check whether the contrast between the text characters and the background of a web page is sufficient for the words to be legible. [Fig. 10.6] The notations are for RGB and HVC color. The tool shows if the color scheme for letters and background is in keeping with the guidelines of the WCAG 2.0 color-contrast formula.[5]

https://snook.ca/technical/colour_contrast/colour.html

Fig. 10.5 The colors selected to represent the blocks and streets surrounding Valencia Parque Central, Spain, are not well chosen. The pastel colors have similar values and not enough contrast. Furthermore, their visual intensity distracts the viewer's focus from the park itself, which is rendered in pale, unsaturated greens.

Lorem ipsum dolor sit amet consectetuer adipiscing elit

Fig. 10.6 Notice how the legibility of the text varies according to the background color. Legibility improves when the difference in value and saturation of the background and figure is greater.

10.6
Why submit design proposals with color yet build without it?

If the landmark buildings of the International Style were designed with colors but disseminated visually through black-and-white photographs, today we find the opposite situation: architectural proposals feature bright, bold colors but end up being built with a different color scheme, often achromatic.

Why submit design proposals with color yet build without it? The conditions of the architectural profession provide some answers.[6]

Architects participating in competitions need to capture the attention of a panel made up of both experts and laypeople. Color focuses attention. Getting through the first round of an architectural competition means capturing, at first glance, the jury's imagination. They may have no time to take a closer look at the architectural content, only enough time to sift through the most eye-catching designs. [Fig. 10.7]

Color can feature in a bid without a commitment to color in the future architectural piece; Rem Koolhaas used color coding in his presentation of the floor plans for the Cordoba Congress Centre in Spain (2002), which made it easy

Fig. 10.7
Gustafson Porter + Bowman, renderings for the winning design of Valencia Parque Central, Spain, 2011

Figs. 10.8–10.11
Comparison of a finished
building and its earlier
graphic representations.
Zaha Hadid, firehouse
for the Vitra factory in
Weil am Rhein, Germany,
1993

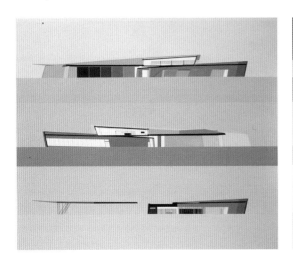

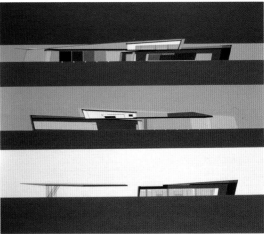

to distinguish the structural form. Of this project, the Spanish architect Ramón Fernández-Alonso commented that "later on, during construction, color was not used, but I believe it to be an essential part of representing the design. In real terms, a competition panel has little time, thus the use of color simplifies one's understanding of the designs."[7]

Fernández-Alonso used this strategy in his own winning competition entry for the Centro de Desarrollo Farmacéutico y Alimentario in Granada, Spain (2010). "Part of the louvers of the roof, used to organize the floor plan into laboratories, were allocated a color code which corresponded to the literal transcription of the one used for the functional plan,"[8] he has explained. The Spanish architects Eva Luque and Alejandro Pascual employed a similar functional color coding in the plan of their winning entry in the Europan Prize 9 competition (2008): "If you look closely, color and program go hand in hand; they make no sense apart. Each element contained within these panels had its own entity: the letters, the modules, the representation of trees and ground."[9]

Colors are used in competition designs to arouse interest, even when the definitive color of the building has not been decided. One strategy to resolve this apparent contradiction is the use of color codes as graphic legends.

On the one hand there is representation; on the other is architecture.

A realized architectural space is a very different thing from the two-dimensional representation that appears before the jury of an architectural competition. To represent the architectural reality of the future, including its lighting and textural possibilities, both colors and lines are valid instruments.

This, at least, is how Zaha Hadid explained the surprising lack of color in her buildings compared to the original designs. [Figs. 10.8, 10.9, 10.10, 10.11] In her early drawings for the firehouse for the Vitra factory, certain wall elevations were painted using saturated colors against a black background, although those colors were not used in the final build. She explained that her paintings were intended to show aspects of the projects' lighting and not meant to be the basis for decisions regarding color.

> [Colors in my paintings] never had anything to do with the final appearance. They have more to do with the quality of the design as well as with the building's light modulation: which wall had to be illuminated or not, and how the building is transformed from day to night.... There is also the question of how to achieve transparency through a solid material. This all came through the paintings.[10]

The British architect Will Alsop similarly affirms that the color in his paintings is not related to the final color in his buildings. "Even though I have described the act of painting as an act of architecture, at the same time there are also some decisions you take to try to make a good painting, which has nothing to do with architecture."[11]

Color acts as a means of graphic expression in the design stage and does not necessarily reflect the finished color of the material. When Sauerbruch Hutton considered color in the architectural competition for the Tokyo International Forum, the architects recalled, "[We] tried to determine how many lines and how much color should be contained in a drawing for one to still be able to understand the space, and capture the concept. Starting from lines and color, we began to think about color and space."[12]

In addition, color plays a fundamental role in transmitting intangible sensations and uncertain aspects that are tied to well-being. As expressed by the Spanish architect Rafael Soler: "Color becomes a valuable instrument in trying to transmit the pursuit, the atmosphere, and the sense of what we want to achieve through architecture."[13]

Color evolves as a design project develops.
From the time of winning an architectural competition to the completion of construction, many factors can affect the budget, execution, and development of the germinal ideas. These same things can affect color usage, which is more flexible than most of the other variables of the design because it has almost no implications for structure or function.

The architects of the Spanish firm MGM Arquitectos, regarding the Níjar Theater, Spain (2008), point out that "it is curious…that certain buildings that are designed using color end up with a white, monochrome appearance, while other buildings that are designed to be white end up tinged with color during the execution process."[14]

The Vitra Fire Station by Zaha Hadid exemplifies this shift in color direction during the construction of the building:

What we wanted to do here was have one reading with no color, so if you look at it one way you see no color but if you look at it the other way you see color. It was another play on things. But when the concrete was finished, I liked the rawness of the concrete inside. I realized the quality of the wall had to be quite cool, and decided to leave it as is."[15]

Deciding on color at the last minute is not necessarily a bad thing, as long as choices are in keeping with the rest of the project's compositional ideas. Remember that even Le Corbusier did so, despite his efforts to rigorously control color (see section 7.4). Often there are aspects of a project that cannot be accurately perceived until the colors are in situ: the relationships among spaces, the orientation and warmth of the lighting, the interaction of color with the surroundings, the overlap with neighboring colors, et cetera. The Mexican architect Luis Barragán fixed the extraordinary colors of his Gilardi House by evaluating painted cartoons on site, where it was possible to test the composition under real lighting conditions (see Fig. 10.8).

Activity 22

Color in Panels for an
Architectural Competition

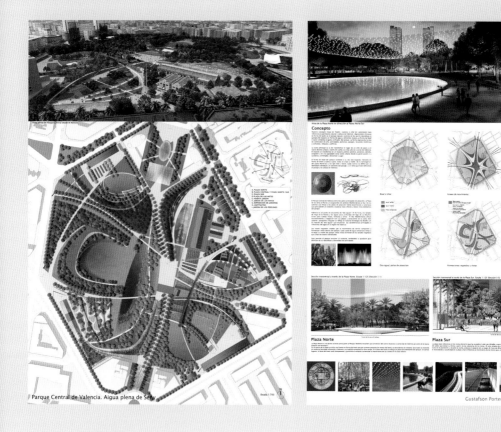

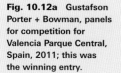

Fig. 10.12a Gustafson
Porter + Bowman, panels
for competition for
Valencia Parque Central,
Spain, 2011; this was
the winning entry.

The city of Valencia had long desired to convert a fifty-seven-
acre (twenty-three-hectare) space into a green park, suturing
two sides of the city that had been divided by railway tracks.
Gustafson Porter + Bowman's design was chosen unanimously
from proposals submitted by five major architecture firms,
with projects of uniformly outstanding levels of quality.

Look at the global character of the panels presented by
some of the most outstanding architectural firms to this
competition and discuss the use of the colors.

[Figs. 10.12a, 10.12b, 10.13, 10.14, 10.15]

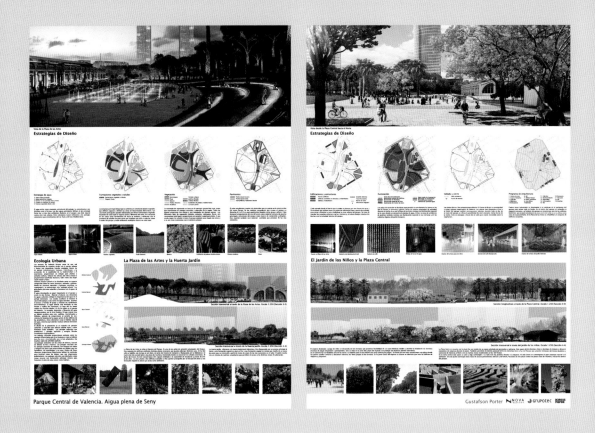

1   Does color help in the reading of the information?

2   Does color codification give meaning or identify the brand
    of the architectural firm? Is there a common color palette
    among the different panels of the same firm?

3   Does color emphasize the main features of the project?

4   Is there a chromatic hierarchy: dominant color, secondary
    colors, and accents?

5   What are the goals, strengths, and weaknesses of how color
    is used in each proposal?

**Fig. 10.12b   Gustafson
Porter + Bowman, panels
for competition for
Valencia Parque Central,
Spain, 2011**

Fig. 10.13
Richard Rogers, panels
for competition for
Valencia Parque Central,
Spain, 2011

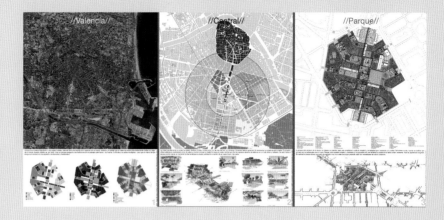

Fig. 10.14
Foreign Office Architects
(FOA) and Alejandro
Zaera-Polo, panels for
competition for Valencia
Parque Central, Spain,
2011

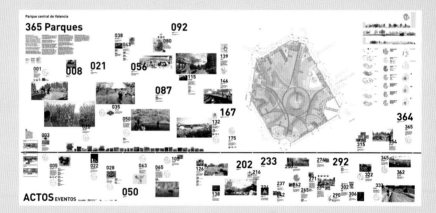

Fig. 10.15
West 8, panels for
competition for Valencia
Parque Central, Spain,
2011

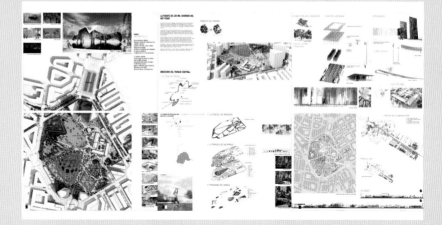

Part Three

Color
and Workflow

11 Color in the Work Process

To maintain reliable color throughout the work process, we must make informed decisions about image file formats and conversions when moving from one device to another. This chapter describes problems of digital color flow and introduces useful concepts, such as color gamut, color profile, color engine, and rendering intent.

11.1
Nondestructive workflow

It is important for color to be consistent from the conception of an architectural project to its final material solution. To establish an adequate workflow for color, you need to understand the variables of your input devices (camera, scanner, existing photographs); your editing tools and devices (software, color spaces, monitors, and screens); and your output devices (office printers, offset printers, viewing screens). [Fig. 11.1] You must then define a logical structure for all these elements, determining where, when, and how to apply color management within the workflow.

The points at which color conversions occur are especially crucial, as well as the profiles and the color settings of the software used to prepare files for the various output devices. Keep the following guidelines in mind:[1]

- The order of decisions is very important. When a TIFF file is converted into a JPEG, for example, any color information that is lost might be irretrievable.
- The maximum quality of the final image will not exceed the lowest quality obtained along the workflow.
- The images' use will guide your decisions. If your photographs will be displayed on a web page, you will be able to work with them as JPEGs; if you might eventually print them in a book or magazine, it's best to use TIFFs.

Fig. 11.1
Color gamut of a RGB
device plotted on the
chromaticity diagram
CIE 1931

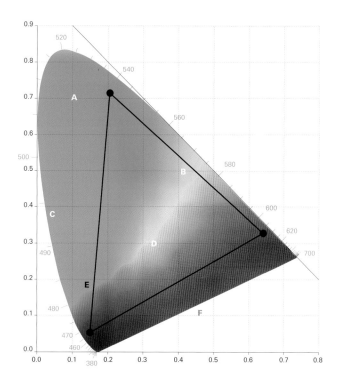

A. All colors visible to the average human eye are contained inside the diagram.

B. The colors along any line between two points can be made by mixing the colors at the end points. In this case, green + red = yellow.

C. The edge of the diagram, called the spectral locus, represents pure, monochromatic light measured by wavelength in nanometers. These are the most saturated colors.

D. The least saturated colors are at the center, emanating from white.

E. Color gamut: subset of colors that can be represented by mixing the fundamental colors of the corners

F. "Line of purples": these colors are fully saturated but can be made only by mixing two colors (red and blue)

11.2
Image file formats

Raw

Raw files retain the most information from the digital camera or scanner. They are akin to digital negatives, having undergone minimal data processing. Raw files cannot be used directly; they need to be converted to a bitmap format that can be edited or printed (such as TIFF or JPEG). Some of the most common formats are CIFF, DNG, and ORF.

Bitmap

A bitmap is a raster image, formed by a grid of color units called pixels. Quality depends on the resolution, or pixels per inch, which refers to the fineness of the pixel grid. Some of the most popular formats are BMP, JPEG, PNG, TGA, TIFF, and WBMP.

Vector image

Vector images are also known as "vector graphics," "geometric modeling," or "object-oriented graphics." They consist of geometric shapes organized by vector (point, line, curve, angle, et cetera), and their quality does not depend on their size; images can be scaled up without losing quality. Some of the most common formats are DXF, EVA, PGML, SVG, and WMF.

Compound files

Files can encompass a description of the document, including text, fonts, graphics, and any other information. Some of the most common compound formats are PDF, PICT, PS, and EPS.

Table 11.1
Typical color profiles for RGB

ProPhoto RGB	Largest gamut. Created by Kodak. Improves the number of colors in green and blue shades; reds are similar to Adobe RGB 1998. Not all current output devices are high-quality enough to accommodate this profile, so it is suitable for postproduction, but the final image will probably be converted into Adobe RGB 1998 / sRGB.
Adobe RGB 1998	Standard profile, useful for shooting and postproduction
sRGB	Smallest color gamut; good for on-screen images. Has fewer intermediate colors and more saturated colors in the edges. It is the preset for low-end scanners and printers. Good for web.

Table 11.2
Recommended file formats for each stage of the workflow

Process	File format	Color Space	Bits
Capture	.tiff	Adobe RGB 1998 / ProPhoto	8 bits
	.raw	—	14 bits
Conversion from raw TIFF	—	Adobe RGB 1998 / ProPhoto	16 bits
Photo editing	.tiff / .psd	Adobe RGB 1998	16 bits
Final files	Photo with layers in .tiff	Adobe RGB 1998	16 bits
	.jpg for printing (RGB)	Adobe RGB 1998	8 bits
	.jpg for web (RGB)	Adobe sRGB	8 bits
	.jpg for printing (CMYK)	CoatedFOGRA39 (Europe)	8 bits
	.jpg for black and white	Gris-CoatedFOGRA39 (Europe)	8 bits

11.3
Recommended image formats

Capture

Take photos at the highest quality that your camera allows by setting your camera to work in the largest possible color profile. The most common are Adobe RGB (1998) and ProPhoto RGB, which are larger than sRGB. [Table 11.1]

When shooting raw images, color profile is not relevant; raw files contain data extracted from the camera sensor with minimal processing, allowing for a maximum range of colors (about 12 to 14 bits per channel). It is possible to manipulate certain variables after the shot, when "developing" the raw image, with more precision: color profile, brightness, white balance, hue, saturation, and so on.

With TIFFs and JPEGs, you must set white balance at the time you shoot the photo. Always bear in mind that a JPEG is a compressed image file. Every time you save the file during editing, the color is compressed and some color information is lost forever; these are accumulative losses. JPEGs consist of only 8 bits per channel.

"Developing"

Raw file information needs to be converted to a TIFF file for editing; you should not edit in raw format, because processing time is extremely slow. However, since you will lose information when you convert to TIFF format, keep master copies of your unconverted image files in raw format, which are the equivalent of film negatives. [Table 11.2]

Camera manufacturers usually provide software for this file conversion: Nikon Capture NX 2, s7raw by Fuji, Digital Photo Professional by Canon, Camedia Master by Olympus, Image Data Converter (IDC) by Sony, Developer Studio/ Digital Camera Utility for Pentax, among others. As alternatives, there are many other generic raw converters: the Camera Raw plug-in for Adobe Photoshop, Cyberlink PhotoDirector, DxO PhotoLab, Corel AfterShot Pro (previously Bibble Labs), Konvertor, IRAW, Zero Noise, Therapee, RawDrop, darktable, et cetera. Adobe Lightroom allows you to make individual copies of each raw file in different folders and with different quality, and it also reduces any **chromatic aberration**.[2]

Photo editing

A good rule of thumb is to work in 16-bit PSDs or TIFFs and keep layers. In theory, 32 bits are better, but these images are processed more slowly. The recommended resolution for printed jobs is 300 ppi at the dimension at which the image will be reproduced.

Final files

For each image, keep an archive of the following files:

- The raw master file
- The edited 16-bit TIFF. It can be useful to keep a PSD as well, but if Photoshop changes in the future, PSDs may not remain editable. Output devices operate at 8 bits, so you would need to convert the TIFF to 8 bits for output.
- The final image converted to JPEG, using maximum quality 12 in Adobe RGB (1998) color space, 8 bits profile. If saved only once, a JPEG loses very little quality. It is common for photo labs to work in sRGB color space; your lab can provide the corresponding ICC color profile (see section 10.5) so that you can preview on-screen how the image will print from the lab's output devices.

Fig. 11.2
Dialog boxes in Adobe Photoshop with information about image and document size

Image size versus file size

Document size (width x height in inches or centimeters) or image size (width x height in pixels) and image resolution (number of pixels per inch) are not exactly the same concepts. [Fig. 11.2] And though they are related, both are independent of the disk space occupied by the file, which depends on its format and compression.

If you resample an image in software like Photoshop, you can increase the number of pixels in the image (pixels per inch). But be careful: the software simply interpolates new pixels between the existing ones. A photo of poor quality will not improve if you artificially increase its resolution (in fact, it will often look worse). For printed images, aim for a resolution of 300 ppi at the size used in the final layout.

11.4
Color gamut of devices

The various input devices (cameras, scanners, et cetera), visual reproduction devices (screens, projectors, et cetera), and output devices (printers, et cetera)

Fig. 11.3
Color gamuts of different
devices plotted on the
chromaticity diagram
CIE 1931

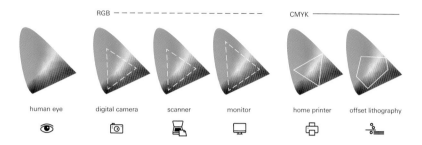

RGB — — — — — — — — — — — — — — — — —   CMYK ——————————

human eye   digital camera   scanner   monitor   home printer   offset lithography

cannot reproduce all the colors that the human eye is able to see, but rather a smaller range of colors that we call **gamut**. [Fig. 11.3] This color gamut depends on factors such as the particular device, its age, its technical features, and the color space in which we are working.

A 1931 CIE diagram displays the gamut of colors that various devices can reproduce. The colors that cannot be displayed are said to be out of gamut. When we transfer information from one device to another, colors that are out of the gamut of the target device are replaced by similar colors that the device can reproduce. Bear in mind that this transformation is not reversible: if you convert an image from ProPhoto to sRGB, you will permanently lose color information, even if you convert the image back to ProPhoto.

The color gamut for input devices (cameras, scanners) and display (monitors) is represented in RGB, with three coordinates that each have a value between 0 and 255. The color gamut for output devices (printers) is represented in CMYK, with four numbers, each with a value between 0 and 100.

11.5
ICC color profiles

An ICC color profile is a set of data describing the color attributes of a particular device (scanner, camera, monitor, et cetera). This profile allows you to compare the colors of such a device with a standard, unambiguous color space known as Profile Connection Space (PCS), based on CIE color spaces (CIE XYZ or CIE Lab) with an illuminant (D50) and standard observers. ("ICC" stands for the International Color Consortium, which was created to develop and manage this standard file format for color.)

ICC input profiles (for scanners and cameras)
An ICC input profile describes the color gamut of a scanner or digital camera. Most input devices read RGB colors and have a one-way profile that converts RGB device coordinates to PCS. It is a matrix or table for the values of the three RGB fundamental colors and white point, to transform them to PCS.

ICC visualization profiles (for monitors and screens of personal devices)

An ICC visualization profile describes the color gamut of a particular device (LCD, LED, IPS-LED, CRT, et cetera) in an ideal RGB working space. This color profile is bidirectional; it can convert PCS to RGB and vice versa. Thus, it can serve as a data source to convert from a monitor to a printing device or as a destination to convert colors from a scanner to a monitor.

An ICC visualization profile usually has a matrix with three hue curves, the XYZ coordinates of the target white point (three numbers), and the XYZ coordinates for each of the three phosphors of the monitor (nine numbers). From this information, the conversion from RGB to PCS XYZ can be calculated and vice versa.

ICC output profiles (printers)

An ICC output profile describes the color gamut for a printing device. All printing devices use CMYK inks (or variations thereof), but some high-end printers with PostScript processors accept only RGB data, which the printer driver converts to CMYK. Using a PostScript raster image processor (RIP) can dramatically reduce the CPU work involved in printing documents by transferring the process of rendering PostScript images from the computer to the printer, which enables faster printing times.

ICC output profiles are bidirectional, as the printer can be the end device (when it converts from the colors of the monitor to those of the printer) or the originating device (when we want to emulate another printing device). The printing profile usually includes three different tables to move from the device to PCS (one for the perceptual rendering, one for colorimetric, and one for saturation) and three more tables for converting from PCS to the final device.

11.6
Correspondence between profiles

Input, visualization, and output ICC profiles are used to ensure that the original color that has been photographed remains consistent when viewed on a monitor and printed.

Converting an image that is displayed on the screen in RGB to one printed in CMYK ink requires two steps:

1   Obtain the PCS XYZ or PCS Lab coordinates corresponding to each RGB value of the image.
2   Locate these PCS XYZ or PCS Lab coordinates in the ICC profile of the printing device, along with the corresponding CMYK percentages.

A color conversion for printing always needs two profiles: an input (source) profile and a destination profile. In the source profile, the table converts from RGB to PCS, and in the destination, it converts from PCS to CMYK.

When you open an image in Photoshop with an embedded color profile (ICC) that does not match the working space, the program will ask if you want to transform the image into the new working color space or maintain the embedded profile. You can do that at any time by choosing "Edit > Convert to Profile." Maintain the embedded color profile if you just want to view the image, but convert to a color space with a broader gamut if you want to edit the image. I recommend working in Adobe RGB 1998, which is the most common workspace for editing images.

To save your image with an embedded profile, assign the profile to your image file. In Photoshop, open "File > Save as…" and check "ICC Profile." Note that you can save PSD, JPEG, TIFF, and PDF files with an embedded profile, although not all image formats permit this.

11.7
Color engine

The color engine is simple software that performs the digital conversion of color from source to destination. A complete RGB table should include more than sixteen million rows, and an ICC color profile cannot include them all. So one of the tasks of the color engine is to interpolate color values between those of the table. If the profile does not contain a table but only the information needed to build it, it is the color engine that carries out this task.[3]

Most image-editing programs include their own color engine—the Adobe Color Engine (ACE), for example—but others use the standard color engines installed in the operating system, such as Apple ColorSync or Microsoft Image Color Management (ICM).

11.8
Rendering intent

When the gamut of the color space of an input device is larger than that of the output device, then those colors located out of range will need to be converted or replaced by similar colors within the gamut of the output device. How that transformation is done depends on the rendering intent.

Rendering intent informs how the color engine translates colors from one color space to another. Imagine a target blue that your digital camera has captured from nature but which does not exist in your printer's color space. How is it printed? Rendering intent provides specific criteria for substituting a similar color that falls within your printer's gamut. There are three main types of rendering: **colorimetric**, **perceptual**, and **saturation**. [Figs. 11.4a–e]

Fig. 11.4a
In this example, the range of colors from the source device (input gamut) does not match that of the destination device (output gamut) when plotted on the chromaticity diagram, so an adequate rendering intent needs to be selected.

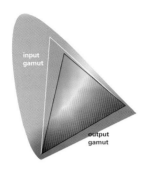

Fig. 11.4b
Relative Colorimetric Rendering Intent keeps the colors that are common to both gamuts and matches the white point of source and destination.

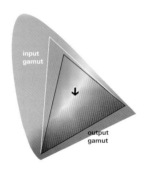

Fig. 11.4c
Absolute Colorimetric Rendering Intent keeps the colors that are common to both gamuts and keeps independent the white point of source and destination.

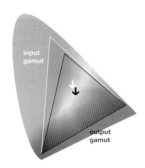

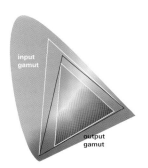

Fig. 11.4d
Perceptual Rendering
Intent, or photo-
graphic, compresses
the size of the original
color gamut to fit
within the destination
color gamut.

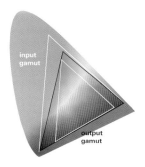

Fig. 11.4e
Saturation Rendering
Intent scales the
input gamut to fit in
the output gamut
and expands to the
edges of the destina-
tion gamut.

Colorimetric Rendering Intent

Fig. 11.4 (all)
Luis Barragán,
Corridor of Gilardi
House, Mexico City,
1976

Colorimetric Rendering Intent keeps the colors that are common to both color gamuts. Those colors that are outside the gamut for the destination color space and therefore cannot be reproduced exactly are replaced by the closest color, preserving the hue and varying only the saturation and brightness. The colors used are those located at the outermost edges of the destination gamut, so there is a tendency toward greater saturation. In general, Colorimetric Rendering Intent is suitable for flat colors and vectors rather than for reproducing photographs.

The color appearance of the brightest white in a color space is called the **white point**. In an electronic visualization device, it is defined by the color temperature of the illuminant taken as a reference for the white. When the color temperature of the white point in the original color space is different from the white point in the destination color space, there are two possibilities:

1   The **Relative Colorimetric Rendering Intent** matches the color temperature of a white point between those of the two spaces so that the white point of the input device changes its position in the output device. To put it simply, the white of the image on the monitor is matched with the white of the paper. The advantage of this method is that a great number of colors can be printed; the disadvantage is that these colors may slightly change when printed on different kind of papers. If your software does not specify whether rendering is **absolute** or **relative**, then relative is used by default. [Fig. 11.4b]

2   The **Absolute Colorimetric Rendering Intent** does not change the color temperature of the white point, so it compares the colors as they are found. To put it simply, the white of the paper is matched with the corresponding color seen on the monitor and not with the white point of the monitor. The advantage is that the printed colors are as faithful as possible to what appears on the screen. The disadvantage is a loss of information, since the system only considers the matching colors. This kind of rendering is useful when you want to print an exact color, as with a logo or a corporate color, for example.[4] [Fig. 11.4c]

Perceptual Rendering Intent (also called Photographic)

Perceptual Rendering Intent compresses the size of the original color gamut to fit within the destination color gamut, transforming the colors of the original color space through scaling. Applying this type of rendering to color spaces with major size differences will cause a loss of color saturation, as the original colors will fall much closer to the central axis of the gray scale.

In general, this rendering intent is suitable for photographs, as the details and proportions among colors are preserved as they are perceived in the original. This is the default setting for Windows color display. It is not recommended, however, if an exact reproduction of a spot color is crucial, since a precise match between the colors of the two spaces is not maintained. [Fig. 11.4d]

Saturation Rendering Intent

Saturation Rendering Intent involves two steps. In the first, the original color gamut is scaled to fit into the destination color gamut, similar to how Perceptual Rendering Intent works. In the second step, the shrunken color space expands to the edges of the destination color gamut, so that it can use 100 percent of the colors that the printer is able to reproduce.

In general, colors that are common to both color spaces (which therefore could be replicated exactly) will be replaced by others that tend to be more saturated, which are located in the outermost parts of the destination space. Moreover, the shades of a gradient tend to be replaced by a single color. Colors become more saturated and lose their relationship to the original versions, so it is recommended for backlit images and large-scale advertisements. [Fig. 11.4e]

Adapting rendering method to situation

The previous paragraphs describe options for converting images from RGB to CMYK, which is the typical sequence if you have captured an image with a digital camera and are planning to print it. But you may instead be interested in converting the image from CMYK to RGB, RGB to RGB, or CMYK to CMYK; each of those cases may require a different rendering intent. [Table 11.3]

Table 11.3
Recommended rendering intent
for each transformation

File	Transformation	Rendering Intent
Images	RGB to CMYK	Perceptual
	RGB to RGB	Relative Colorimetric
	CMYK to RGB	Perceptual
	CMYK to CMYK	Relative Colorimetric
Vector/ plain tints	RGB to CMYK	Relative Colorimetric
	RGB to RGB	Absolute Colorimetric
	CMYK to RGB	Relative Colorimetric
	CMYK to CMYK	Absolute Colorimetric

Table 11.3 source: Miguel Ángel Muñoz Pellicer, "Curso flujos de trabajo avanzados" (lecture, Valencia: AIDO, Instituto Tecnológico de Óptica, Color e Imagen, April 30, 2013).

12 Calibrating a Monitor

The monitor is one the most important devices in the workflow, as many
architectural decisions are made by observing colors on the monitor—often
among people working with different monitors placed under different visual
conditions. Many variables affect the perception of colors seen on the monitor;
it is crucial to control them as much as possible, starting with accurate color
calibration and characterization.

12.1
Calibration is different from characterization

Calibration is the process of adjusting a device to match a reference state
specified by the manufacturer. Calibration enables the device to respond
predictably.

In contrast, **characterization** refers to measuring the inherent limitations in
color reproduction of a device and recording that behavior in a color profile
(ICC or LUT). Characterization allows us to identify the reproducibility of color
without changing the device's response. It describes the behavior when the
profile was created; if that behavior varies, the profile is no longer valid.

So first we calibrate, then we characterize. However, for both calibration and
characterization, we need to send a standardized stimulus to a device, measure
the resulting color (its **response**), and enter that result into the device.

12.2
Monitor calibration

As a monitor ages, its white point becomes less bright. Calibrating the monitor resets its parameters to display color as similarly as possible to when it was new. The parameters that can be calibrated on a monitor are:[1]

- The **white point**. This is the color appearance of the brightest white seen on the device; it is the same as its color temperature (see section 1.5). It is adjusted by the monitor contrast control. Standard white point settings vary between countries and industries, with 5,000 and 6,500 Kelvin being the most common viewing standards. Note that a temperature of 5,000 K will appear more dim or yellow than 6,500 K.
- The **black point**. This is the hardest to adjust consistently: it refers to the minimum voltage of signal that is sent to the screen. It is adjusted with the monitor brightness control.
- The **gamma**, or **response curve**. Until recently, gamma was adjusted using the settings of the graphics card. The monitor was not really calibrated; rather, the settings of the graphics card were adjusted. The recommended ranges were Macintosh = 1.8; Windows = 2.2. Nowadays, most monitors have an internal LUT (Look Up Table), and the parameters of the graphic card do not need to be modified during the calibration process.[2]

Wait for the device to stabilize

Wait a few minutes for the monitor to warm up and to stabilize: ten to fifteen minutes for TFT and LED displays and at least half an hour for CRT monitors.

Room lighting

Monitors perform best in low ambient light. Indirect lighting that does not fall onto the monitor is recommended, corresponding roughly to levels between 32 and 64 lux. Using a digital camera, you can measure the ambient light level and adjust it to 4 EV (exposure value), which equals about 40 lux. A reading of 4 EV is equivalent to 1/2 EV f/2.8, ISO 100 on your camera. Consider using a protective monitor visor, which can considerably improve the appearance of colors on the monitor, particularly dark ones.

Calibrating the monitor

Before calibrating the monitor, check the characteristics of your display settings: its resolution, screen refresh rate, color depth, and color temperature.

In Windows 10, you can find these in "Control Panel > Appearance and Personalization > Display." Windows 10, like previous versions, includes a color calibration utility to make sure your monitor displays the most accurate colors

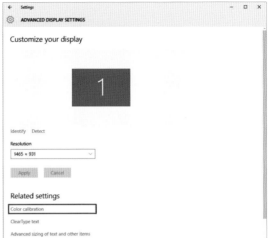

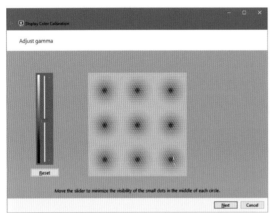

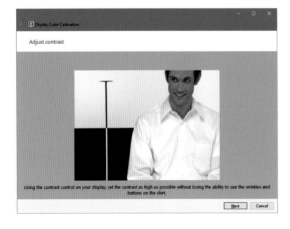

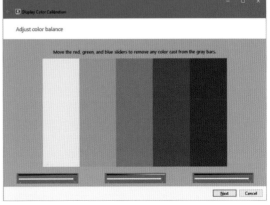

Fig. 12.1
Windows 10 allows users
to calibrate the monitor
with a simple plug-in.

and black levels. Choose "Control Panel > Appearance and Personalization > Color calibration" to launch the utility. This wizard will walk you through the steps of specifying color settings: gamma adjustment, higher and lower levels of brightness, and the color balance for RGB channels. [Fig. 12.1].

In Mac OS, you can find these options in "Apple menu > System Preferences > Displays." Choose the resolution and set the brightness with the slider. Choose "Color > Calibrate" to launch the display calibrator assistant, to set the gamma and white point.

Resolution

The recommended **resolution** for a LCD or LED monitor is usually the highest it permits (approximately 1600 × 1200 pp for a standard twenty-inch monitor or 1400 × 1050 pp for thirteen- to fifteen-inch laptops).[3] A higher resolution will make elements rendered on the monitor smaller, but more material will fit on the screen and the display will appear sharper.

Screen refresh rate

The recommended minimum value for **screen refresh rate** is 60 hertz (Hz); between 75 Hz and 85 Hz is best. Screen refresh can be changed by right-clicking on the Windows desktop and selecting "Screen Resolution > Advanced Configuration > Monitor > Refresh."

Color depth

Set the color depth to at least 32 bits to avoid a banding effect.

Setting the color temperature

Most monitors have several choices for color temperature, usually the following (see section 1.5):

- Three different settings: 5,000, 6,500, and 9,300 K
- Adjustable temperature without presets
- A fine adjustment with three separate channels (RGB). This is the most difficult setting to tune without a hardware device. If you do not have a calibration device, set the temperature to 6,500 K.

Gamma adjustment

Gamma adjustment sets the intermediate grays. The higher the gamma value, the darker the colors appear on a monitor. The typical value for Windows is 2.2; the standard for Macintosh is 1.8. Ideally, when working in mixed environments with both Mac and PC, all monitors should use the same gamma settings. [Figs. 12.2, 12.3]

Adjusting the black point

Adjusting the **black point** determines the minimum voltage sent to monitor channels. This voltage must be set so that when a signal corresponding to pure black is sent to the screen, it appears as black as possible. This adjustment can be difficult because if the black point is set too high, some RGB values that are slightly higher than R = 0, G = 0, and B = 0 (pure black) will also be displayed as black.[4]

Adjusting primary color

Following the calibration wizard, you can adjust your monitor's color balance by moving the sliders for the red, green, and blue colors until you no longer can see any color cast in the gray bars, but calibrations by eye are quite inaccurate if you do not have a calibration device like an Eye-One (see section 12.3). For more precision, you could find the coordinates in CIE XYZ color space of the three monitor primary colors (red, green, and blue) and specify them using the Monitor Calibration Wizard to complete the calibration.

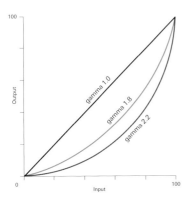

Fig. 12.2 The gamma curve shows the relationship between the brightness of the data captured (input) and the brightness of the output device to match the human perception of color.

Fig. 12.3 Images in RGB observed with gamma 1.0, 1.8, 2.2, and 4.0. Santiago Calatrava, main entrance to the Príncipe Felipe Science Museum in the City of Arts and Sciences, Valencia, Spain, 1998

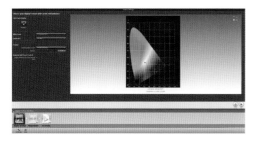

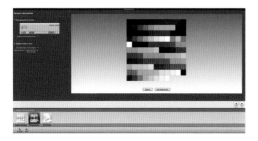

Figs. 12.4–12.7
Eye-One hardware
characterization of
the monitor

12.3
Monitor characterization

To characterize is to create a color profile that describes
the color characteristics of a particular device—in this
case, the monitor. To do so, you will need to measure
several aspects, such as the white point, the color
characteristics of the primaries (red, green, and blue),
or the response curve (gamma). Most calibration
devices (which are small, plug-in hardware items) allow
you to calibrate and measure to create a monitor profile.
These devices are similar to spectrocolorimeters and
can measure the physical characteristics of a color—
in other words, the light reflected or emitted by a
colored surface in the visual spectrum. We will briefly
explain the process working with the Eye-One hardware
device from X-Rite.

Eye-One hardware characterization
Be sure your Eye-One is plugged in and open the
Eye-One Match software.[5] Then, select the device you
wish to profile. [Fig. 12.4] In easy mode, Eye-One
will build the profile quickly, but you will not have the
option to change brightness, contrasts, gamma, or
white point. Once you choose your monitor type (LCD,
LED, or CRT), the software will run by default with the
native settings for your operating system, video card,
and display. In advanced mode, you can manually
change other options supported by the monitor, such
as brightness, contrast, RGB, white point, or color
temperature. First, the Eye-One device has to be calibrated with the white plate provided. [Fig. 12.5] Then
the device has to be held against the monitor. [Fig. 12.6]
Place it as close to the center of the screen as possible.
The software will flash different colors onto the monitor,
taking readings of each. [Fig. 12.7] A progress bar will
appear, and in a couple of minutes, the monitor will be
calibrated and profiled. The profile will automatically be
saved in the operating system folder:

Mac: Macintosh HD > Library > Colorsync > Profiles
Windows: C:\Windows\System32\spool\drivers\color

13 Photographing and Editing Colors

A knowledge of certain camera settings is important to accurately represent color in photographs. This chapter outlines some basic concepts about photography (depth of field, aperture, shutter speed, exposure, et cetera) and provides guidance on characterizing your camera with a color profile to ensure that colors recorded in RGB are as faithful as possible to the original ones. Finally, a calibrated visual device is necessary to check the color consistency of your photos.

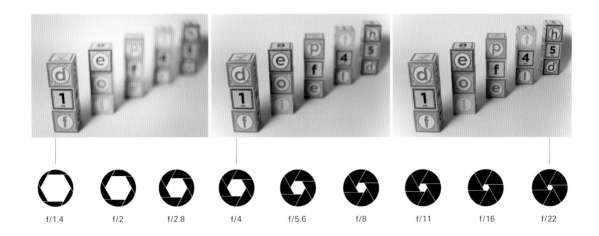

f/1.4   f/2   f/2.8   f/4   f/5.6   f/8   f/11   f/16   f/22

Fig. 13.1 Depth of field in a photograph

13.1
Basic concepts

Depth of field

Depth of field refers to the distance between the closest and farthest elements that appear focused or crisp in a photograph. [Fig. 13.1] The depth of field depends on the camera's aperture, the focal length, and the actual distance between the camera and the focal point.

Aperture/brightness

Aperture describes the diameter of the opening through which light penetrates the image sensor. It is measured in values called f-stops; on a basic camera these will range from f/2 (largest aperture) to f/11 (smallest aperture).

A larger aperture means:

- More light will pass through the lens.
- Less exposure time is required because of the greater illumination.
- The depth of field will be shallower, meaning that less of the image will be in focus.

If you would like everything in the photograph to be in focus, you should choose a higher f-stop of f/8 or f/11. The aperture scale is as follows: f/1, f/1.4, f/2, f/2.8, f/4, f/5.6, f/8, f/11, f/16, f/22, f/32, f/45, f/64, f/90. An aperture of f/4 will admit half as much light as the previous aperture, f/2.8, and twice the light of f/5.6.

Shutter speed/exposure time

Shutter speed is the time it takes for the camera's diaphragm to open and close to let the light pass through. A faster shutter speed means:

- Less exposure time is required.
- Images will be less bright (unless a larger aperture is chosen to allow more light in).
- You will be able to take crisp photographs of moving objects.

Exposure value

The **exposure value** (EV) is a number that represents the variables that exposure depends on: aperture, shutter speed, and ISO sensitivity. It is based on a series of aperture f numbers and shutter speeds.

ISO sensitivity

ISO sensitivity is a concept inherited from analog photography, which depends on the sensitivity of the film negative to light, based on its silver halide content. [Fig. 13.2] Roughly speaking, it indicates the amount of light the CCD (charge-coupled device) image sensor requires to generate an electric pulse. A base value would be 100 ISO for outdoor photography and 400 to 1600 ISO for indoor or nighttime photography.

A higher ISO value means:

- Greater sensitivity to light
- Greater **visual noise** in dark areas (that is, random variations of brightness or color information)

Fig. 13.2 Comparison between approximate human eye sensitivity and Sony A7S camera at 25,600 ISO

Focal length (zoom)

The **focal length** is the distance between the focus (sensor) and the plane of the lens. Each lens has a minimum focal length in relation to the camera, below which focus cannot be achieved. The standard optics for a 35 mm reflex camera range from 28 to 85 mm. Shorter focal lengths produce wide-angle photographs; telephoto lenses (with longer focal lengths of 55 to 250 mm) allow you to take photographs from a greater distance. Greater focal length means more zoom and consequently a narrower viewing angle. [Fig. 13.3]

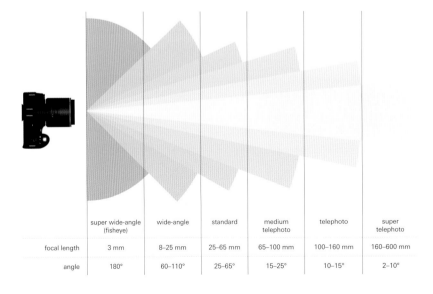

	super wide-angle (fisheye)	wide-angle	standard	medium telephoto	telephoto	super telephoto
focal length	3 mm	8–25 mm	25–65 mm	65–100 mm	100–160 mm	160–600 mm
angle	180°	60–110°	25–65°	15–25°	10–15°	2–10°

Fig. 13.3
Focal length (zoom)

13.2
White balance

Different light sources have different spectral distributions, or hues. As a result, colors appear to change according to the type of lighting. Daylight might appear yellowish at midday and bluish when the sky is overcast; accordingly, objects might appear slightly yellowish or bluish depending on these lighting conditions (see section 1.1). The human eye can very efficiently offset the effect of different-colored light sources, making adjustments to our perception without us even being aware of them.

We want the white in a photograph to appear white, which means we need to artificially "heat" or "cool" the image to ensure that there is an adequate color balance. This process is known as **white balance adjustment**.

White balance adjustment in the camera

Digital cameras make white balance automatic and easy, but the process is not perfect. Most digital cameras come with a series of default settings for white balance based on standard lighting conditions, such as tungsten, fluorescent, daylight, flash, overcast, and hue. These parameters are based on statistical averaging. If you are shooting in JPEG or TIFF format, the best way to achieve neutral, accurate colors is to customize the white balance prior to taking shots. Without a customized white balance, it will be quite tricky to offset any color defects.

To optimally adjust white balance, include a calibration chart in the shot, such as the X-Rite ColorChecker Classic (see section 13.3). [Fig. 13.4] This provides a reference for later color correction. Another method, though not quite as accurate, is to include a piece of white paper. The ColorChecker or paper should be under the same illumination as the rest of the shoot, and lighting should be kept as consistent as possible. Should you change the illumination, you will need to reshoot the calibration chart.

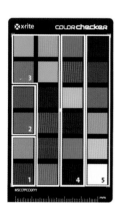

Fig. 13.4 Description of the color swatches in ColorChecker Classic:
1. Skin hues
2. Blue of the sky and green grass
3. Some usual natural and secondary hues
4. Hues from RGB and CMY color systems
5. Neutral grays

Adjustments to white balance during image processing

You can manage the white balance when processing a raw photo in Photoshop with the help of the Camera Raw plug-in or in the Adobe Lightroom application. Select the eyedropper tool in the "White Balance" tab and click on the white reference in the photograph.

13.3
DNG color profiles for the camera

The creation of a color profile for the camera is useful to assure that the colors photographed and electronically recorded by the camera are rendered as similar as possible to the perception of the physical ones. A DNG color profile for the camera is similar to the color profiles of other devices and contains a set of data to determine the correspondence between the colors recorded by the sensor of the camera and a standard color space that is unambiguous (see section 11.5). In short, a camera profile assures that the colors recorded in the digital file are reliably consistent with those seen in nature so that they will look identical when observed on a calibrated display.

A DNG profile describes the camera performance for a specific lighting condition and can be assigned to all the shots belonging to the same photographic session in the moment you develop the photos from .raw to .tiff. In the following section, you will learn how to create a color profile for your camera using a ColorChecker color-calibration target.

Creating a color profile for the camera with ColorChecker

The Munsell ColorChecker color-calibration target, first produced as the Macbeth ColorChecker in 1976 and still widely known as the Gretag Macbeth ColorChecker, is a framed cardboard arrangement of twenty-four squares of painted samples based on Munsell colors (see section 2.4).[1]

To create a color profile for your photographic session, make sure you take a shot with the ColorChecker centered in the image, under the same lighting conditions as the rest of the photos in the session, saved in raw format. You will need to convert the raw file into DNG (Digital Negative) format to be processed using the ColorChecker Passport software. Follow these steps:

1   Open the raw image file for the shot containing the ColorChecker Classic, using the Photoshop Camera Raw plug-in. A white-balance adjustment is not required, because the ColorChecker Passport application will review the image and will automatically make any necessary changes. [Fig. 13.5]

2   Without modifying the image, check that the exposure level is suitable.

3   Select "Save Image"; a new dialogue box will appear. Select "Format > DNG (Digital Negative)." Saving the image in DNG format will allow you to open it in the ColorChecker Passport application.

4   Open ColorChecker Passport. [Fig. 13.6] Select your image or drag and drop the DNG archive into the window.

5   Click on "Create Profile." The application will automatically search for the ColorChecker within the image and will create an ICC profile. If the application is unable to find the ColorChecker, you will be requested to crop the image manually to its edges.

6   Give the profile a name that describes the lighting conditions and click on "Save." By default, the profile will be saved to the directory or folder in which Photoshop, Photoshop Elements, and Lightroom store DNG profiles (C:\Users \[User Name]\AppData\Roaming\Adobe\CameraRaw\Camera Profiles).

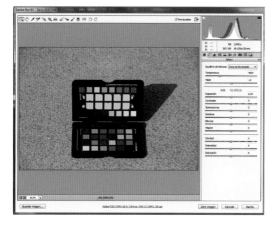 

Fig. 13.5
Photoshop Camera Raw plug-in allows the user to edit different camera adjustments after the shot.

Fig. 13.6
Camera Profiling with ColorChecker Passport

7   Reboot the Adobe applications to use the new DNG profile. It should be available in the Camera Calibration panel in the Lightroom and Camera Raw applications.

8   In Camera Raw, open another image taken during the same photographic session. Click on the Camera icon to see the Camera Calibration file.

9   In the drop-down menu, select and add the new profile.

Customized dual illuminant profiles

The ColorChecker Passport and Lightroom application can create customized dual illuminant DNG profiles. The dual-illuminant profile enables you to make adjustments to photographs taken under two different lighting conditions—for example, one indoors and one outdoors. The colors of the same object photographed indoors and outdoors will have the same appearance, despite the fact that the images have been taken under different lighting conditions. Dual-illuminant DNG profiles can be created with any two illuminants from the list of fifteen compatible conditions provided by default in ColorChecker Passport software.[2] However, the two must have different correlated color temperatures (CCT); to obtain the best results, the CCT (in Kelvin) should not be too close (see section 6.2). This is why Adobe profiles use incandescent (tungsten) light and daylight as defaults.

13.4
Color swatches

You may need to perform the same color correction on a large group of photographs. It is possible to make that correction to a few primary photographs and then apply the same changes to the remaining images.

To color correct all the photos from one photographic session taken under the same lighting conditions, include a calibration chart with color swatches in one of the photos. This will allow you to later compare the image on the screen with the physical color chart.

Most photo-editing programs include controls for making specific changes to the three visual attributes: hue, saturation, and luminance (HSL). In the Camera Raw application, these controls can be found in the "Hue-Saturation-Luminance" file or tab. In the Lightroom application, these are found within the "Develop" panel. It's best to start with the default profile for your camera, then use the chromatic and tonal controls for making specific changes.

Visual comparison

Comparing the colors of an image on your monitor with a physical object helps to make well-grounded decisions about color. Follow these steps using the Lightroom application to match the colors on the monitor to those of your physical object:

1   Choose "Develop > Target" in the upper-left margin of the HSL panel.
2   Go to "Colors." The colors roughly correspond to the HSL arrow keys in the Develop dialogue box in the Lightroom plug-in.
3   To select a color and make changes, click and drag the Target tool up or down or use the arrow keys or the values in the HSL panel.

Additional color matching can be accomplished using color swatches. When matching colors, be sure to use a properly calibrated monitor and controlled lighting conditions, such as a light booth, to illuminate your physical object.

You can save the Hue, Saturation, and Luminance settings and apply them to the rest of the images from the same photographic session, as long as they were taken under the same lighting conditions as the color chart. Color profiles in Windows are saved to C:\Windows\System32\spool\drivers\color.

A number of applications can be used to color correct images in raw format, including Lightroom 2, Capture One by Phase One, and Bibble by Bibble Lab. These applications are specifically designed to make it easy for photographers to perform color correction, make adjustments to exposure and contrast, trim images, and create image collections. They also include functions for quickly importing, processing, and manipulating images, one at a time or as a group, from the photography session.

When these applications are used with ColorChecker Passport, you can be sure that corrections are based on accurate chromatic data. The main difference between these programs is that Bibble and Capture One are compatible with ICC profiles, whereas Lightroom functions with Adobe DNG profiles.

Customized profiles can be particularly useful for quickly and precisely matching exact colors. ICC and DNG profiles can represent camera, lens, and lighting conditions, but there are differences in the way in which you create and use them. X-Rite offers other applications that can be used to create customized ICC profiles. For more information, see http://www.xritephoto.com.

13.5
Photo editing in Photoshop

Photoshop is a powerful photo editing tool; it allows users to modify many aspects related to the color of an image after it has been shot. The quality of a bad image can be easily improved using Photoshop's many options, with the advantage that they can be applied to just a part of the photo and are reversible when working in mask mode. Below is a brief introduction to photo editing; for further information about specific tools for color correction, matching or replacing colors, and useful filters, please refer to Appendix B.

Histogram control

Photoshop allows us to adjust images by using a graph called a **histogram.** Open an image in Photoshop and select "Window > Properties," "Image > Adjustments > Curves," or "Window > Adjustments > 'curves' or 'levels' icon." [Fig. 13.7] The histogram is a graph that displays the distribution of shades in an image, providing the number of pixels at each intensity level. By examining the histogram we can check the exposure—that is, whether an image includes enough details in its dark, medium, and light areas. We can also select a specific area to check the tonal range of a portion of the document.

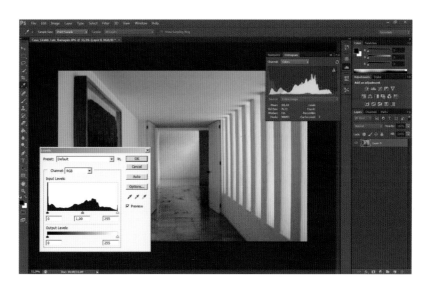

Fig. 13.7
Histogram of an image

Fig. 13.8a
Original image:
Will Alsop, Colorium,
Dusseldorf, Germany,
2001.

Fig. 13.8b
Excess backlighting:
the histogram shows
crests in the extremes

Fig. 13.8c
Overexposed image with
too much whiteness

The histogram displays a graph for each RGB color channel; its horizontal axis is on a scale from 0 to 255 with all possible levels of brightness. Sometimes the horizontal axis is divided into five areas that we can call, from left to right, black, gray, medium gray, light gray, and white. The vertical axis shows the total number of pixels that exist at each brightness level.[3] You can easily edit the histogram curve to modify the exposure of the image, which is the distribution of the *value* (dark/light) of the colors.

A good image contrast: high, medium, and low color ranges

In general, a picture is considered to have a good contrast if its histogram covers almost the entire range of shades. [Fig. 13.8a] But it should be noted that a night-time image (low value ranges of color) will have a histogram with a strong shift to the left-hand side (the area of dark shades), while for an image with light colors (high value ranges of color), the histogram will be higher in the light gray and white areas.

Correct exposure

The height of the histogram graph depends on the composition of the scene. Normally, using the wrong exposure when shooting a photograph leads to a straight cut in the curve. Ideally, if an image has a correct exposure, with enough shades, the transitions between shades should be continuous and the distribution of intensity levels will not display high points at its extremities. [Figs. 13.8b, 13.8c]

Edition of colors in mask mode

A mask is useful for making a color correction in just one area of an image. It also makes it possible to undo the editing at any moment by turning the corresponding layer on or off. When a selection is used to define a mask, a supplementary channel appears in the Channels panel with the default name "mask."

Create a selection and click on the bottom button of the tools panel to switch to "quick mask" mode. Double-click on the icon and the display options will appear. By default, the protected part of the mask is colored red. The foreground color in the tool panel will automatically change to white, and the background to black. If you use any drawing tool to draw in white, that area will be added to the selection; if you draw in black, it will be subtracted.

Masks can be designated as either "layer" or "vector." Layer masks are bitmap images that are dependent on the image's resolution; they are edited using the painting and selection tools. Vector masks are independent of resolution and are created using a shape tool or pen tool. Layer masks and vector masks are not destructive: you can always go back and edit them without losing the pixels that they cover.

14 Printing Color Accurately

When we print an image we have been viewing on a computer monitor, we often are disappointed by an obvious color shift. Although a printed color will always appear somewhat different from one viewed on-screen, good printer profiling will save us from unpleasant surprises. Further, a printer profile makes it possible to preview on the screen a soft proof of the image as it would look printed on various different output devices.

14.1
Soft proofing printed colors

The colors that come out of your printer should match the ones that you see on your computer screen. To ensure this as much as possible, you will need to adjust your printer's color profile parameters.

Printing adjustments
First, check whether your printer or output device comes with a specific color profile, provided by its manufacturer. Many companies have published specific (ICC) color management profiles for each type of paper.[1] To install these profiles, download them from the printer manufacturer's website and save them in your computer's ICC profile folder:

*   Windows: C:\Window\System32\spool\drivers\color
*   Mac OS: Systems Folder/ColorSync/Profile

Print preview
In Photoshop, you can display an on-screen preview of how your document's colors will look when reproduced on a particular output device. The reliability

of this "soft proof" depends upon the quality of your monitor, the profiles of your monitor and output devices, and the ambient lighting conditions of your work environment. Go to "View > Proof Setup." You can choose from a list of soft-proof presets or you can load a custom proof setup.

To create a custom proof setup, select the output profile that corresponds to your printer and the type of paper you will use. Certain printing houses provide ICC printer profiles for their printers and paper types. These can be used to simulate the output colors but should not be embedded in the image itself. Remember that you can embed a color profile by going to the window "Edit > Assign Profile" or, at the moment you save the file, in the window "File > Save As" under "Color," checking the box with the color profile.

Rendering intent

In Photoshop's "View > Proof Setup > Custom" options, select the correct rendering intent for your profile. Your choice will depend on the type of image you are working with (see section 11.8). "Black Point Compensation" ensures that the shadow detail in the image is preserved by simulating the full dynamic range of the output device. Select this option if you plan to use black point compensation when printing (which is recommended in most situations).

"Simulate Paper Color" mimics the tone of real paper, which is not truly white, based on the proof profile. "Simulate Black Ink" simulates the dark gray of many printers in place of a solid black, according to the proof profile. Not all profiles support these two options.

Click "OK," and you will immediately see the final result on the screen. Note that in the bar where the image title appears, there is also an indication of how it is being previewed.[2]

14.2
Printer profiling

A number of variables affect printed colors:[3]

- the brand and specific model of printer
- the ink
- the paper
- the RIP component
- the resolution, printing speed, and printer properties

Despite the fact that printer manufacturers provide suitable ICC profiles for each model, it is always much better to obtain custom printer profiles by using a hardware device, such as an Eye-One profiler by X-Rite. [Figs. 14.1, 14.2] Remember that each type of printer, RIP, paper, and combination of inks requires its own color profile.

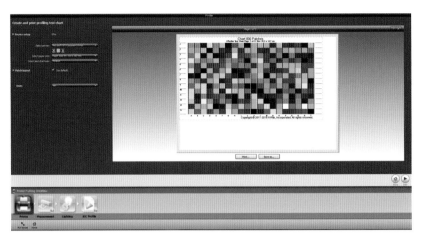

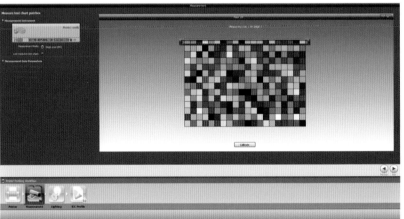

Figs. 14.1 and 14.2
Creating printer profiles
with Eye-One

What is a printer RIP?

RIP stands for Raster Image Processor, which is the mechanism for interpreting and converting the pixels of an image for accurate printing. It can be incorporated into the printer's hardware system or into the software that controls the printer. If you create a profile using hardware, notify the printer drivers to deactivate color management, as this will be carried out by specific software. Before characterizing your printer, make sure that the color management of the manufacturer's printer RIP is deactivated, so as not to interfere in the printing of swatches. If you are printing using software like Photoshop, you can do this in "File > Print"; under "Color Management," in the "Color Handling" drop-down menu, select "Photoshop manages color" to avoid having the printer manage the color.

Calibrating or linearizing a printer

Calibration optimizes printer functioning. You can carry this out via the printer's control panel, the printer driver, or RIP Postscript software. Calibration is required before you create a color profile for your printer and should be carried out periodically.

Characterizing or creating the color profiles for a printer

Open the Eye-One interface and select the printer icon to begin creating the profile. Select your printer from the drop-down menu; the Eye-One will automatically detect the color mode used by the printer (RGB, CMYK). If the printer uses six inks (CMYK + light blue + light magenta), its profile will be equivalent to CMYK. For printers with more ink cartridges (orange and green), other specific software should be used, such as X-Rite's Profile Maker Pro.[4]

Fig. 14.3
IT8 calibration targets

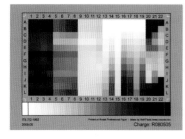

Based on the color mode, Eye-One provides a color chart with a specific number of color swatches (Eye-One RGB Target 1.5, Eye-One TC 9.18 RGB, et cetera). These target color charts must be printed from the printer to be profiled, matching the characteristics of the final work to be printed (print quality, resolution, paper, et cetera). [Fig. 14.3]

Measurement mode for the Eye-One instrument

The measurement mode of an Eye-One device determines the type of measurement to be made and the number of readings. Some Eye-One devices measure a single target color; others are able to read a whole row of various colors, which is faster.

Lighting conditions

The Eye-One Profiler software allows you to create profiles for different lighting conditions. On the lighting page, you can choose standard D50 lighting or other CIE illuminants, or even create custom settings for your workplace's specific lighting conditions, since a printed image will appear different under different lighting conditions (see section 1.1). By using the lighting options in the Eye-One Profiler software, you will be able to produce printouts that are customized to be accurate under various lighting conditions.

Creation of the custom color profile

After measuring the physical target colors printed on the paper, the Eye-One software generates an ICC color profile. You will be asked to give a name and save the new profile in your computer's ICC profile folder. Remember that a soft-proof comparison with other profiles is also possible in Photoshop by going to "View > Proof Setup" and selecting the specific printer color profile.

15 Color in Building

Sometimes it is crucial to find out the specific color of a building or physical material. We may need to repaint an ancient facade or introduce a new element that matches a preexisting color, or we just want to check the accuracy of the final color with respect to the one chosen. In any of these cases, we can bring a physical color atlas to the site and try to visually match the target color with the swatches, but difficult-to-control variables, such as the lighting conditions and our own subjectivity, might bias the result. Using technology like colorimeters or spectrophotometers improves accuracy and avoids subjective imprecision. In addition, spectrophotometers allow us to accurately interpret metameric colors and anticipate the perceptual aspect of a color under different lighting conditions.

These instruments measure colors visible on the surface of the material, but if the aim is to recover the color of a historical building in ancient times, when different layers of paint or materials exist, other analytical techniques might be necessary, such as extracting the plaster to analyze with a microscope.

15.1
Technology for measuring color

To accurately measure color on a surface, consider the following aspects:

- Use standard lighting: D50 for graphics and D65 for architecture. In other words, you need to know the spectral distribution of the light.
- Decide the angle of observation of the sample. A two-degree angle of observation is used for small samples and ten-degree for large ones (see section 1.1).
- Decide whether measurements will include specularly reflected light. This is light that reflects from the equal but opposite angle to the light

source. If it is excluded (Specular Component Excluded SCE), only the diffuse reflectance light, which is scattered in many directions, will be considered. When we observe a glossy surface, we tend to ignore reflections when we identify its inherent color, so SCE is the best way to measure a color if we do not want to consider the brightness of the surface. If specular reflection is included (SCI), the total reflectance will be considered, specular and diffuse.

- Decide the inclination angle for the light source. Usually 0/45 (illuminant perpendicular to sample and observer at 45 degrees) or 45/0 (45-degree illuminant and observer perpendicular to the sample) are used. Alternately, you can use diffuse lighting, conferring the advantage of being able to calculate an average color, should the samples be heterogeneous.
- Measure a sample area that is representative of the whole. (Some instruments enable you to automatically calculate the average of more than one area of measurement.)

15.2
Instruments for measuring color

Colorimeters

Colorimeters measure the visual appearance of a color, providing the color notation of a sample in various desired color spaces (NCS, Munsell, Lab, et cetera). [Figs. 15.1, 15.2] Colorimeters have three photosensitive sensors that

Fig. 15.1
NCS Colour Scan
contact colorimeter

measure short wavelengths (violets/blues), medium wavelengths (greens/yellows), and long wavelengths (reds). The limitation of a colorimeter is that it does not provide a preview of how a color will look under changes to lighting or observation conditions. In other words, it cannot be used to detect metameric colors (those which appear the same under some lighting conditions but different under others; see Activity 3).

Fig. 15.2
NCS Colourpin II
colorimeter

Spectrophotometers

The **spectrophotometer** calculates and draws the spectral reflectance curve of a color sample with a complete sweep of the whole visible spectrum (between 400 and 700 nm) with a pass every 5, 10, or 20 nm, regardless of the illuminant. [Fig. 15.3] It has great advantages over colorimeters and densitometers:

- It is much more precise.
- Readings are independent of the lighting conditions of the sample.
- Readings are independent of the standard observer used.
- You can compare the appearance of the sample under different lighting and observer conditions, to observe metamerism.

Fig. 15.3
Konica Minolta
CM-2600d
spectrophotometer

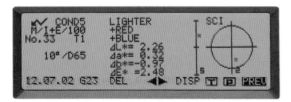

Fig. 15.4
Identification of a target color and statistical information about color differences of the rest of the measurements. SpectraMagic software by Konica Minolta

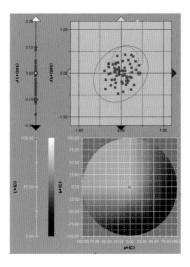

15.3
Software

The software programs packaged with spectrophotometers allow you to download and edit the data on your computer.

SpectraMagic NX
Konica Minolta packages this software with its instruments; it permits the user to collect very precise technical assessment data. [Fig. 15.4] SpectraMagic NX allows you to:

- Review and edit spectral reflectance curves for each material.
- Produce color notation for the different color spaces: Lab, Munsell, XYZ, CIE Lab, et cetera.
- Evaluate color appearance using different illuminants and observers.
- Draw colors using different graphics: chromaticity diagram, CIE Lab, et cetera.
- Compare colors, with a target color as a reference, using dE, dL, da, db, et cetera.

Appendix A:
Tables Relating to Visual Ergonomics

Table A.1
Standard values for lighting of indoor workplaces

	Em	UGRL	Uo	Ra
Filing, copying, etc.	300	19	0.40	80
Writing, typing, reading, data processing	500	19	0.60	80
Technical drawing	750	16	0.70	80
CAD workstations	500	19	0.60	80
Conference and meeting rooms	500	19	0.60	80
Reception desks	300	22	0.60	80
Archives	200	25	0.40	80

- Illuminance levels must not fall below the Em maintenance values in the visual task area. If the precise location is not known, the limit should be applied to the whole room or a specific working area.
- The maintenance factors can be determined on a case-by-case basis, according to the manufacturer's specifications. Where no individual maintenance data is available, the following values are recommended as reference maintenance factors for modern technology and three-times-a-year maintenance: 0.67 in a clean atmosphere, and 0.50 in very dirty environments. EN 12464 specifies that the lighting designer must document the maintenance factor and maintenance schedule.
- UGRL is the upper limit for direct glare. The UGR value calculated in the design process must lie below this.
- Uniformity Uo is the ratio between the lowest (Emin) and the mean illuminance level (E) in the area to be evaluated. The result is a minimum level.
- Ra is the lower limit for the color rendering index. The Ra of the selected lamp must be equal to or greater than this value.

Table A.2
Color performance of lamps according to working environments

Group	Range of Ra	Color Appearance	Preferred Use	Acceptable Use
1A	[90, 100]	warm neutral cold	color matching, clinical explorations, art galleries	
1B	[80, 90]	warm neutral	homes, hotels, shops, offices, schools, hospitals	
		neutral cold	graphic arts, textile and paper industry, industrial work	sports facilities
2	[60, 80]	warm neutral cold	industrial work	offices, schools
3	[40, 60]		industries handling large objects	industrial work
4	[20, 40]			none

Tables A.1, A.2, and A.3 source: Tables and figures were taken from the European standards: "Lighting of indoor workplaces," EN12464-1 (June 2011), "Lighting of outdoor workplaces," EN 12464-2 (October 2007); "Sports facility lighting," EN 12193 (April 2008), Table A.4 source: Alliance for Solid-State Illumination Systems and Technologies (ASSIST), Recommendations for Specifying Color Properties of Light Sources for Retail Merchandising 8, no. 2 (March 2010): 7, http://www.lrc.rpi.edu/

Table A.3
Color rendering index Ra or CRI for different types of lighting

Source	Ra or CRI						
	90	80–89	70–79	60–69	40–59	20–39	
Daylight	+						
LED	+	+	+				
Halogen lamp	+	+					+ Recommended
Compact fluorescent lamp	+	+					
Fluorescent lamp	+	+	–	–	–		– No longer recommended due to low efficiency and inappropriate color rendering
High-pressure mercury lamp				–	–		
Metal halide lamp	+	+		–			
High-pressure sodium lamp		+		–	–	–	

Table A.4
Examples of light sources that meet the criteria for CRI (≥80 and ≤100)

Light source	Manufacturer	Product Model	CCT (K)	CRI	GAI
Xenon	Osram Sylvania	1000W	5,853	97	91
PC-LED phosphor-converted white light–emitting diode	Cree	XR-E lamp	4,154	84	82
	Sharp	Zenigata	5,097	95	99
RGB-LED red, green, and blue LEDs mixed to create white light	Various	Peak wavelengths of 465 nm, 545 nm and 614 nm	4,000	89	82
T8 linear fluorescent, 25 mm diameter	General Electric	F32T8 / SPX50	4,751	87	86
	Lumiram	Lumichrome 1XX	5,960	93	95
	Verilux	F32T8SPX50	6,369	85	96
T12 linear fluorescent, 38 mm diameter	Osram Sylvania	Design50, 40W	4,861	90	84
	General Electric	Sunshine F40C50	4,944	92	87
	Duro-Test	Vita-Lite 5500K	5,159	88	90
	Lumiram	Lumichrome 1XC	5,207	92	93
	Philips	Colortone 75	6,217	90	85
	Duro-Test	DAYLITE 65, 40W	6,588	93	95
MH metal halide	Philips	CDM100W / 4K	4,075	93	80
	Philips	CDM150W / 4K	4,197	92	83
Daylight		CIE D50	5,000	100	88
		CIE D65	6,500	100	98

Appendix B:
Editing Images in Photoshop

1
Color corrections in Photoshop using the Adjustments panel

Open an image in Photoshop and select "Window > Adjustments." This panel contains many different icons for color corrections. These corrections are applied to a new layer and those underneath; you can edit, activate, or deactivate these changes by updating the adjustment layer (or deleting it altogether) at any stage. Presets are available for Levels, Curves, Exposure, Hue/Saturation, Black & White, Channel Mixer, and Selective Color. You can do the same by going to the panel "Layer > New Adjustment Layer," selecting the desired adjustment, and clicking "OK" in the New Layer dialogue box.

Note that you can make these same corrections in "Image > Adjustments"; however, this method makes direct changes to the image instead of adding an adjustment layer, so once you save the image, these changes are not reversible.

Brightness/Contrast
Enter values for brightness (–150 to 150) and contrast (–50 to 100) or drag the sliders back and forth. You can restore the original setting by checking "Use Legacy."

Levels
The histogram in the Levels window represents the number of pixels for each intensity level of the image, from the darkest pixels on the left to the lightest on the right. The input level displays information about shadows, midtones, and highlights, while the output level indicates the values of corrections.

The input levels are defined in three fields, with three sliders under the histogram: the black shadow slider (default value = 0), the midtone slider

(default =1), and the highlight slider (default = 255). The output levels are shown in the two fields at the bottom. The black slider, on the left, is the first field and regulates the shadows (default value = 0), while the white slider, on the right, is the second field and controls the lights (default value 255).

You can darken or lighten an image by adjusting the input and output sliders. All those pixels with a value equal to or less than the shadow input level will have the value of the shadow output level. All those pixels with a value equal to or higher than the highlight input level will be set to the highlight output level. Adjustments can be made to all three RGB channels simultaneously or one by one.

Curves
This function allows you to adjust the tonal area of an image by using an adjustment curve. The horizontal axis represents the original brightness values of the pixels 0–255 (input level). [Fig. B.1] The vertical axis represents the changed values (output levels). The diagonal line represents the value of different tones (shadows to the left, midtones in the center, and lights to the right).

When you select the hand icon, the cursor turns into an eyedropper; clicking on any pixel of the image displays it on the curve. You can adjust the shape of the curve by selecting that point, then clicking and dragging. The output curve can be edited using the icons on the left-hand side of the panel. These allow you to locate checkpoints, draw a curve manually, adjust the curve, et cetera. It is also possible to select presets from a drop-down menu.

Exposure
This setting allows you to correct underexposure or overexposure by lightening or darkening the entire

image. The Exposure slider modifies the lightness or darkness, primarily intervening in the highlights. The Offset slider primarily involves the midtones and shadows. The Gamma Correction slider manages the midtones of the image. The command "Image > Adjustments > Shadows/Highlights," also lets you retouch photos that have too much backlighting.

Vibrance

Drag the Vibrance slider to increase or decrease color saturation without clipping. (Color clipping is produced when the intensity of a color is too high or too low, so it is set out of gamut and is shifted to the closest color in gamut.) Vibrance increases the saturation of colors that are less saturated more than those that are already saturated. Then, do one of the following:

- To further adjust less saturated colors and prevent colors clipping as they reach total saturation, move the Vibrance slider to the right.
- To apply the same amount of saturation adjustment to all colors regardless of their current saturation, move the Saturation slider. In some situations, this may produce less banding than the Saturation slider in the Hue/Saturation Adjustments panel or Hue/Saturation dialog box.
- To decrease saturation, move either the Vibrance or the Saturation slider to the left.

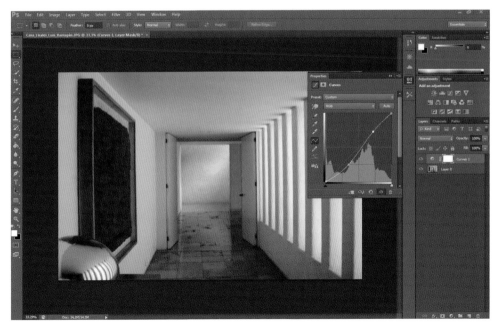

Fig. B.1 Adjusting the curves

Hue/Saturation

Hue/Saturation alters the hue, saturation, and brightness of the color components of a document or selection. [Fig. B.2] This operation is similar to previous ones, but the lower slider is particularly useful because the full color spectrum is indicated for both input and output. If you are working in RGB channels, the range of colors under consideration is displayed and can be edited. Use the eyedroppers to select a specific color within the image to select, enlarge, or reduce the range of colors affected.

Color Balance

Color Balance changes the overall mixture of colors in an image. It allows you to modify the hues of shadows, midtones, and highlights by dragging the slider to the right or left. The values beside the color bars show the color changes for the red, green, and blue channels. (For Lab images, values are for the a and b channels.) Values can range from −100 to +100. Check "Preserve Luminosity" to prevent shifting the color values in the image while changing the color hue. This option maintains the lightness balance in the image.

Black & White

This option is recommended for converting from color to black and white, instead of "Image > Mode > Grayscale," where you have less control over the transformation. In addition, each of these transformations is done in a separate layer that you can turn on or off, to which you can apply a layer mask. In the Preset drop-down menu, you can apply specific settings [Fig. B.3].

By checking Tint and selecting a color, you can tint the entire image in a chiaroscuro scale. But be aware that the image will still be in RGB mode— it is not a duotone image. To convert the image to a true duotone, change the image to gray scale, then apply "Image > Mode > Duotone," which will result in a loss of color information.

Photo Filter

Choose a preset filter to simulate the effect of a warming or cooling filter or to create a customized one. The Density slider controls the effect of the filter; check Preserve Luminosity to maintain lightness.

Channel Mixer

The Channel Mixer allows you to modify a specific RGB output channel depending on the settings of the active channels of the document and also to create gray scale images. Sliders for each channel range between −200% and +200%. A negative value inverts the input channel before adding it to the output channel. Settings can be saved as presets for future images.

Color Lookup

With this setting you can replace the entire color space of an image with that of a source file. The recognized profiles are Device Link, Abstract, or 3D LUT [Fig. B.4]. Device Link applies an ICC, ICM color profile that transforms the image from one device's color space to another without using an intermediate color space. These are useful when specific mappings of device values (like 100 percent black) are required. Abstract profiles enable custom image effects. Abstract profiles can have Lab/XYZ values as both input and output values, which enables generation of a custom LUT to achieve the desired special effect.

A 3D LUT file (3-D lookup table) is used in the film industry to calculate a color correction (also known as color grading or sweetening) for achieving the final result seen on the big screen. Every film has a visual aspect; for example, blue ranges to represent cold, red ranges for warmth, gradations of colors to represent emotions, or even bluish finishing in scary movies. It is similar to the "white balance" in traditional photography, but much more powerful, because 3D LUT can work simultaneously on lights and shadows. The program comes with a small library of "color table aspect" 3D LUTs.

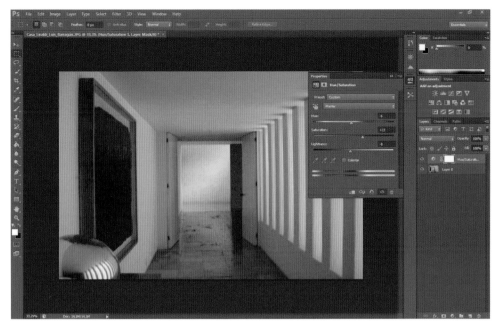

Fig. B.2 Hue/Saturation

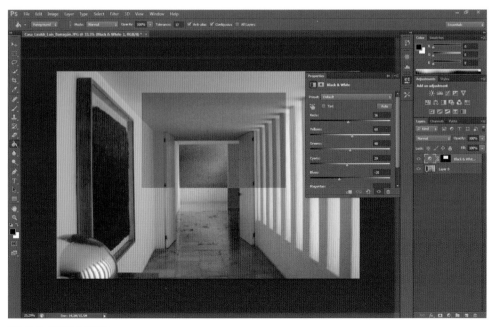

Fig. B.3 Black & White

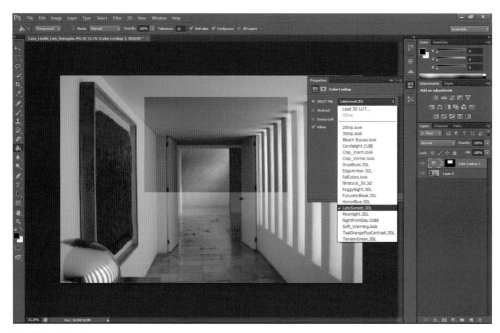

Fig. B.4 Color Lookup

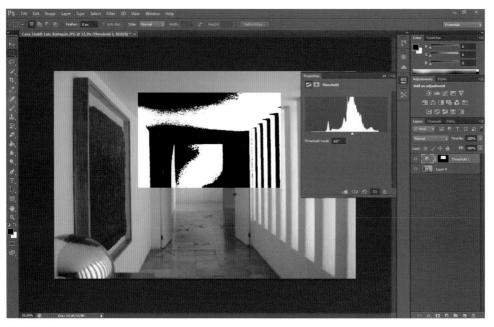

Fig. B.5 Threshold

Invert

Reversing the colors and brightness of the pixels achieves the effect of a photographic negative. When you invert an image, the brightness value of each pixel is converted into the inverse value on the 256-step color-values scale. For example, a pixel in a positive image with a value of 255 is changed to 0. This option is equivalent to "Image > Adjustments > Invert," with the advantage that the effect is applied on a separate layer that can be enabled/disabled, used as a mask, et cetera. Note that the effects of inverting vary depending on whether the color space of the initial image is RGB, Lab, or CMYK.

Posterize

Posterize lets you specify the number of tonal levels (or brightness values) for each channel in an image. It then maps pixels to the closest matching level. For example, choosing two tonal levels in an RGB image gives six colors: two for red, two for green, and two for blue. This setting is used to create special effects, such as large flat areas in a photograph. Its effects are most evident when you reduce the number of gray levels in a gray scale image, but it also produces interesting effects in color images. If you want your image to contain a specific number of colors, convert the image to gray scale and specify that number of levels. Then convert the image back to the previous color mode and replace the various gray tones with the colors you want.

Threshold

Threshold converts a color image into a high-contrast black-and-white image. When you specify a certain level as a threshold, all pixels lighter than the threshold are converted to white, and all pixels darker are converted to black [Fig. B.5]. The Threshold command is useful for determining the lightest and darkest areas of an image.

Selective Color

Selective color correction is a technique used by high-end scanners and separation programs to change the amount of each process color in the primary color components in an image. You can modify the amount of a process color in any primary color selectively—without affecting the other primary colors. For example, you can use selective color correction to dramatically decrease the cyan in the green component of an image while leaving the cyan in the blue component unaltered. Even though Selective Color uses CMYK colors to correct an image, you can use it on RGB images.

This allows you to individually modify each color range of the image. Each original color is selected from a drop-down menu, and the values of the output percentage in CMYK can be modified. When you select "Relative," the existing amount of cyan, magenta, yellow, or black is modified by its percentage of the total. For example, if the original image is 50 percent red and we add 10 percent more, a total of 55 percent will be added (that is, the current percentage of 50 percent, plus 10 percent of the current percentage, which is 5 percent). If you select "Absolute," the modification percentage is adjusted to the color in absolute values. For example, if the original image is 50 percent red and we add 10 percent more, the total will be 60 percent.

Gradient Map

The Gradient Map maps the gray scale range of an image to the colors of a specified gradient. The left color of the gradient is applied to the shadows, and the right one to the highlights. The midtones are distributed according to the hues of the gradient. Dither adds random noise to smooth the appearance of the gradient fill and reduce banding effects; Reverse switches the direction of the gradient fill, reversing the gradient map.

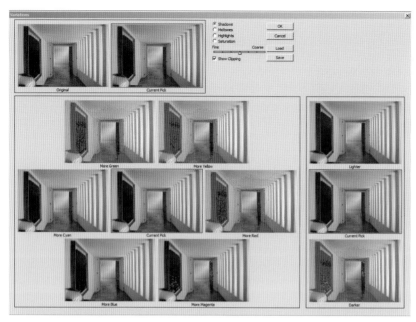

Fig. B.6 Variations of shadows and lights

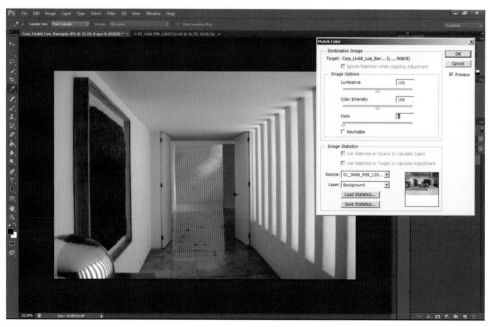

Fig. B.7 Match Color

2
Color corrections in Photoshop using "Image > Adjustments"

Note that these changes are applied directly to the original set of colors of the layer—not to a mask—so the original color information is lost. Some of the same commands appear that are described above; below are additional ones.

Shadows/Highlights

Shadows/Highlights is one method for correcting photos in which objects appear silhouetted due to strong backlighting; it is also useful for correcting subjects that have been washed out because they were too close to the camera flash. This adjustment can also be used for brightening areas of shadow in an otherwise well-lit image. The Shadows/Highlights command does not simply lighten or darken an overall image; it lightens or darkens based on the surrounding pixels in the shadows or highlights, using separate controls for shadows and highlights. The defaults are set to fix images with backlighting problems.

The Shadows/Highlights command also has a Midtone slider, a Black Clip option and a White Clip option for adjusting the overall contrast of the image, and a Color slider for adjusting saturation.

Adjust the amount of lighting correction by moving the Amount slider or entering a value in the Shadows or Highlights percentage box. Larger values provide either greater lightening of shadows or greater darkening of highlights. You can adjust both Shadows and Highlights in the same image. Choose "Save Defaults" to save your current settings and make them the default settings for the Shadows/Highlights command. To restore the original default settings, hold down the Shift key while clicking the Save Defaults button.

HDR Toning

Although it does not produce a real High Dynamic Range image, this effect provides similar results by permitting you to choose format settings, as well as the method to be used, with many possibilities for modifying colors that can be saved and then applied to other images.

Variations

Variations allows you to preview certain presets on the original image, to facilitate adjusting the color settings [Fig. B.6].

Desaturate

Desaturate converts the image to gray scale, although it is more precise to use the tools described above.

Equalize

Equalize establishes uniform brightness values throughout the image by defining the intermediate values between black and white. It is helpful to use this option when you want to lighten a dark picture, but generally, the tools described above will provide more control.

3
Match and replace colors in Photoshop

Match Color

Choose "Image > Adjustments > Match Color." This powerful adjustment allows you to apply the colors of one image, layer, or selection to a different image.

To match the colors of two images, both should be open. If necessary, select the portion of the image that will serve as a reference for color matching. [Fig. B.7] Target indicates the document to be changed (by default the current document). If you have selected a layer, its name will appear in brackets. In the pull-down menu "Source," select the image whose colors will be applied to the target document. If this image includes different layers, the desired source layer can be specified.

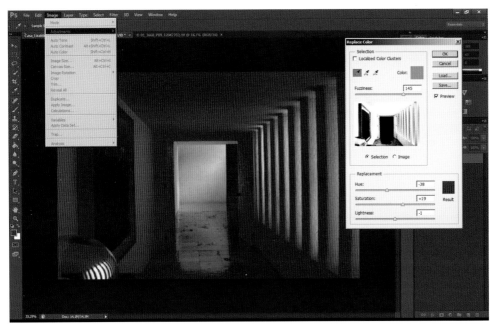

Fig. B.8 Replace Color

To remove a color cast in the target image, select the Neutralize option. Make sure that Preview is selected so that your image is updated on-screen as you make adjustments. To increase or decrease the brightness of the target image, move the Luminance slider or enter a value in the Luminance box. The maximum value is 200, the minimum is 1, and the default is 100. To adjust the color saturation in the target image, move the Color Intensity slider or enter a value in the Color Intensity box. The maximum value is 200, the minimum is 1 (which produces a gray scale image), and the default is 100. To control the amount of adjustment applied to the image, move the Fade slider; moving the slider to the right reduces the adjustment.

Replace Color

Choose "Image > Adjustments > Replace Color." The Replace Color dialog box combines tools for selecting a color range with Hue, Saturation, and Lightness sliders for replacing that color. You can also choose the replacement color in the Color picker. The Replace Color command is good for global color changes—especially changing out-of-gamut colors for printing. [Fig. B.8]

To create a mask defining the colors that you want to replace, use the eyedropper tool to click in the image or in the preview box. To refine the selection, do any of the following: (1) Shift-click or use the Add to Sample eyedropper tool to add areas. (2) Alt-click (Windows), Option-click (Mac OS), or use the Subtract from Sample eyedropper tool to remove areas. (3) Click the Color swatch to open the Color Picker and target the color you want replaced. As you select a color in the Color Picker, the mask in the preview box is updated.

Drag the Fuzziness slider or enter a Fuzziness value to control the degree to which related colors are included in the selection. Specify a replacement color by doing either of the following: (1) drag the Hue, Saturation, and Lightness sliders (or enter values in the text boxes); (2) click the Result swatch and use the Color Picker to select the replacement color.

You can also replace color using the Color Replacement Tool available on the Tools window. If the tool isn't visible, access it by holding down the Brush Tool.

4
Applying Photoshop effects using Filters

Filters let you apply various artistic effects to an image. These filters are not available for Bitmap or Indexed Color images, and some can be applied only in RGB mode. Any type of filter should be applied at the end of the editing process, as some color information is always lost. Below is a selection of Photoshop's numerous filters that have close ties to color and architecture.

Blur

Select among various preset options under "Filter > Blur Gallery" to blur the entire image ("Field Blur") or a partial area. With "Iris Blur" you can protect one or more areas of the image, where the filter will not be applied. [Fig. B.9] The display in the Iris Blur panel includes a large blur preview ring and several dots. In the middle of the ring is a pin that resembles a target. At the center of the target, the image is sharp and clear; further away from the target, the image increases in blurriness.

Sharpen

The various filters in "Filter > Sharpen" correct the contrast of contours to sharpen images, drawing a lighter or darker line on one side or another of the contour of a shape. The "Shake Reduction" filter can reduce blurring resulting from several types of camera motion, including linear motion, arc-shaped motion, rotational motion, and zigzag motion.

A blur trace represents the shape and extent of a blur that affects a selected region of an image. Different regions of an image may have differently shaped blurs. Automatic camera shake reduction takes into account the blur trace for just the default region of the image that Photoshop has determined as most suitable for blur estimation. To further fine-tune the image, you can have Photoshop compute and consider blur traces for multiple regions. Available blur traces are listed in the Advanced panel of the Shake Reduction dialog. Photoshop provides several ways to create and modify blur traces; you can click a blur trace to zoom in on it. For best results, create blur traces in regions of the image that have edge contrast.

Lighting

Choose "Filter > Render > Lighting Effects." In the preview window, select individual lights to adjust. Then, in the upper half of the Properties panel, do any of the following: (1) choose a light type from the top menu: Point, which emits light with a spherical form within the image; Spot, which emits light with a cone shape; or Infinite, which approximately corresponds to sunlight at a specific angle; (2) adjust color, intensity, and hot spot size.

Fig. B.9 Blur filters

In the lower half of the Properties panel, adjust the entire set of lights with these options: (1) Colorize tints the overall lighting; (2) Exposure controls highlight and shadow detail; (3) Gloss determines how much surfaces reflect light; (4) Metallic determines which is more reflective: the light or the object on which the light is cast; (5) Ambience diffuses the light as if it were combined with other light in a room, such as sunlight or fluorescent light—choose a value of 100 to use only the light source or a value of –100 to remove the light source; (6) texture applies a texture channel. [Fig. B.10]

Create and manage smart filters

Smart filters allow you to return to previous settings and add successive filters. [Fig. B.11] Select the appropriate layer and go to "Filter > Convert for Smart Filters." When you accept, a default intelligent layer called "layer 2" will appear. You can then apply the filter to the layer or to a selected area of the layer. Intelligent filters can be hidden, shown, or disabled. The smart filter has a filter mask similar to a mask layer, whereby anything painted in white will be included in the selection (shown), anything painted in black will be excluded (hidden), and grays will be partially shown. The mask filters can be activated/deactivated.

References

Adobe. "Photoshop User Guide." Accessed March 5, 2018. https://helpx.adobe.com/photoshop/user-guide.html.

Atienza Vanacloig, Vicente. "El histograma de una imagen digital." *Informática de sistemas y computadores (DISCA), Universitat Politècnica de València*, 2011. https://riunet.upv.es/bitstream/handle/10251/12711/El%20histograma%20una%20imagen%20digital.pdf.

Mytherapy, "Mytherapy," 2017, accessed July 20, 2018, http://www.mytherapy.tv/.

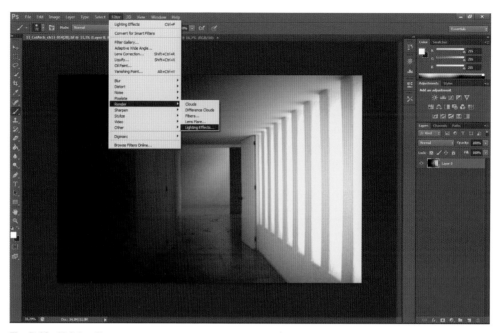

Fig. B.10 Lighting filters

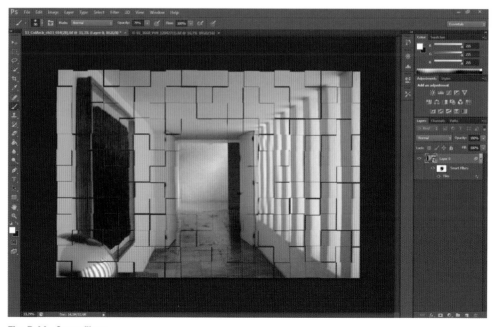

Fig. B.11 Smart filters

Notes

1

What Is Color?

Epigraphs
Anna Bofill and Ricardo Bofill, quoted in *Colour for Architecture*, ed. Tom Porter and Byron Mikellides (London: Studio Vista, 1976), 49.
Paul Green-Armytage, "Seven Kinds of Colour," in *Colour for Architecture Today*, ed. Tom Porter and Byron Mikellides (London: Taylor & Francis, 2009), 64.

1 Real Academia Española (RAE), Diccionario de la lengua española, s.v. "color," 2017, http://dle.rae.es/?id =9qYXXhD. For specific vocabulary about color in Spanish, see Comité Español de Color, *Vocabulario de color* (Terrassa, Spain: Sociedad Española de Óptica, 2002), http://www.sedoptica.es/SEDO/color/docs/publicaciones/vocabulario-del-color.pdf.

2 Ludwig Wittgenstein and G. E. M. Anscombe, *Remarks on Colour* (Oxford, UK: Blackwell, 1977), 2e–3e.

3 Manuel Melgosa and Claudio Oleari, "De términos de color a emociones suscitadas por el color," in *El color en la arquitectura y en el diseño*, ed. Ana Torres Barchino and Ángela García Codoñer (Valencia, Spain: Universitat Politècnica de València, 2010), 41–52.

4 Luigina De Grandis, *Teoría y uso del color* (Madrid: Cátedra, 1985), 80–81.

5 You can experience the absence of vision in the blind spot by doing the following exercise: (1) draw two spots on a piece of paper separated the width of a credit card, approximately 3 1/4 in. (8.3 cm); (2) hold the paper approximately 10 in. (25.4 cm) away from your eyes; (3) close your left eye and focus your gaze on the left spot; (4) notice how the right spot suddenly disappears (if this does not occur, gently shake your head until it does).

6 De Grandis, *Teoría y uso del color*, 69–74.

7 Humberto Moreira Villega and Julio Lillo Jover, "Uso de términos de color básicos en daltónicos dicrómatas y personas de edad avanzada" (PhD diss., Universidad Complutense de Madrid, 2011), http://eprints.ucm.es/12200/1/T32429.pdf, 33.

8 David Robson, "The Women with Superhuman Vision," BBC, September 5, 2014, http://www.bbc.com/future/story/20140905-the-women-with-super-human-vision.

9 Juan Carlos Sanz and Rosa Gallego, *Diccionario Akal del color*, s.v. "tono" (Madrid: Akal, 2001).

10 Luminance is the amount of visible light that comes to the eye from a surface. Lightness is the perceived reflectance of a surface. It represents the visual system's attempt to extract reflectance based on the luminance of the scene. Brightness is the perceived

intensity of light coming from the image itself, rather than any property of the portrayed scene. Brightness is sometimes defined as perceived luminance. See Harald Arnkil, ed., *Colour and Light: Concepts and Confusions* (Helsinki: Aalto University, 2015), 70.

11 Perceptually speaking, magenta is a red that tends slightly toward purple, and cyan is a blue that tends slightly toward green.

12 Ángela García Codoñer, *Apuntes de color: Teoría básica* (Valencia, Spain: Servicio de Publicaciones Universitat Politècnica de València, 1998), 10.

13 Johannes Itten, *The Elements of Color: A Treatise on the Color System of Johannes Itten Based on His Book "The Art of Color,"* ed. Faber Birren (Wokingham, UK: Van Nostrand Reinhold, 1970), 31.

14 You can find the correlation between color temperature and light source, coordinates in the chromaticity diagram (x, y), and approximate RGB color appearance in Mitchell Charity, "Blackbody color datafile," Vendian .org, June 22, 2001, accessed July 20, 2018, http://www.vendian.org/mncharity/dir3/blackbody/UnstableURLs/bbr_color.html.

15 Manuel Melgosa, Luis Gómez-Robledo, María Isabel Suero, and Mark D. Fairchild, "What Can We Learn from a Dress with Ambiguous Colors?" *Color Research and Application* 40, no. 5 (2015): 525–29, https://doi .org/10.1002/col.21966.

16 Eduardo Cordero, María Isabel Suero, Pedro José Pardo, and Ángel Luis Pérez, "Estudio de la variabilidad de color de muestras cromáticas del atlas NCS ante cambios de iluminante," in *Actas del IX Congreso Nacional del Color* (Alicante, Spain: Publicaciones de la Universidad de Alicante, 2010), 58–60.

2

Naming Colors

1 In Photoshop, hexadecimal notation is given in the color palette together with RGB decimal notation. Various hexadecimal to decimal converters are available online; see, for example, http://www.psyclops.com/tools/rgb/.

2 "Colorimetry—Part 4: CIE 1976 L*A*B* Colour Space," CIE International Commission on Illumination, http://www.cie.co.at/publications/colorimetry-part-4-cie-1976-lab-colour-space-0.

3 Bruce Lindbloom, "Useful Color Information, Studies and Files: Information About RGB Working Spaces," accessed June 12, 2018, http://www.brucelindbloom.com/index.html?LabGamutDisplay.

4 Yolanda Sanjuán, *"Apuntes curso gestión de flujos de color en artes gráficas (TF070089)"* (course text, Instituto Tecnológico de Óptica Color e Imagen Aido, Valencia, Spain, 2007).

5 Jaume Pujol, "Sistemas de ordenación del color," in *Fundamentos de colorimetría*, ed. Pascual Capilla, José M. Artigas, and Jaume Pujol (Valencia, Spain: Universitat de València, 2002), 91–117.

6 Anders Hård and Lars Sivik, "NCS— Natural Color System: A Swedish Standard for Color Notation," *Color Research and Application* 6, no. 3 (1981): 129–38, https://doi.org/10.1002/col.5080060303.

7 According to Hård and Sivik, the lines for constant NCS *lightness identity* or *value* in the NCS triangle converge with increasing chromaticness. See Anders Hård and Lars Sivik, "A Theory of Colors in Combination—A Descriptive Model Related to the NCS Color-Order System," *Color Research and Application* 26, no. 1 (2001): 10, https://doi.org/10.1002/1520-6378 (200102)26:1<4::AID-COL3>3.0.CO ;2-T.

8 Arnkil, *Colour and Light*, 71.

9 According to Hård and Sivik, the term *saturation* in NCS is a constant relation between chromaticness and whiteness. See Hård and Sivik, "Theory of Colors in Combination," 21–22.

10 Munsell Color Lab is located at the Rochester Institute of Technology. For more information about Munsell Color, see http://munsell.com/about-munsell-color/. For an online version of the Munsell color atlas, visit http://www.colormunki.com/munsell.

11 For more information about Pantone color systems, see https://www.pantone.com/color-systems-intro.

12 For more information about NCS Colour, see http://ncscolour.com/.

13 For more information about the NCS-Munsell Translation Key, see https://www.yumpu.com/en/document/view/20020651/munsell-ncspdf.

14 For Pantone conversion into RGB, HEX/HTML, CMYK, see https://www.pantone.com/color-finder.

15 For RAL conversion using rgb.to, see http://rgb.to/ral/page/1.

16 For Munsell color tables, see WallkillColor, http://wallkillcolor.com/.

3

Color and Perception

1 Josef Albers, *Interaction of Color*, 4th ed. (New Haven, CT: Yale University Press, 2013), 22–24.

2 De Grandis, *Teoría y uso del color*, 107.

3 Will Alsop quoted in Cordula Rau, ed., *Why Do Architects Wear Black?* (Vienna: Springer Vienna Architecture, 2008).

4 Karin Fridell Anter, "What Colour Is the Red House? Perceived Colour of Painted Facades," PhD thesis, Department of Architectural Forms, School of Architecture, KTH Royal Institute of Technology, 2000, http://www.diva-portal.org/smash/get/diva2:8790/FULLTEXT01.pdf, 103–7.

5 Kaida Xiao, M. Ronnier Luo, Changjun Li, and Guowei Hong, "Colour Appearance of Room Colours," *Color Research and Application* 35, no. 4 (2010): 284–93, doi.org/10.1002/col.20575.

6 De Grandis, *Teoría y uso del color*, 99.

7 García Codoñer, *Apuntes de color*, 12.

8 Albers, *Interaction of Color*.

9 Anders Hård demonstrates this by observing the leaves of a forest at different distances, which evolve from green to blue. Cited in Michael Lancaster, *Colourscape* (London: Academy Editions, 1996), 30.

10 Lois Swirnoff, "Color Structure: A Perceptual Techtonic," in Porter and Mikellides, *Colour for Architecture Today*, 82.

11 *Interaction of Color*, digital app (Yale University, 2013), adapted from Albers, *Interaction of Color*.

4

Combining Colors

1 Egon G. Guba and Yvonna S. Lincoln, "Competing Paradigms in Qualitative Research," in *The SAGE Handbook of Qualitative Research*, ed. Norman K. Denzin and Yvonna S. Lincoln (Thousand Oaks, CA: Sage, 1994).

2 Zena O'Connor, "Color Harmony Revisited," *Color Research and Application* 35, no. 4 (2010), https://doi.org/10.1002/col.20578.

3 For more information about sounds and colors in history, see John Gage, *Color and Culture: Practice and Meaning from Antiquity to Abstraction* (Berkeley: University of California Press, 1999), 227–46.

4 For the latest research about the physical relationship between color and music, see Joaquín Pérez Fuster and Eduardo Gilabert Pérez, "Color y música: Relaciones físicas entre tonos de color y notas musicales," in *Actas del IX Congreso Nacional del Color* (Alicante, Spain: Publicaciones de la Universidad de Alicante, 2010), 445–48.

5 Occam's (or Ockham's) razor is the methodological and philosophical principle attributed to William of Ockham (1285–1347/49) that given two theories, the simpler explanation is usually the right one.

6 Zena O'Connor, "Façade Colour and Aesthetic Response: Examining Patterns of Response within the Context of Urban Design and Planning Policy in Sydney" (PhD diss., Faculty

of Architecture, Design & Planning, University of Sydney, 2008), 38.
7 Guba and Lincoln, "Competing Paradigms in Qualitative Research," 109.
8 Ibid., 110.
9 José Luis Caivano, "Armonías de color," *Revista GAC: Grupo Argentino de color* 19 (2004): 2.
10 T. M. Cleland, *A Practical Description of the Munsell Color System with Suggestions for Its Use*, 3rd ed. (Baltimore: Munsell Color, 1937), 18.
11 Carl E. Foss, Dorothy Nickerson, and Walter C. Granville, "Analysis of the Ostwald Color System," *Journal of the Optical Society of America* 34, no. 7 (1944): 361–81, https://doi.org/10.1364/JOSA.34.000361.
12 Caivano, "Armonías de color," 3–6.
13 Johannes Itten, *The Art of Color: The Subjective Experience and Objective Rationale of Color* (New York: Van Nostrand Reinhold, 1974).
14 O'Connor, "Façade Colour and Aesthetic Response," 40.
15 Hård and Sivik, "Theory of Colors in Combination."
16 Gage, *Color and Culture*, 37.
17 Amy Dempsey, *Styles, Schools and Movements: The Essential Encyclopaedic Guide to Modern Art* (London: Thames & Hudson, 2011), 26–30.
18 Albert Munsell, *A Grammar of Color* (Mittineague, MA: Strathmore Paper, 1921).
19 The nine rules for the grammar of color combinations using the Munsell system can be summarized as follows: (1) gray colors equidistant from N5 (N2, N5, N8); (2) monochromatic colors belonging to the same hue family and centered in a shade with middle value and chroma (YR 7/6, YR 5/4, YR 3/2); (3) complementary colors (opposing hues) centered in N5 (GY 5/8, P 5/8); (4) complementary colors (opposing hues) with the same value but different chroma displayed in inverse proportion to chroma (12 parts of BG 5/6, 6 parts of R 5/12); (5) complementary colors (opposing hues) with the same chroma and different value but centered in N5 (R 4/8, BG 6/8); (6) complementary colors (opposing hues) with different value and chroma but displayed in inverse proportion to chroma (12 p. B 3/6, 6 p. YR 7/12); (7) three colors with neighboring hues or complementary colors divided, assuming that the curve that links the three colors in the Munsell solid is centered in any of them (R 6/12, B 2/6, G 4/6); (8) a sequence of colors in diminution, drawing a kind of spiral with the gray N5 as a center (4 p. Y 8/9, 5 p. GY 7/8, 6 p. G 6/7, 7 p. BG 5/6, 8 p. B 4/5, 9 p. PB 3/4); (9) a sequence of colors equidistant in an ellipse that has its center in N5 (3 p. G 5/5, 4 p. BG 5/4, 5 p. B 5/3, 5 p. PB 5/3, 4 p. P 5/4, 3 p. RP 5/5, 4 p. R 5/4, 5 p. YR 5/3, 5 p. Y 5/3, 4 p. GY 5/4). Caivano, "Armonías de color," 2–11.
20 Itten, *Elements of Color*, 32.
21 Juan Serra, "Projects Born by Colours: An Interview with British Architect William Alsop," *EGA revista de expresión gráfica arquitectónica* 15 (2010): 197.
22 Gary T. Moore, "Toward Environment—Behavior Theories of the Middle Range," in *Toward the Integration of Theory, Methods, Research, and Utilization*, ed. Gary T. Moore and Robert W. Marans (New York: Plenum Press, 1997).
23 Fernando Távora quoted in Francisco Bethencourt, *Cosmopolitanism in the Portuguese-speaking World* (Lieden, the Netherlands: Kononklijke Brill, 2018), 169.
24 Arthur Schopenhauer and David E. Cartwright, *On Vision and Colors: An Essay* (Oxford, UK: Berg, 1994), 70.
25 Itten, *Elements of Color*, 60.
26 *"Monsieur Le Corbusier determinant lui même sur place la distribution des différentes couleurs et ceci au moment ou l'entrepreneur devra commencer les travaux, il est donc impossible de definir à l'avance avec précision l'emploi des couleurs. Il convient que l'entrepreneur évalue à 50% la partie en blanc et à 50% la partie peinte en couleur, dont 15% de teintes vives. Ces évaluations n'engagent pas l'entrepreneur, les quantités réelles seront seules prises en compte au moment du règlement du marché."* Fondation Le Corbusier FLC 408, CUB-Doc F Pe -5.
27 Also see Lisa Charlotte Rost, "Your Friendly Guide to Colors in Data Visualisation," April 22, 2016, https://lisacharlotterost.github.io/2016/04/22/Colors-for-DataVis/.
28 Juan Serra, Jorge Llopis, Ana Torres, and Manuel Giménez, "Color Combination Criteria in Le Corbusier's Purist Architecture Based on Salubra Claviers from 1931," *Color Research and Application* 41, no. 1 (February 2016): 85, https://doi.org/10.1002/col.21940.

5
Choosing the Color That Fits the Form

1 The content of this chapter is based on Juan Serra, "Three Color Strategies in Architectural Composition," *Color Research and Application* 38, no. 4 (August 2013): 238–50, https://doi.org/10.1002/col.21717.
2 Josep Maria Montaner, *Sistemas arquitectónicos contemporáneos* (Barcelona: Gustavo Gili, 2008), 223–24.
3 MVRDV, "Projects Realized: Studio Thonik," accessed October 2, 2018, https://www.mvrdv.nl/en/projects/thonik#!#archive.
4 Ángela García Codoñer Jorge Llopis Verdú, Ana María Torres Barchino, and Juan Serra Lluch, "Color as a Structural Variable of Historical Urban Form," *Color Research and Application* 34, no. 3 (2009): 253–65, https://doi.org/10.1002/col.20491.
5 Aaron Betsky, "Pleasurable and Essential: Color and Content in the Work of Sauerbruch & Hutton," in *Sauerbruch Hutton Architects, 1997/2003* (Madrid: El Croquis, 2003), 8–9.
6 Ibid., 12–13.
7 Grete Smedal, "The Longyearbyen Project: Approach and Method," in Porter and Mikellides, *Colour for Architecture Today*, 73.
8 Donis A. Dondis, *A Primer of Visual Literacy* (Cambridge, MA: MIT Press, 1973).
9 Rüegg, *Polychromie Architecturale: Le Corbusier's Farbenklaviaturen*, 27–28.
10 Lois Swirnoff, *Dimensional Color*, 2nd ed. (New York: W. W. Norton, 2003), 77–78.
11 Peter J. Hayten, *El color en la arquitectura y decoración* (Barcelona: LEDA Las Ediciones de Arte, 1960), 22–23.
12 Le Corbusier, "Architectural Polychromy," 1932, in Rüegg, *Polychromie Architecturale: Le Corbusier's Farbenklaviaturen*, 114–15.
13 Ibid., 116–17.
14 Frank H. Mahnke, *Color, Environment, and Human Response: An Interdisciplinary Understanding of Color and Its Use as a Beneficial Element in the Design of the Architectural Environment* (New York: Van Nostrand Reinhold, 1996), 72–73.
15 Mary C. Miller, *Color for Interior Architecture* (Chichester, UK: John Wiley & Sons, 1997).
16 Niels Luning Prak, *The Visual Perception of the Built Environment* (Delft, the Netherlands: Delft University Press, 1977), 33–34.
17 Waldron Faulkner, *Architecture and Color* (New York: Wiley-Interscience, 1972), 6.
18 Mahnke, *Color, Environment, and Human Response*, 72–73.
19 Piero Bottoni, "Cromatismi architettonici," *Architettura e arti decorative* 6, no. 1–2 (1927): 219–21.
20 Piero Bottoni, "Note illustrative ai cromatismi architettonici" in Graziella Tonon, *Una nuova antichissima bellezza. Scriti editi e inediti 1927–1973* (Bari, Italy: Laterza & Figli, 1995), 91.
21 Wassily Kandinsky, *Concerning the Spiritual Art*, trans. M. T. H. Sadler (New York: Dover Publications, 1977), 25.
22 Rem Koolhaas, *OMA 30: 30 Colors* (Blaricum, the Netherlands: V+K Publishing, 1999), 12–13.
23 Juan Serra, Jorge Llopis Verdú, and Ángela García Codoñer, "Ruskin Revisited: Material Truth in Modern and Contemporary Architecture," in *Color*
& *Light in Architecture* (Venice: Università Iuav di Venezia, 2010).
24 Giovanni Brino, "Italian Color Plans (1978–2007)," in Porter and Mikellides, *Colour for Architecture Today*, 30–35.
25 Per Arnoldi, *"Color Is Communication": Selected Projects for Foster+Partners, 1996–2006* (Basel: Birkhäuser, 2007), 7–8.
26 Werner Spillmann, "Unity in Diversity at Kirchsteigfeld, Postdam," in Porter and Mikellides, *Colour for Architecture Today*, 36–38.
27 Matthias Sauerbruch and Louisa Hutton, "Fire and Police Station Berlin," 2004, http://www.sauerbruchhutton.de/images/FPR_fire_and_policestation_en.pdf.
28 Matthias Sauerbruch and Louisa Hutton, "Museum Brandhorst Munich," 2009, http://www.sauerbruchhutton.de/images/SAB_brandhorst_museum_en.pdf.

6
Visual Ergonomics

1 Francisco Miguel Martínez Verdú and Dolores de Fez Sáiz, "La ergonomía del color: Influencia en el rendimiento y la salud del trabajador," *Gestión Práctica de Riesgos Laborales* no. 30 (September 2006): 34–45, http://pdfs.wke.es/8/3/9/5/pd0000018395.pdf.
2 International Commission on Illumination (CIE) and CIE Technical Committee 1–19 of Division 1, "Vision and Color," in "The Correlation of Models for Vision and Visual Performance," *CIE* 145 (2002), http://www.cie.co.at/publications/correlation-models-vision-and-visual-performance.
3 De Grandis, *Teoría y uso del color*, 99.
4 Julio Lillo Jover, *Ergonomía: Evaluación y diseño del entorno visual* (Madrid: Alianza, 2000); Peter Robert Boyce, *Human Factors in Lighting*, 2nd ed. (London: CRC Press, 2013).
5 The illuminance is the level of light falling onto a surface, represented by the quotient between the luminous flux incident onto a surface and its area. Illuminance is usually measured in lux (1 lumen/m^2) or phot (1 lumen/cm^2).
6 International Commission on Illumination (CIE), "Method of Measuring and Specifying Color Rendering Properties of Light Sources," *CIE* 13.3-1995.
7 The CIE describes the method of measuring and specifying color rendering properties of light sources in ibid.
8 Pablo Martín Andrade and Soledad Luengo Jusdado, *Accesibilidad para personas con ceguera y deficiencia visual* (Madrid: ONCE, 2003), 36–40.
9 Asociación Española de Normalización y Certificación (Aenor), "UNE 170002: 2009 Requisitos de accesibilidad para la rotulación" (Madrid, 2009).

7

Does Architecture
Need to Be White?

1 Juan Serra, Ángela García, Ana Torres, and Jorge Llopis, "Color Composition Features in Modern Architecture," *Color Research and Application* 37, no. 2 (2012): 126–33, https://doi.org /10.1002/col.20657.

2 César Pelli, quoted in José Luis Caivano, "Research on Color in Architecture and Environmental Design: Brief History, Current Developments, and Possible Future," *Color Research and Application* 31, no. 4 (2006): 356, https://doi.org/10.1002/col.20224.

3 Manuel de las Casas, quoted in Teresa Táboas Veleiro, *El color en arquitectura* (Sada, La Coruña, Spain: Ediciós do Castro, 1991), 109.

4 Montaner, *Arquitectura y crítica*, (Barcelona: Gustavo Gili, 1999), 40.

5 Henry-Russell Hitchcock Jr. and Philip Johnson, *The International Style: Architecture Since 1922* (New York: W. W. Norton, 1932).

6 Juan Antonio Ramírez, *Arte y arquitectura en la época del capitalismo triunfante* (Madrid: Visor Libros, 1992), 258.

7 Mark Wigley, *White Walls, Designer Dresses: The Fashioning of Modern Architecture* (Cambridge, MA: MIT Press, 1995), 424.

8 David Batchelor, *Chromophobia* (London: Reaktion Books, 2000), 124.

9 Tom Wolfe, *From Bauhaus to Our House* (New York: Picador, 1981), 24.

10 Sean Kisby, *Bruno Taut: Architecture and Colour,* Cardiff, Wales: Welsh School of Architecture Year 3, accessed May 29, 2018, http://www .kisbyism.com/write/bruno-taut -architecture-and-colour.htm.

11 Katrin Simons, "Farbe in der Architektur," *Detail* 12 (2003): 1400.

12 Richard Meier, "Ceremony Acceptance Speech," the Pritzker Architecture Prize, National Gallery of Art, Washington, DC, 1984, http://www .pritzkerprize.com/laureates/1984.

13 Le Corbusier, *Towards a New Architecture*, 2nd ed. (NY: Dover, 1986), 29.

14 Rüegg, *Polychromie Architecturale: Le Corbusier's Farbenklaviaturen,* 95.

15 Bruno Taut, "Renacimiento del color," extracted in "Farbe Am Hause," 1st German Colorist Congress, Hamburg, 1925, in *El color en la arquitectura*, ed. Martina Düttmann, Friedrich Schmuck, and Johannes Uhl (Barcelona: Gustavo Gili, 1982), 13.

16 Ibid., 13.

17 Ibid., 13.

18 Piet Mondrian, "Plastic Art and Pure Plastic Art" (1937), reprinted in *Modern Artists on Art,* ed. Robert L. Herbert, 2nd enl. ed. (NY: Dover Publications, 1999), 165.

19 Bart van der Leck, "The Place of Modern Painting in Architecture," in *De Stijl*, trans. Hans L. C. Jaffe (New York: Harry N. Abrams, 1971), previously published in *De Stijl* 1, no. 1 (1918): 6–7.

20 Fernand Léger, *Functions of Painting* (New York: Viking, 1973), 158.

21 Le Corbusier, "Fragment VIII from 'Notes à la suite,'" *Cahiers d'art*, no. 3 (1926): 49, quoted in Jan de Heer, *The Architectonic Colour: Polychromy in the Purist Architecture of Le Corbusier* (Rotterdam: 010 Publishers, 2009), 215.

22 Le Corbusier, *Modulor 2: 1955 (Let the User Speak Next)*, 2nd printing (Cambridge, MA: MIT Press), 233.

23 Le Corbusier, "Architectural Polychromy," 1932, in Rüegg, *Polychromie Architecturale: Le Corbusier's Farbenklaviaturen*, 95.

24 Luisa Martina Colli, "Hacia una policromía arquitectónica," in *Le Corbusier, Une Encyclopédie* (Paris: Centre Pompidou, 1987), 97.

25 Robert Carro, "Le Corbusier Nos Hizo El Regalo Del Muro Blanco," *VIA Arquitectura* 13 (2003): 8–17.

26 Wassily Kandinsky, *Concerning the Spiritual in Art*, trans. M. T. H. Sadler (New York: Dover, 1977), 18.

27 Taut, "Renacimiento del color," 12.

28 Hitchcock and Johnson, *International Style*, 65–66.

29 Bottoni, "Cromatismi architettonici," 220.

30 Ángela Garcia Codoñer, Jorge Llopis Verdú, and Juan Serra Lluch, "Aportaciones al colorido de la modernidad Made in Italy, Piero Bottoni y la gradación cromática que nunca Ffe," *EGA: Revista de Expresión Gráfica Arquitectónica*, no. 14 (1993): 180–87.

31 Caivano, "Research on Colorn," 356.

32 Kandinsky, *Concerning the Spiritual in Art*, 35.

33 J. J. P. Oud, quoted in Leonardo Benevolo, *History of Modern Architecture*, vol. 2, 6th ed. (Cambridge, MA: MIT Press, 1999), 411.

34 Theo van Doesburg, "Towards White Painting," *Art concret* (April 1930), quoted in *Theo van Doesburg*, ed. Joost Baljeu (London: Studio Vista, 1974), 183.

35 Larissa Noury, *La couleur dans la ville,* (Paris: Moniteur, 2008), 168.

36 Isabel Ramírez Luque, "Mucho más que una cuestión de piel: La experiencia del color en la arquitectura contemporánea," in *Variaciones sobre el color*, ed. Diego Romero de Solís, Inmaculada Murcia Serrano, and Jorge López Lloret (Seville, Spain: Universidad de Sevilla, 2007), 371.

37 Amy Dempsey, *Styles, Schools and Movements: The Essential Encyclopaedic Guide to Modern Art* (London: Thames and Hudson, 2002), 119–21.

38 Bruno Taut, "Beobachtungen über Farbenwinkürgen Aus Meiner Praxis,"

Die Wauelt, no. 38 (1919): 13, quoted in Düttmann, Schmuck, and Uhl, *El color en la arquitectura*, 20.

39 Wolfgang Pehnt, *Expressionist Architecture* (New York: Praeger, 1973), 88.

40 Piet Mondrian, "Plastic Art and Pure Plastic Art," in *Theories of Modern Art: A Source Book by Artists and Critics*, ed. Herschel B. Chipp (Berkeley: University of California, 1968), 350.

41 M. J. H. Schoenmaekers, "Het Niewe Wereldbeeld," in *Modern Architecture: A Critical History*, ed. Kenneth Frampton, 3rd ed. (London: Thames and Hudson, 1992), 117.

42 Le Corbusier and Amédée Ozenfant, "After Cubism," trans. M. T. H. Sadler, in *L'Esprit Nouveau: Purism in Paris, 1918–1925*, ed. Carol S. Eliel (New York: Harry N. Abrams in association with Los Angeles County Museum of Art, 2001), 165.

43 Batchelor, *Chromophobia*, 124.

44 Rüegg, *Polychromie Architecturale: Le Corbusier's Farbenklaviaturen*, 113.

45 Taut, quoted in Düttmann, Schmuck, and Uhl, *El color en la arquitectura*, 191.

46 Le Corbusier, *Journey to the East*, ed. Ivan Zaknic, 2nd ed. (Cambridge, MA: MIT Press, 2007), 14.

47 John Ruskin, *The Seven Lamps of Architecture* (London: Smith, Elder, 1849), Project Gutenberg, published April 18, 2011, 54, https://www .gutenberg.org/files/35898/35898-h /35898-h.htm.

48 Claire Beck-Loos, *Adolf Loos: A Private Portrait*, ed. Carrie Paterson (Los Angeles: DoppelHouse Press, 2011), 63.

49 Rem Koolhaas, "The Future of Colours Is Looking Bright," in *Colours,* ed. Rem Koolhaas, Norman Foster, and Alessandro Mendini (Basel: Birkhäuser, 2001), 11–13.

50 Michiel Riedijk, "Code, Space and Light," in *Colour in Contemporary Architecture: Projects, Essays, Calendar, Manifestoes*, ed. Susanne Komossa, Kees Rouw, and Joost Hillen (Amsterdam: SUN, 2009), 419.

8

The Meaning
of Color

1 Nicolas Humphrey, "Colour Currency of Nature," in Porter and Mikellides, *Colour for Architecture Today*, 9–10.

2 Ibid., 12.

3 Dirk Meyhöfer, *In Full Color: Recent Buildings and Interiors* (Berlin: Verlagshaus Braun, 2008), 7–8.

4 Michael Caesar, *Umberto Eco: Philosophy, Semiotics and the Work of Fiction* (Cambridge, UK: Polity, 1999).

5 José Luis Caivano, "Color and Semiotics: A Two-Way Street," *Color*

Research and Application 23, no. 6 (1998): 395–97, doi:10.1002/(SICI)1520 -6378(199812)23:6<390::AID-COL7> 3.0.CO;2-#.

6 Arnoldi, *Colour Is Communication*, 13.

7 Rudolf Arnheim, *Art and Visual Perception: A Psychology of the Creative Eye* (Berkeley: University of California Press, 1974), 333.

8 Aaris Sherin, *Design Elements: Color Fundamentals* (Beverly, MA: Rockport, 2012).

9 Randi Priluck Grossman and Joseph Z. Wisenblit, "What We Know about Consumers' Color Choices," *Journal of Marketing Practice: Applied Marketing Science* 5, no. 3 (June 12, 1999): 78–88, https://doi.org/10.1108 /EUM0000000004565.

10 Cordula Rau, *Why Do Architects Wear Black?* (New York: Springer Vienna Architecture, 2008).

11 Heinz's introduction of green and purple ketchup to the marketplace in 2000 and Pepsi's release of a transparent soda, Crystal Pepsi, in the early 1990s were initially a success, albeit but short-lived; after the novelty wore off, customers returned to the traditional colors.

12 For an in-depth examination of meaning and color that links the art, symbolism, and science of various historical moments, see John Gage, *Color and Meaning: Art, Science, and Symbolism* (Berkeley: University of California Press, 1999).

13 Xiao-Ping Gao and John H. Xin, "Investigation of Human's Emotional Responses on Colors," *Color Research & Application* 31, no. 5 (October 2006): 411, https://doi.org/10.1002/col.20246.

14 Charles E. Osgood, George J. Suci, and Percy H. Tannenbaum, *The Measurement of Meaning* (Urbana: University of Illinois Press, 1967).

15 Gao and Xin, "Investigation of Human's Emotional Responses on Colors," 411–12.

16 Banu Manav, "Color-Emotion Associations and Color Preferences: A Case Study for Residences,"*Color Research and Application* 32, no. 2 (2007): 144– 50, https://doi.org/10.1002/col.20294.

17 Nancy Kwallek, Kokyung Soon, and Carol M. Lewis, "Work Week Productivity, Visual Complexity, and Individual Environmental Sensitivity in Three Offices of Different Color Interiors," *Color Research and Application* 32, no. 2 (2007): 130–43, https://doi.org/10.1002/col.20298.

18 Zena O'Connor, "Colour Psychology and Colour Therapy: Caveat Emptor," *Color Research and Application* 36, no. 3 (2011): 229–30, https://doi.org /10.1002/col.20597.

19 Byron Mikellides, "Colour, Arousal, Hue-Heat and Time Estimation," in Porter and Mikellides, *Colour for Architecture Today*, 128.

20 Eva Heller, *Psicología del color: Cómo actúan los colores sobre los*

sentimientos y la razón (Barcelona: Gustavo Gili, 2004).

21 Mei-Yun Hsu, Li-Chen Ou, and Shing-Sheng Guan, "Colour Preference for Taiwanese Floral Pattern Fabrics," Color Research and Application 41, no. 1 (2016): 43–55, https://doi.org/10.1002 /col.21947.

22 Karen B. Schloss and Stephen E. Palmer, "An Ecological Valence Theory of Human Color Preferences," Journal of Vision 9 (2009): 2663–68.

23 Cooper B. Holmes, Jo Ann Buchanan, and Stephen F. Davis, "Color Preference as a Function of the Object Described," Bulletin of the Psychonomic Society 22, no. 5 (1984): 423–25, https://link.springer.com/content/pdf /10.3758/BF03333865.pdf.

24 Charles Taft, "Color Meaning and Context: Comparisons of Semantic Ratings of Colors on Samples and Objects," Color Research and Application 22, no. 1 (1997): 41, https://doi.org/10.1002/(SICI)1520 -6378(199702)22:1<40::AID -COL7>3.0.CO;2-4.

25 T. R. Lee, D. L. Tang, and C. M. Tsai, "Exploring Color Preference through Eye Tracking," AIC Colour 05 — 10th Congress of the International Colour Association, 2005, 333–36, https:// www.researchgate.net/publication /228394046_Exploring_color _preference_through_eye_tracking.

26 H. J. Eysenck, "A Critical and Experimental Study of Colour Preferences," American Journal of Psychology 54, no. 3 (July 1941): 385–94, https://doi .org/10.2307/1417683.

27 Manav, "Color-Emotion Associations and Color Preferences," 144.

28 Helle Wijk, Stig Berg, Lars Sivik, and Bertil Steen, "Colour Discrimination, Colour Naming and Colour Preferences among Individuals with Alzheimer's Disease," International Journal of Geriatric Psychiatry 14, no. 12 (December 1, 1999): 1000–1005. https://doi.org /10.1002/(SICI)1099-1166(199912)14: 12<1000::AID-GPS46>3.0.CO;2-E; J. P. Guilford and P. C. Smith, "A System of Color-Preferences," American Journal of Psychology 72 (1959): 487–502, http://dx.doi.org/10.2307 /1419491; J. P. Guilford, "The Affective Value of Color as a Function of Hue, Tint, and Chroma," Journal of Experimental Psychology 17, no. 3 (1934): 342–70, https://doi.org/10.1037 /h0071517; Heller, Psicología del color; Byron Mikellides, "Colour Preference: The Longitudinal Perspective," in Porter and Mikellides, Colour for Architecture Today, 120; Nilgün Camgöz, Cengiz Yener, and Dilek Güvenç, "Effects of Hue, Saturation, and Brightness on Preference," Color Research and Application 27, no. 3 (2002): 199–207. https://doi.org/10.1002/col.10051.

29 Camgöz, Yener, and Güvenç, "Effects of Hue, Saturation, and Brightness on Preference," 204.

30 Giovanni Moretti, Paul Lyons, and Stephen Marsland, "Computational Production of Colour Harmony. Part 1: A Prototype Colour Harmonization Tool," Color Research and Application 38, no. 3 (2011): 6, https://doi.org /10.1002/col.20736.

31 See Colors of the Social World (Wide Web), https://wiki.digitalmethods.net /Dmi/WebFlags.

32 Camgöz, Yener, and Güvenç, "Effects of Hue, Saturation, and Brightness on Preference."

33 Anya C. Hurlbert and Yazhu Ling, "Biological Components of Sex Differences in Color Preference," Current Biology 17, no. 16 (August 21, 2007): R623–25, https://doi.org/10.1016/j.cub .2007.06.022.

34 Jin Gyu Park, "Correlations between Color Attributes and Children's Color Preferences," Color Research and Application 39, no. 5 (2014): 452–62, https://doi.org/10.1002/col.21801.

35 Maurice Déribéré, El color en las actividades humanas (Madrid: Tecnos, 1964).

36 John Nash Ott, Health and Light: The Effects of Natural and Artificial Light on Man and Other Living Things (Old Greenwich, CT: Devin-Adair, 1973).

37 Roger S. Ulrich, "View through a Window May Influence Recovery from Surgery," Science 224, no. 4647 (April 27, 1984): 420–21.

38 Frank H. Mahnke, Color, Environment, and Human Response: An Interdisciplinary Understanding of Color and Its Use as a Beneficial Element in the Design of the Architectural Environment (New York: Van Nostrand Reinhold, 1996).

39 O'Connor, "Colour Psychology and Colour Therapy," 229.

40 Richard G. Stevens, David E. Blask, George C. Brainard, Johnni Hansen, Steven W. Lockley, Ignacio Provencio, Mark S. Rea, and Leslie Reinlib, "Meeting Report: The Role of Environmental Lighting and Circadian Disruption in Cancer and Other Diseases," Environmental Health Perspectives 115, no. 9 (2007): 1357–62, https://doi.org/10.1289/ehp .10200; Morton G. Harmatz, Arnold D. Well, Christopher E. Overtree, Kathleen Y. Kawamura, Milagros Rosal, and Ira S. Ockene, "Seasonal Variation of Depression and Other Moods: A Longitudinal Approach," Journal of Biological Rhythms 15, no. 4 (2000): 344–50, https://doi.org/10.1177 /074873000129001350.

41 D. J. Skene, S. W. Lockley, K. Thapan, and J. Arendt, "Effects of Light on Human Circadian Rhythms," Reproduction, Nutrition, Development 39, no. 3: 295–304, http://www.ncbi.nlm.nih.gov /pubmed/10420432.

42 B. Lawson and M. Phiri, "Architectural Environment and Its Effect on Patient Health Outcomes" (Sheffield, UK: University of Sheffield, 2002).

43 M. G. Shogan and L. L. Schumann, "The Effect of Environmental Lighting on the Oxygen Saturation of Pre-Term Infants in the NICU," Natal Network 12, no. 5 (1993): 7–13, https://www.ncbi .nlm.nih.gov/pubmed/8350854.

44 Faber Birren, Color and Human Response (New York: John Wiley & Sons, 1984).

45 A. G. Schauss, "Tranquilizing Effect of Color Reduces Aggressive Behaviour and Potential Violence," Journal of Orthomolecular Psychiatry 4 (1979): 218–21.

46 Elif Öztürk, Semiha Yilmazer, and Sibel Ertez Ural, "The Effects of Achromatic and Chromatic Color Schemes on Participants' Task Performance in and Appraisals of an Office Environment," Color Research and Application 37, no. 5 (2012): 359–66, https://doi.org/10 .1002/col.20697.

47 Kwallek, Soon, and Lewis, "Work Week Productivity," 130–43.

48 Debora Niero and Alessandro Premier, "Colour in the Schools," Colour and Light in Architecture: First International Conference, Venice, 2010, 475–81, http://rice.iuav.it/249/1/05_niero -premier.pdf.

49 N. Kwallek, C. M. Lewis, J. W. D. Lin-Hsiao, and H. Woodson, "Effects of Nine Monochromatic Office Interior Colors on Clerical Tasks and Worker Mood," Color Research and Application 21, no. 6 (1996): 448–58, https://doi.org/10.1002/(SICI)1520-6378(199612)21:6<448::AID-COL7> 3.0.CO;2-W.

50 Nancy J. Stone, "Environmental View and Color for a Simulated Telemarketing Task," Journal of Environmental Psychology 23, no. 1 (2003): 63–78.

51 I. M. Cockerill and B. P. Miller, "Children's Color Preferences and Motor Skill Performance with Variation in Environmental Color," Perceptual and Motor Skills 56 (1983): 845–46.

52 Jacob S. Nakshian, "The Effects of Red and Green Surroundings on Behavior," Journal of General Psychology 70, no. 1 (January 1964): 143–61, https://doi.org /10.1080/00221309.1964.9920584.

53 Aseel Al-Ayash, Robert T. Kane, Dianne Smith, and Paul Green-Armytage, "The Influence of Color on Student Emotion, Heart Rate, and Performance in Learning Environments," Color Research and Application 41, no. 2 (2015): 196–205, https://doi .org/10.1002/col.21949.

54 Richard Rogers, "The Colour Approach of Piano and Rogers," in Porter and Mikellides, Colour for Architecture, 61.

55 For more information about the Color Research Group, see http://grupocolor .webs.upv.es/WEB/; Ángela García Codoñer, Jorge Llopis Verdú, Ana Maria Torres Barchino, and Juan Serra Lluch, "Colour as a Structural Variable of Historical Urban Form," Color Research & Applications 34, no. 3

(2009): 253–65, https://doi.org/10.1002 /col.20491; Ángela García Codoñer, Jorge Llopis Verdú, José Vicente Masiá León, Ana Torres Barchino, and Ramón Villaplana Guillém, El color de Valencia: El centro histórico (Valencia, Spain: Excmo. Ayuntamiento de Valencia y Generalitat Valenciana, 2012).

56 Heller, Psicología del color.

57 Daniela Späth, "The Psychological and Physiological Effect of 'Cool Down Pink' on Human Behavior," in AIC 2011 Midterm Meeting: Interaction of Colour & Light in the Arts and Sciences, ed. Verena M. Schindler and Stephan Cuber (Zurich: AIC, 2011), 751–54, https://aic-color.org/resources /Documents/aic2011proc-reduced.pdf.

58 James E. Gilliam and David Unruh, "The Effects of Baker-Miller Pink on Biological, Physical and Cognitive Behaviour," Journal of Orthomolecular Medicine 3, no. 4 (1988): 202–6.

59 Paolo Frassanito, and Benedetta Pettorini, "Pink and Blue: The Color of Gender," Child's Nervous System 24, (2008): 881–82.

60 Samyn and Partners, Project Selection, Built, "373-Fire Station Houten," https:// samynandpartners.com/portfolio/fire -station-houten/.

61 Boa Mistura, "Projects: Luz nas Vielas (Light in the Alleyways)," http://www .boamistura.com/#/project/luz-nas -vielas-2.

9
Trends in Color and Architecture

1 Juan Serra, "Colores virtuales en arquitecturas reales," in Actas del 13 Congreso de Expresión Gráfica Arquitectónica (Valencia, Spain: Universitat Politècnica de València, 2010).

2 Koolhaas, "The Future of Colours," 12.

3 Rem Koolhaas, "junk-space," in Content (Köln, Germany: Taschen, 2004), 171.

4 Mohsen Mostafavi, "Landscape as Plan [a conversation with Zaha Hadid]," in Zaha Hadid 1996–2001 (Madrid: El Croquis, 2001), 17.

5 Robert Venturi, Steven Izenour, and Denise Scott Brown, Learning from Las Vegas: The Forgotten Symbolism of Architectural Form, 1972, facsimile ed. (Cambridge, MA: MIT Press, 2017).

6 Juan Serra, "The Versatility of Color in Contemporary Architecture," Color Research and Application 38, no. 5 (2013): 344–55, doi.org/10.1002 /col.21734.

7 emmanuelle moureaux architecture + design, http://www.emmanuelle moureaux.com/sugamo-shinkin-bank -shimura.

10

Color in Proposals for Architectural Competitions

1 E. Boganelli, "Colore e segnalazione di pericoli nei luoghi di lavoro," in *Actas oficiales del II Congreso Nacional del color*, ed. Feria de Padua, 328–31 (Padua, Italy: INCO, 1985); cited in De Grandis, *Teoría y uso del color*, 96.
2 Francisco Marchori Ortíz, Juan Serra Lluch, and Susana Iñarra Abad, "Evaluación del contraste del color para dirigir la atención en el render de arquitectura," Universitat Politècnica de València, 2015, https://riunet.upv.es /handle/10251/54400.
3 Rüegg, *Polychromie Architecturale: Le Corbusier's Farbenklaviaturen*.
4 José Luis Caivano, Ingrid Menghi, and Nicolás ladisernia, "Cesia and Paints: An Atlas of Cesia with Painted Samples," 113–16, AIC 2004 Color and Paints, Interim Meeting of the International Color Association, Proceedings, 2004.
5 The tool is structured following the "Accessibility guidelines for web-based content," as recommended by the Web Accessibility Initiative (W3C) in its initial version in 1999. In 2013 the "Guidance on Applying WCAG 2.0 to Non-Web Information and Communications Technologies (WCAG2ICT)" was published for non-web-based media.
6 Juan Serra, Ana Torres, and Ángela García, "¿Por qué se concursa con colores y se construye sin ellos?" in *Actas Del 14 Congreso EGA de Expresión Gráfica Arquitectónica*, (Oporto, Portugal: Universidad de Valladolid, 2012), 995–1000.
7 Ramón Fernández-Alonso, "Enseñar el color," in *Tras el muro blanco*, ed. Jesús Marina and Elena Morón (Madrid: Lampreave, 2010).
8 Ibid.
9 Eva Luque and Alejandro Pascual, "Los Del Desierto," in Marina and Morón, *Tras el muro blanco*.
10 Zaha Hadid and Yukio Futagawa, *Zaha M. Hadid* (Tokyo: A.D.A. Edita, 1995), 75.
11 Juan Serra, "Projects Born by Colours," 196.
12 Matthias Sauerbruch and Louisa Hutton, *Sauerbruch Hutton Archive* (Baden, Switzerland: Lars Müller, 2006), 22.
13 Rafael Soler, "Rafael Soler," in Marina and Morón, *Tras el muro blanco*.
14 José Morales and Sara de Giles, "MGM," in Marina and Morón, *Tras El Muro Blanco*.
15 Hadid and Futagawa, *Zaha M. Hadid*, 75.

11

Color in the Work Process

1 Miguel Ángel Muñoz Pellicer, "Curso flujos de trabajo avanzados" (lecture, AIDO, Instituto Tecnológico de Óptica, Color e Imagen, Valencia, Spain, April 30, 2013).
2 Aberration is the tendency of some lenses to produce color fringing at the corners of the image. Chromatic aberration can be corrected in Photoshop for red/cyan, green/magenta, or blue/yellow.
3 Hugo Rodríguez, *"Gestión del Color en Photoshop," El blog de Hugo Rodríguez: Píldoras diarias de técnica fotográfica* (blog), 2003, accessed June 19, 2018, http://www.hugorodriguez .com/calibracion/gc_photoshop_01 .htm.
4 Emilio Pérez Picazo and Vicente De Gracia, "Rendering Intent: Diferentes tipos de rendering y su función," *CMYK: Publicación técnica de AIDO, Instituto de Óptica, Color e Imagen* 4 (2001): 10–19.

12

Calibrating a Monitor

1 Hugo Rodríguez, "Calibración del monitor," *El blog de Hugo Rodríguez: Píldoras diarias de técnica fotográfica* (blog), 2004, accessed June 5, 2018, http://www.hugorodriguez.com /index_calibrar_el_monitor.php.
2 ICC profiles generally are tied to CIE L*a*b* or CIE XYZ, while LUTs can be designed for linear, log, or Rec709 encodings and many different primaries and white points.
3 In CRT monitors, the recommended resolution is 1024 x 768 pixels for fifteen inches and 1280 x 1024 pixels for seventeen to nineteen inches.
4 Hugo Rodríguez, *Calibrar el monitor*, 3rd ed. (Barcelona: Marcombo, 2013), 96.
5 X-Rite, "How to Calibrate your Monitor in 10 Steps," *X-Rite Color Blog*, October 25, 2016, accessed July 19, 2018, https://www.xrite.com/blog/how-to -calibrate-your-monitor.

13

Photographing and Editing Colors

1 Wikipedia, s.v. "ColorChecker," last modified March 5, 2018, 10:45, https:// en.wikipedia.org/wiki/ColorChecker.
2 The correlated color temperatures used by ColorChecker are: 0 = Unknown, 1 = Daylight, 2 = Fluorescent, 3 = Tungsten (incandescent light), 4 = Flash, 9 = Fine weather, 10 = Cloudy weather, 11 = Shade, 12 = Daylight fluorescent (D 5,700–7,100 K), 13 = Day white fluorescent (N 4,600–5,400 K), 14 = Cool white fluorescent (W 3,900–4,500 K), 15 = White fluorescent (WW 3,200–3,700 K), 17 = Standard light A, 18 = Standard light B, 19 = Standard light C, 20 = D55, 21 = D65, 22 = D75, 23 = D50, 24 = ISO studio tungsten, 25 = Other light sources.
3 Vicente Atienza Vanacloig, "El histograma de una imagen digital" (Valencia, Spain: Informática de Sistemas y Computadores DISCA, Universitat Politècnica de València, 2011), https://riunet.upv.es/bitstream /handle/10251/12711/El%20 histograma%20una%20imagen %20digital.pdf.

14

Printing Color Accurately

1 Epson, "Premium ICC Printer Profiles for the Epson SureColor P400," accessed June 14, 2018, https://epson .com/Support/wa00793.
2 Adobe, "About Soft-Proofing Colors," accessed June 14, 2018, https://helpx .adobe.com/photoshop/using/proofing -colors.html.
3 X-Rite, "Eye-One Training Modules: Creating Profiles for Your Output Devices," software help menu.
4 X-Rite, "i1 Profiler," software help menu.

Selected Bibliography

Books

Albers, Josef. *Interaction of Color.* 4th edition. New Haven, CT: Yale University Press, 2013.

Arnheim, Rudolf. *Art and Visual Perception: A Psychology of the Creative Eye.* Berkeley: University of California Press, 1974.

Arnkil, Harald, ed. *Colour and Light: Concepts and Confusions.* Helsinki: Aalto University, 2015.

Arnoldi, Per. *Colour Is Communication: Selected Projects for Foster+Partners, 1996–2006.* Basel: Birkhäuser, 2007.

Batchelor, David. *Chromophobia.* London: Reaktion Books, 2000.

Birren, Faber. *Color and Human Response.* New York: John Wiley & Sons, 1984.

Bottoni, Piero. "Cromatismi architettonici." *Architettura e arti decorative* 6, no. 1–2 (1927).

Cleland, T. M., *A Grammar of Color.* Mittineague, MA: Strathmore Paper, 1921.

De Grandis, Luigina. *Teoría y uso del color.* Madrid: Cátedra, 1985.

de Heer, Jan. *The Architectonic Colour: Polychromy in the Purist Architecture of Le Corbusier.* Rotterdam, the Netherlands: 010 Publishers, 2009.

Déribéré, Maurice. *El color en las actividades humanas.* Madrid: Tecnos, 1964.

Dondis, Donis A. *A Primer of Visual Literacy.* Cambridge, MA: MIT Press, 1973.

Düttmann, Martina, Friedrich Schmuck, and Johannes Uhl. *El color en la arquitectura.* Barcelona: Gustavo Gili, 1982.

Faulkner, Waldron. *Architecture and Color.* New York: Wiley-Interscience, 1972.

Fridell Anter, Karin. "What Colour Is the Red House? Perceived Colour of Painted Facades." PhD diss., Department of Architectural Forms, School of Architecture, KTH Royal Institute of Technology, 2000. http://www.diva-portal.org/smash/get/diva2:8790/FULLTEXT01.pdf.

Gage, John. *Color and Culture: Practice and Meaning from Antiquity to Abstraction.* Berkeley: University of California Press, 1999.

———. *Color and Meaning: Art, Science, and Symbolism.* Berkeley: University of California Press, 1999.

García Codoñer, Ángela, Jorge Llopis Verdú, José Vicente Masiá León, Ana Torres Barchino, and Ramón Villaplana Guillém. *El color de Valencia: El centro histórico.* Valencia: Excmo. Ayuntamiento de Valencia y Generalitat Valenciana, 2012.

Hayten, Peter J. *El color en arquitectura y decoración.* Barcelona: LEDA Las Ediciones De Arte, 1960.

Heller, Eva. *Psicología del color: Cómo actúan los colores sobre los sentimientos y la razón.* Barcelona: Gustavo Gili, 2004.

Hitchcock, Henry-Russell Jr., and Philip Johnson. *The International Style: Architecture Since 1922.* New York: W. W. Norton, 1932.

Itten, Johannes. *The Art of Color: The Subjective Experience and Objective Rationale of Color.* New York: Van Nostrand Reinhold, 1974.

Itten, Johannes. *The Elements of Color: A Treatise on the Color System of Johannes Itten Based on His Book "The Art of Color."* Edited by Faber Birren. Wokingham, UK: Van Nostrand Reinhold, 1970.

Kandinsky, Wassily. *Concerning the Spiritual in Art.* 1914. Translated by M. T. H. Sadler. New York: Dover Publications, 1977.

Komossa, Susanne, Kees Rouw, and Joost Hillen. *Colour in Contemporary Architecture: Projects, Essays, Calendar, Manifestoes.* Amsterdam: SUN, 2009.

Koolhaas, Rem, Norman Foster, and Alessandro Mendini. *Colours.* Basel: Birkhäuser, 2001.

Lancaster, Michael. *Colourscape.* London: Academy Editions, 1996.

Lillo Jover, Julio. *Ergonomía: Evaluación y diseño del entorno visual.* Madrid: Alianza, 2000.

Mahnke, Frank H. *Color, Environment, and Human Response: An Interdisciplinary Understanding of Color and Its Use as a Beneficial Element in the Design of the Architectural Environment.* New York: Van Nostrand Reinhold, 1996.

Martín Andrade, Pablo, and Soledad Luengo Jusdado. *Accesibilidad para personas con ceguera y deficiencia visual.* Madrid: ONCE, 2003.

Meyhöfer, Dirk. *In Full Colour: Recent Buildings and Interiors.* Berlin: Verlagshaus Braun, 2008.

Miller, Mary C. *Color for Interior Architecture.* Chichester, UK: John Wiley & Sons, 1997.

Noury, Larissa. *La couleur dans la ville.* Paris: Moniteur, 2008.

O'Connor, Zena. "Façade Colour and Aesthetic Response: Examining Patterns of Response within the Context of Urban Design and Planning Policy in Sydney." PhD diss., Faculty of Architecture, Design & Planning, University of Sydney, 2008.

Porter, Tom, and Byron Mikellides, eds. *Colour for Architecture.* London: Studio Vista, 1976.

———. *Colour for Architecture Today.* London: Taylor & Francis, 2009.

Rau, Cordula, ed. *Why Do Architects Wear Black?* Vienna: Springer Vienna Architecture, 2008.

Rüegg, Arthur, ed. *Polychromie Architecturale: Le Corbusier's Farbenklaviaturen von 1931 und 1959* [Architectural Polychromy: Le Corbusier's color keyboards from 1931 and 1959]. Basel: Birkhäuser, 1997.

Sanz, Juan Carlos, and Rosa Gallego. *Diccionario Akal del color*. Madrid: Akal, 2001.

Sauerbruch, Matthias, and Louisa Hutton. *Sauerbruch Hutton Archive*. Baden, Switzerland: Lars Müller, 2006.

Schopenhauer, Arthur, and David E. Cartwright. *On Vision and Colors: An Essay*. Oxford, UK: Berg, 1994.

Sherin, Aaris. *Design Elements: Color Fundamentals*. Beverly, MA: Rockport, 2012.

Smedal, Grete. *Colours of Longyearbyen: An Ongoing Project*. Bergen, Norway: Eget forlag, 2009.

Swirnoff, Lois. *Dimensional Color*. 2nd ed. New York: W. W. Norton, 2003.

Táboas Veleiro, Teresa. *El color en arquitectura*. Sada, La Coruña, Spain: Ediciós do Castro, 1991.

Venturi, Robert, Steven Izenour, and Denise Scott Brown. *Learning from Las Vegas: The Forgotten Symbolism of Architectural Form*. 1972. Facsimile ed. Cambridge, MA: MIT Press, 2017.

Wigley, Mark. *White Walls, Designer Dresses: The Fashioning of Modern Architecture*. Cambridge, MA: MIT Press, 1995.

Wittgenstein, Ludwig, and G. E. M. Anscombe. *Remarks on Colour*. Oxford, UK: Blackwell, 1977.

Wolfe, Tom. *From Bauhaus to Our House*. New York: Picador, 1981.

Periodicals

AIC (International Color Association). *Proceedings of the International Congresses and Midterm Meetings of the AIC*. http://www.aic-color.org/.

Color Research and Application. Wiley Science, ISSN:1520-6378. https://onlinelibrary.wiley.com/journal/15206378.

EGA: Expresión Gráfica Arquitectónica. https://polipapers.upv.es/index.php/EGA.

JAIC: Journal of the International Color Association. http://www.aic-color.org/journal.htm.

MIX Magazine. http://colourhive.com/.

Websites

Boa Mistura. http://www.boamistura.com.

The Bold Collective (blog). http://theboldcollective.com.au/blog.

Color Group Universitat Politècnica de València. http://grupocolor.webs.upv.es/WEB/.

Colour Lovers. http://www.colourlovers.com.

Colour Marketing Group. https://colormarketing.org.

Bruce Lindbloom. http://www.brucelindbloom.com/index.html?LabGamutDisplay.html.

emmanuelle moureaux architecture + design. http://www.emmanuellemoureaux.com.

Munsell Color. http://munsell.com.

NCS Colour. http://ncscolour.com.

Pantone. https://www.pantone.com.

Rodríguez, Hugo. *El blog de Hugo Rodriguez: Píldoras diarias de técnica fotográfica* (blog). http://www.hugorodriguez.com/blog.

Sauerbruch Hutton. http://www.sauerbruchhutton.de.

Serra, Juan. Color y Arquitectura Contemporánea. http://juaserl1.blogs.upv.es/.

Serra, Juan. Graphic and Chromatic Design for Architecture. http://graphicandchromaticdesign.blogs.upv.es.

X-Rite. https://www.xrite.com/en.

Index

Illustration Credits

Many of the images in this book have been redrawn for clarity and consistency; however, the original sources of their content are listed here.

1.1 Image by author
1.2 Translated by author from an original by Horst Frank, Wikimedia Commons, CC BY-SA
1.3 Kelvingsong, Wikimedia Commons
1.4 Image by author
1.5 Based on an image by National Eye Institute, NIH National Institutes of Health in Bethesda, Maryland, CC BY 2.0
1.6 Dr. Robert Fariss, National Eye Institute, NIH National Institutes of Health, Bethesda, Maryland, CC BY 2.0
1.7 Image by author
1.8 © Konica Minolta Inc.
1.9 Marco Polo, Wikimedia Commons
1.10 Image by author based on a graph by Kevin Houser (Loucetios), Wikimedia Commons
1.11–1.12 Image by author
1.13 https://pxhere.com/es/photo/664930
1.14 Image by author based on J. Itten, Wikimedia Commons
1.15 Courtesy of Sean Scully and Galerie Lelong, New York
1.16 Collection of Art Institute of Chicago, Wikimedia Commons
1.17 Collection of Minneapolis Institute of Arts, Wikimedia Commons
1.18 Image by author
1.19 Photograph © The State Hermitage Museum, photograph by Vladimir Terebenin
1.20 Science Museum of London, CC BY 4.0
1.21 Courtesy of Anna Delcampo
1.22 carlinhos75 in Flickr, CC BY 2.0
1.23 Image by author based on thedailyenglishshow.com, Flickr, CC BY 2.0
1.24 © Konica Minolta Inc.

2.1 Peter Halasz, Wikimedia Commons, CC BY-SA 3.0
2.2 Photograph by author
2.3 Paulschou, Wikimedia Commons, CC BY-SA 3.0
2.4 Wikimedia Commons, CC BY-SA 3.0
2.5–2.6 © Konica Minolta Inc.
2.7 Courtesy of Bruce J. Lindbloom
2.8–2.9 Natural Colour System® © property of and used on license from NCS Colour AB, Stockholm 2017
2.10 Thenoizz, Wikimedia Commons, CC BY-SA 3.0
2.11 Jacob Rus, Wikimedia Commons, CC BY-SA 3.0
2.12 SharkD, Wikimedia Commons, CC BY-SA 3.0
2.13–2.14 © 2018, Adobe Systems Incorporated. All rights reserved. Adobe and Adobe Photoshop CS are registered trademarks of Adobe Systems Incorporated in the United States and/or other countries.
2.15 Courtesy of Yves Charnay
2.16–2.17 Brad Feinknopf / OTTO
3.1 Photographs by author

3.2 C2RMF, Wikimedia Commons
3.3–3.4 Courtesy of Karin Fridell Anter
3.5–3.10 Image by author
3.11 Courtesy of Archiv Geiger GbR, Munich, 2009
3.12 Private collection © 2018 The Josef and Anni Albers Foundation / Artists Rights Society (ARS), New York; photograph: Tim Nighswander / Imaging4Art
3.13 Image by author, based on the app Interaction of Color, © Yale University.
3.14–3.15 L. Gehse
3.16 ScagliolaBrakkee / © Neutelings Riedijk Architects
3.17 David Evers, Wikimedia Commons, CC BY 2.0
3.18–3.19 Courtesy of Yasutaka Yoshimura Architects
3.20 © Jasper Johns and ULAE / licensed by VAGA, New York, NY, published by ULAE, photograph: Imaging Department © President and Fellows of Harvard College
3.21 Piotr Bodzek, Wikimedia Commons, CC SA-BY 3.0
3.22–3.23 Photomontage by the author over a photograph by Ossip van Duivenbode, courtesy of MVRDV

4.1 https://archive.org/details/gri_c00033125006531145
4.2–4.4 Courtesy of José Luis Caivano
4.5 Johannes Itten, *Kunst der Farbe Studienausgabe. Subjektives Erleben und objektives Erkennen als Wege zur Kunst.* © 2009 Christophorus Verlag GmbH & Co. KG, Freiburg, 39, 57
4.6– 4.7 Courtesy of i29 interior architects
4.8 Bibliothèque nationale de France, département Réserve des livres rares
4.9 Johannes Itten, *Kunst der Farbe Studienausgabe: Subjektives Erleben und objektives Erkennen als Wege zur Kunst.* © 2009 Christophorus Verlag GmbH & Co. KG, Freiburg, 39, 57.
4.10 Collection of Metropolitan Museum of Art, New York, Wikimedia Commons
4.11 Image by Muntsa Gisbert
4.12 Wikimedia Commons
4.13 Natural Colour System®© property of and used on license from NCS Colour AB, Stockholm 2017. References to NCS®© in this publication are used with permission from the NCS Colour AB.
4.14 Courtesy of Yeong Hao Han
4.15–4.16 Courtesy of Emilio Tuñón Architects
4.17, 4.19–4.21 E. Rimalova
4.18 Leopold Museum, Vienna, Wikimedia Commons
4.22 © F.L.C. / VEGAP, Valencia, 2018
4.23 Image by author

5.1 Friedrich Ernst von Garnier
5.2 Courtesy of MVRDV architects
5.3 Courtesy of Campo Baeza Architects
5.4 Courtesy of Annette Kisling and Sauerbruch Hutton
5.5 Courtesy of Grete Smedal and Kristina Emberg

5.6–5.7 © Florentijn Hoffman
5.8–5.9 Photograph by Mar Añó Nadal
5.10 Photograph by Kristof Lemp
5.11 Claire Saxby, Wikimedia Commons, CC BY-SA 3.0
5.12 Friedrich Ernst von Garnier
5.13 Photomontage by author based on an image from Friedrich Ernst von Garnier
5.14 Claude Truon-Ngoc, Wikimedia Commons, CC BY-SA 3.0
5.15 Cacophony - Own work, Wikimedia Commons, CC BY-SA 3.0
5.16 Courtesy of Thomas Kesseler, Düsseldorf.
5.17 Courtesy of Richard Davies Photographer
5.18–5.19 Courtesy of MVRDV. Photograph by Rob't Hart Photography
5.20–5.21 Courtesy of Eugeni Pons Photography
5.22–5.24 Photograph by Jan Bitter
5.25–5.28 Image by author
Table 5.1 Top, Pablo Alberto Salguero Quiles, Wikimedia Commons, CC BY-SA 3.0; bottom, Roberto Latxaga. Flickr, CC BY 2.0
5.29 Photograph by Schlaier
5.30 René Spitz. CC BY 2.0
5.31 Image by author

6.1 Courtesy of The Bold Collective; photograph by Cameron Zegers
6.2 Courtesy of The Bold Collective
6.3 Image by author
6.4 Image by author, based on a graph by Jean Paul Freyssinier and Mark Rea
6.5–6.7 Courtesy of The Bold Collective. Photograph by Andrew Worssam

7.1 Jchancerel, Wikimedia Commons
7.2 © F.L.C. / VEGAP, Valencia, 2018
7.3 © 2012 Artists Rights Society (ARS) © F.L.C. / VEGAP, Valencia, 2018.
7.4 M-Louis /LeonL in Flickr, CC BY 2.0
7.5 Wikimedia Commons, CC BY-SA 3.0
7.6 Daderot, Wikimedia Commons
7.7 Radomir Cernoch, Wikimedia Commons, CC BY-SA 2.0
7.8 Chair of Arthur Rüegg, ETH Zürich, Stephan Bleuel, © F.L.C. / VEGAP, Valencia, 2018
7.9 Courtesy of Mar Añó Nadal
7.10 © F.L.C. / VEGAP, Valencia, 2018
7.11–7.12 Wikimedia Commons
7.13 Courtesy of Mar Añó Nadal
7.14 Onbekend, Wikimedia Commons
7.15 Ad from the Netherlands, Wikimedia Commons, CC BY-SA 2.0
7.16 Wikimedia Commons

8.1 M_H.DE - Own work, Wikimedia Commons, CC BY 3.0
8.2 Courtesy of Richard Rogers
8.3 Courtesy of Zaha Hadid
8.4 (all) Courtesy of Marina Valero Martínez
8.5 Courtesy of Foster and Partners
8.6 Arnaud 25, Wikimedia Commons, CC BY-SA 3.0
8.7 Morio, Wikimedia Commons, CC BY-SA 3.0

8.8 Jean-Pierre Dalbéra, CC BY 2.0
8.9–8.10 Watercolors by Ana Torres Barchino
8.11 Courtesy of Prof. Dr. D. Prokop
8.12 Edited image based on a photograph by Rainerzufall1234, Wikimedia Commons, CC BY-SA 4.0
8.13 Courtesy of British Airways
8.14–8.15 Courtesy of Samyn and Partners. Image by Ch. Richters
8.16–8.17 Courtesy of Joan Fontcuberta
8.18 Photograph by author
8.19–8.21 Courtesy of Boa Mistura Urban Art Group
8.22–8.23 Image by author

9.1 Courtesy of BIG architects
9.2 Image by Another Believe, Wikimedia Commons, CC BY-SA 3.0
9.3–9.4 Courtesy of © Fundació Enric Miralles
9.5–9.6 Courtesy of NO.MAD Architecture Office
9.7 Courtesy of MVRDV architects
9.8 Courtesy of Rafael Vargas
9.9 Courtesy of UNstudio, photograph by Christian Richters
9.10 Marion Schneider & Christoph Aistleitner, Wikimedia Commons, CC BY-SA 2.5
9.11 Courtesy of Pantone® LLC, 2018
9.12–9.15 Photograph by Nacasa & Partners Inc.
9.16 Metropolitan Museum of Art, The Elisha Whittelsey Collection, The Elisha Whittelsey Fund, 1959, CC0 1.0 UPD
9.17 Courtesy of Langarita Navarro. Photograph by Luis Díaz Díaz
9.18–9.19 Courtesy of Langarita Navarro. Photograph by Miguel de Guzmán
9.20–9.21 Courtesy of Mas Que Espacio. Photograph by Cualiti
9.22 Courtesy of MVRDV Architects
9.23–9.24 Courtesy of Supermachine Studio. Photograph by Wison Tungthunya

10.1 Courtesy of Susana Iñarra Abad and bg studio
10.2 Based on images by Ángel Rodas Jordá, Francisco Marchori Ortíz, and Susana Iñarra Abad
10.3 Wikimedia Commons
10.4 Courtesy of Richard Rogers
10.5 Courtesy of West 8
10.6 Image by author
10.7 Courtesy of Gustafson Porter + Bowman
10.8 Andreas Schwarzkopf, Wikimedia Commons, CC BY-SA 3.0
10.9–10.11 Courtesy of Zaha Hadid Architects
10.12a–b Courtesy of Gustafson Porter + Bowman
10.13 Courtesy of Richard Rogers
10.14 Courtesy of Foreign Office Architects (FOA) and Alejandro Zaera-Polo
10.15 Courtesy of West 8

Acknowledgments

11.1 Image by Cpesacreta, Wikimedia, CC BY 2.5
11.2 © 2018, Adobe Systems Incorporated. All rights reserved. Adobe and Adobe Photoshop CS are registered trademarks of Adobe Systems Incorporated in the United States and/or other countries.
11.3 Edited image based on an image © 2018, Adobe Systems Incorporated. All rights reserved. Adobe and Adobe Photoshop CS are registered trademarks of Adobe System Incorporated in the United States and/or other countries.
11.4a–e Images edited by author, based on an image by Ulises00, Wikimedia Commons

12.1 Used with permission from Microsoft
12.2 Image by author
12.3 Images edited by author based on a photograph from https://www.maxpixel.net/Architecture-Water-Reflection-Santiago-Calatrava-1297680
12.4–12.7 Courtesy of X-Rite Incorporated

13.1 Image by author based on Alex1ruff, Wikimedia Commons, CC BY-SA 4.0
13.2 Courtesy of PhilipBloom.Net
13.3 Image by author
13.4–13.6 Courtesy of X-Rite Incorporated
13.7 © 2018, Adobe Systems Incorporated. All rights reserved. Adobe and Adobe Photoshop CS are registered trademarks of Adobe Systems Incorporated in the United States and/or other countries.
13.8a–c Edited on an image by Bert Kaufmann, Wikimedia Commons, CC BY-SA 2.0

14.1–14.2 Courtesy of X-Rite Incorporated
14.3 Image by CosticÐ Acsinte

15.1–15.2 NCS. Natural Colour System®© property of and used on license from NCS Colour AB, Stockholm 2017. References to NCS®© in this publication are used with permission from the NCS Colour AB.
15.3–15.4 © Konica Minolta Inc.

B.1–B.11 © 2018, Adobe Systems Incorporated. All rights reserved. Adobe and Adobe Photoshop CS are registered trademarks of Adobe Systems Incorporated in the United States and/or other countries.

To my colleagues at Universitat Politècnica de València: thanks to Ángela García Codoñer, senior professor of architectural graphic expression, who has passed on to me her knowledge of and enthusiasm for color. To my Color Research Group colleagues, particularly Ana Torres Barchino and Jorge Llopis Verdú, with whom I experience challenging projects about color. To all the teachers of Architectural Formal Analysis, particularly Manolo Giménez, who addresses my concerns day by day, and also Irene de la Torre and Javier Cortina, who get roped into our color dilemmas. Be careful: there is no way back! To our other colleagues in the Architectural Graphic Expression Department, particularly Pedro Cabezos for his help in proofreading and Susana Iñarra for her concerns with observers. To Anna Delcampo and Luis Querol for their assistance on the edition management of this book.

To the many members of the National Group of Color in Spain (SEDO) and the International Color Association (AIC), who have given me their support from time to time or have kindly collaborated at any moment on this publication: Professor Manuel Melgosa of Granada; Associate Professor Karin Fridell of Sweden; Verena Schindler, the Swiss head of the Study Group on Environmental Color Design in AIC; and Professor José Luis Caivano of Argentina. To Ellen C. Carter, editor of *Color Research and Application*, for her determination in advancing research about color and architecture. And to all the architects and artists who have kindly agreed to collaborate on this book, providing images and comments.

This book is yours in part!

When did I first love color in buildings?
Paz, Miguel, Irene, and Juan…
You've built my life in full colors!

Answers to questions
in the Activities:

Activity 1 (page 23)
1: Those with normal color vision see a 45. The
majority of color-blind people cannot see this number
clearly. (Ishihara's plate 9)
2: Those with normal color vision should see a 42.
Red-color-blind (protanopia) people will see a 2, mild
red-color-blind people (prontanomaly) will also faintly
see a number 4. Green-color-blind (deuteranopia)
people will see a 4, mild green-color-blind people
(deuteranomaly) may also faintly see
a number 2. (Ishihara's plate 17)
3: Those with normal color vision see a 74. Those
with red green color blindness see a 21. Those with
total color blindness see nothing. (Ishihara's plate 7)
4: Those with normal color vision see a 6. The
majority of color-blind people cannot see this number
clearly. (Ishihara's plate 8)
5: Those with normal color vision see a 3. Those with
red green color blindness see a 5. Those with total
color blindness see nothing. (Ishihara's plate 5)

Activity 3 (page 27)
1: C, 2: D, 3: B, 4: A, 5: C, 6: B, 7: A, 8: D, 9: C, 10: D

Activity 7 (page 52)
1: Medical professionals are exposed for several
hours to the red color of blood and might perceive
a disturbing negative afterimage in a greenish color.
This annoying successive color contrast is not
perceived when the green afterimage of red is seen
against a green surface, as it blends in.

Activity 16 (page 133)
1: C, 2: B, 3: D, 4: A, 5: E

Activity 17 (page 134)
1: A, 2: F, 3: A, 4: H, 5: C, 6: G, 7: D, 8: B, 9: E

Published by Princeton Architectural Press
A McEvoy Group company
202 Warren Street, Hudson, New York 12534
www.papress.com

Princeton Architectural Press is a leading publisher
in architecture, design, photography, landscape, and
visual culture. We create fine books and stationery
of unsurpassed quality and production values.
With more than one thousand titles published, we find
design everywhere and in the most unlikely places.

© 2019 Juan Serra Lluch
All rights reserved
Printed and bound in China
22 21 20 19 4 3 2 1 First edition

No part of this book may be used or reproduced in
any manner without written permission from the
publisher, except in the context of reviews.
Every reasonable attempt has been made to identify
owners of copyright. Errors or omissions will be
corrected in subsequent editions.

Translation assistance: Stephen E. C. McCullough
Editor: Sara Stemen
Designer: Benjamin English

Special thanks to: Paula Baver, Janet Behning,
Abby Bussel, Jan Cigliano Hartman, Susan Hershberg,
Kristen Hewitt, Lia Hunt, Valerie Kamen, Jennifer Lippert,
Sara McKay, Parker Menzimer, Eliana Miller, Wes Seeley,
Rob Shaeffer, Marisa Tesoro, Paul Wagner, and
Joseph Weston of Princeton Architectural Press
—Kevin C. Lippert, publisher

Library of Congress Cataloging-in-Publication Data
Names: Serra Lluch, Juan, author.
Title: Color for architects / Juan Serra Lluch.
Description: First edition. | New York : Princeton
  Architectural Press, 2019. | Includes bibliographical
  references and index.
Identifiers: LCCN 2018026555 | ISBN 9781616897949
  (pbk. : alk. paper)
Subjects: LCSH: Color in architecture.
Classification: LCC NA2795 .S46 2019 | DDC 729/.4—dc23
LC record available at https://lccn.loc.gov/2018026555